Mortal Remains

Mortal Remains

Death in Early America

Edited by
NANCY ISENBERG and
ANDREW BURSTEIN

PENN

University of Pennsylvania Press

Philadelphia

10   9   8   7   6   5   4   3   2   1

Published by
University of Pennsylvania Press
Philadelphia, Pennsylvania 19104-4011

Library of Congress Cataloging-in-Publication Data
   Mortal remains : death in early America / edited by Nancy Isenberg and Andrew Burstein.
      p.   cm.
   Includes bibliographical references and index.
   ISBN 0-8122-3678-5 (cloth : alk. paper)—ISBN 0-8122-1823-X (paper : alk. paper)
   1. Death—Social aspects—United States.   2. Funeral rites and ceremonies—United
States—History.   3. United States—Social life and customs—To 1775.   4. United States—
Social life and customs—19th century.   I. Isenberg, Nancy.   II. Burstein, Andrew.
HQ1073.5.U6 M67 2003
306.9—dc21

                                                                    2002074221

All things must pass
None of life's strings can last.
　　　　　—George Harrison

Contents

Illustrations

Introduction

How is the culturally learned fear of finality explained? That is the essential question behind this book, which began as a symposium titled "Mortal Remains," underwritten by the Mary Frances Barnard Chair endowment at the University of Tulsa and held April 19–22, 2001. Historians and literary scholars met and gave papers on a variety of subjects relating to individual and community experiences with death during the formative period in America's modern history, 1620–1860. The combined purpose of the symposium participants, and of this collection, is to emphasize America's beginnings in terms that are a bit different from the way the story is generally told. We write of life as lived in relation to death as felt.

How death touched the lives of early Americans emerges most plainly from the pages of their personal correspondence. When men and women reported on the passing of relatives and friends, they bequeathed a rich record to historical investigators. In demographic terms, we are led by facts to reevaluate the past: there was a gradual increase in life expectancy between 1750 and 1790, in spite of the Revolutionary War; yet, while survival statistics vary among geographic regions, we have also learned that the average American's life span *declined* after 1790, from approximately fifty-six to forty-eight years by the time of the Civil War. Geographical mobility helped to spread infectious diseases, and many more Americans suffered from scarlet fever, typhoid, and tuberculosis. Growing urban areas like New York, Philadelphia, and Boston faced periodic epidemics—yellow fever was perhaps the most ravaging among these. The towering image of six foot four inch Abraham Lincoln was anomalous: the U.S. population was weaker, shorter, and less robust by the mid-nineteenth century because fighting childhood diseases took a tremendous toll.

Mortal Remains studies neglected aspects of American culture, illustrating the profound ways in which experiences with death and the imagery associated with death influenced not only something as obvious as religious practice, but also national and gender politics, race relations, and other notions which are easy to relate to our own contemporary concerns. As they struggled to survive and grow in a medically primitive and politically evolving environment, early Americans reveal in their texts that mortality was, for them, inseparable from national self-definition. They combated personal dissolution and attempted to make sense of their suffering and loss while projecting a future of cultural permanence and spiritual value.

Understandings are gleaned from stark images and subtle metaphors. In this study, "great white men" share the stage with murder victims, desecrated Indian burial sites, and threatened slaves. This is a book about embattled ministers and comforting angels, about a harsh reality softened by sensual visions. *Mortal Remains* presents a series of vignettes that encompass a range of human responses. Just as people cannot seem to avoid looking at and contemplating terror, they cannot avoid seeking out comfort and desiring reconciliation in the afterlife.

Private and public rituals and private and public shrines reanimate departed persons, idealistically projecting the renewal of life—this is as true in the imagined national family as it is in the "typical" family. Visual and written records keep the dead alive. From the Vietnam Veterans Memorial in Washington, D.C., to television retrospectives and popular biographies of "heroes," or journalistic rediscoveries of white relatives by the curious descendents of African American slaves, death's finality is never quite acknowledged. When we say, "life goes on," we are doing more than sighing in the acceptance of some passage, we are also asserting the power of the living to rationalize and remember death in new ways.

Since the death of George Washington in 1799, the passing of presidents has transformed the ancient rituals of mourning for a king into celebrations of democratic rule. Yet even for the average individual, death is followed by a series of cultural rituals. A corpse is prepared for burial, and then in a public ceremony the community honors the deceased. Afterward, the body is hidden from view: it is interred in the ground, in a crypt, or it is cremated (a common modern practice in the United States, but traditionally performed in many older cultures). Traces of a life—the headstone, obituaries, genealogies in family bibles, portraits or photographs, locks of hair, church and state documents—systematically leave a record for posterity, that is, for as long as the official record, newspaper, cherished family memento, or cenotaph survives.

As of this writing, death looms especially large in the popular imagination. Although few people beyond clergy, healthcare professionals, police, and morticians deal with death on a regular basis, still the dead are always "with us." After her fatal car accident, the celebrated Princess Diana continued to live on in *People* magazine. For much of 2001, a missing Washington intern, Chandra Levy, though presumed dead, was kept alive, smiling and happy, in home movies and photographs constantly broadcast in the saturation coverage of cable network news. Popular television shows as "Forensic Files" (part of the genre called "Reality TV") exhaustively reconstruct the dying moments of murder victims from hair, blood residue, and bones. From the *New York Times Magazine* to extended network news features, reports on the unusual experimental laboratory known as the "Body Farm" have offered the reading and viewing public uncensored images of human remains in various stages of decomposition. On September 11, 2001, the airborne attacks on New York and Washington landmarks most shockingly brought home the old notion of death as the metaphorical King of Terrors.

For most Americans, death is mediated. It is carefully packaged, programmed, and formulated in familiar scripts that seek to entertain rather than alarm audiences. The driving force behind many video games, for example, has been the fantasy of death—its imaginary features: animated action figures hunt and kill their enemies in dystopic environments ambiguously set in the netherworld of the distant past or future. Dark humor and satire about death are routinely circulated on the Internet. On a commercially lavish scale, Michael Jackson's *Thriller* cleverly choreographed the undead as the dancing dead in one of the most famous music videos ever produced.

Hollywood has been the master of mass-produced cultural illusion and fantasy, constantly reinventing older plots that present death in a recognizable register of emotional and visual cues, such as oblique camera angles, musical crescendos, or close-ups of the anguished face of a victim. Heroic and sacrificial deaths are common tropes in war films, such as Willem Dafoe's Christlike death in *Platoon* (1986) and Tom Hanks's fraternal sacrifice in *Saving Private Ryan* (2000). Soldiers dying in each other's arms, or a grim view of corpses in a heap in the aftermath of battle, have long been staple images of war films and can be traced back to *The Birth of a Nation* (1915), D. W. Griffith's silent epic about the Civil War. Tragic, romantic partings of lovers and family members have long centered on the deathbed scene. One of the most memorable of these is Olivia de Havilland portraying the unfailingly self-sacrificing Melanie in *Gone with the Wind* (1939). Dying in childbirth, the devoted wife and mother is a moral exemplar, her perfect death heralding the regeneration of the South and the reunion of the nation as a whole.

The inverse of this formula can be found in film plots about supernatural encounters. In *Ghost* (1990), a murdered husband's undying love allows him to protect his new wife even from the grave, while a dead man is given a second chance at life and redemption in *Heaven Can Wait* (1943 and 1978). Divine intervention by a kindly if bungling angel, like Clarence Oddbody in *It's a Wonderful Life* (1939), disrupt the natural law of death's unpredictability, exposing the cultural desire that death is surmountable.

Why are these plots so compelling? Perhaps because they have arisen out of Americans' experience over centuries. There is a history behind death's contested meanings which speaks to Americans' responses to various forms of social disorder, especially war, but also to the fantasized angst of racial and sexual conflict. So, the historian has an important role to play in connecting death to defining moments in cultural evolution.

Philippe Ariès's scholarship has cast a long shadow on the historical subject of death. In *Hour of Our Death* (1977) and *Images of Man and Death* (1985), he emphasized the centrality of death in daily life before the twentieth century and the dramatic shift in the aesthetics of death. By the early nineteenth century the corpse was made desirable—inviting to the eye and senses. Since Ariès wrote, historians have returned to the issue of the symbolic and social meaning of the corpse. Gary Laderman's *The Sacred Remains: American Attitudes Toward Death, 1799–1883* (1996) looks at the manner in which the interests of survivors dominated the treatment of dead bodies. From the Civil War era forward, the science of embalming preserved and reconstructed the corpse for a more pleasing public viewing. This took on a particular national significance when the martyred Abraham Lincoln was laid out before citizens during his posthumous train ride back to Springfield, Illinois, where he was interred.

In the pursuit of new methods of social geography and literary analysis, scholars have also paid attention to cemeteries and epitaphs, as well as the role of photography in the tradition of memento mori, the keepsakes of death. Recent historical studies have also concentrated on the politics of grief, particularly through the memorialization of the dead. Still others have reexamined death and the culture of crime, raising issues related to racial and gender tensions in society. In *Mortal Remains*, we incorporate many of these approaches, and offer a comprehensive survey of the latest methodologies used by social, cultural, and art historians, literary scholars, and students of material culture.[1]

In Part I of this collection, "Mortality for the Masses," Laura M. Stevens, Daniel A. Cohen, and Robert V. Wells explore the tension between death as a personal, individual experience, and death as an experience of collective loss. Stevens focuses on America's preoccupation with the image of the vanishing Indian. She locates the origins of this phenomenon in the writings of English missionaries of the seventeenth century, for whom two types of narratives prevailed: accounts of wartime blood and carnage, and singular accounts of the "good death" enacted by Christianized Indians. The first type features a divine providence in support of the mass extermination of native peoples, while the latter conjures a "pleasing melancholy," suffusing native demise with sorrow and salvation's grace.

It is that melancholic image which evolved into the ironic conception among the race responsible for Indian removal that the vanishing Indian was to be mourned. The English project of conquest was deceptively construed as an "act of kindness," leaving the fate of the Indians to the invisible forces of divine will or progress. English missionaries linked their religious purposes to a Protestant model of colonization based on husbandry and trade. In this grand scheme, the English claimed that they were saving the Indians from the Spanish (who were "cruel and inefficient managers of colonial wealth") and saving the heathen Indians from themselves. As Stevens pointedly explains, the potent themes of "waste" and "conservation" cast the English as caretakers of both unsaved Indian "souls" and the vast unsettled land of North America. The Indians "waste away . . . like the snow against the sun," missionary Thoroughgood Moore wrote in 1705. Inducing grief without moral accountability, the English, and later the Americans, saw Indian death as a sign of productivity and progress.

The English influence on early American culture also encompassed murder and crime literature. In "Blood Will Out," Daniel A. Cohen uncovers the antecedents of modern American notions of "gothic horror" or crime as "mystery," by analyzing popular English murder publications of the early to mid-seventeenth century. As Cohen carefully demonstrates, readers responded to this genre not with compassion but with outrage and the desire to see capital punishment enacted. They read of horrific murders involving dismemberment and of unnatural mothers who slew their own children. Sons killed their mothers, too: in one account, a son divided his mother's head "from that breast, and those paps which gave suck unto him." Unlike the case of dying Indians who quietly and poetically "wasted away," Cohen identifies a voyeuristic, as well as moralistic, fascination with violent death.

Both Stevens and Cohen prove that early modern literary forms persisted into the nineteenth century and continue to resonate in our contemporary culture. Giving us opposite sides of the same doctrinal and devotional coin, they separately show the enduring influence of the Protestant ars moriendi, or art of dying; it is equally apparent in the "good death" (dying at peace with the world) and in the "bad death" (dying amid terror and as a result of murder). Both scholars link older Protestant conventions to emerging literary genres—missionary tracts and crime literature—both of which were marketed and disseminated among the masses.

In a more personal, but no less literary, mode, early Americans kept diaries in which they wrote about death. In his "Tale of Two Cities," Robert V. Wells examines three traumatic epidemics, comparing the responses of Cotton Mather, a Puritan minister, and Elizabeth Drinker, a Quaker matron. Mather lived through two terrifying epidemics in Boston, measles in 1713 and smallpox in 1721. Drinker endured the yellow fever epidemic in Philadelphia in 1793. Once again, the contrast between a good death and bad death is starkly apparent. Epidemics disrupted normal death rituals, as Wells shows, producing social chaos and a constant fear, "induced by unfamiliar and loathsome forms of death."

As a minister, Mather recognized the pedagogic value of death. During the two epidemics he experienced, he aggressively enlarged his role in instructing his flock in the proper way of preparing for death and dealing with the dying. After his wife succumbed to measles, he gave a sermon at her burial that he later published: "What Should be the Behavior of a Christian at a Funeral." Mather and Drinker both understood death to involve three stages: spiritual preparation, physical preparation ("laying out" the corpse), and recovery, that is, helping the survivors to grieve, to remember the dead, and to return to the normal routine of the living. Drinker described how Philadelphia was devastated by the yellow fever epidemic: bodies were left in the street, people died alone, corpses were dumped in graveyards, and racial and ethnic fears were fed—foreign invasions, on the one hand, and blacks poisoning well water on the other. The horror of being buried alive—bodies were placed in coffins too quickly and without care—is another observation that appears in Drinker's 1793 diary, which she later dubbed her "Book of Mortality."

The first three essays in the volume tap into primal fears. Death was conceived as an arbitrary, invisible, and evil force that randomly took victims, leaving mutilated or disfigured corpses in its wake. In response, the Protestant religion offered a variety of cultural rituals and literary discourses for containing and channeling fear and disciplining death. In his sermons, as well as in his personal spiritual exercises, Cotton Mather asserted that death demanded resignation, acceptance, and preparation. English missionaries used the same religious framework to elevate dying Indians into models of Christian conversion, while infusing Indian deaths with a sense of pleasing melancholy and nostalgic loss. "Affective control," in Stevens's words, advanced imperialist agendas, making death serve the process of American colonization. Sensational tales of domestic murder likewise empowered the state to cleanse itself of "unnatural monsters," dispatching ruthless killers at the gallows to avenge a decidedly Protestant God as well as a mortified reading public.

In Part II, "The Politics of Death," Nancy Isenberg, Andrew Burstein, and Julia Stern examine how the dead were used figuratively to embody the new republic in the late eighteenth and early nineteenth centuries. In "Death and Satire," Isenberg assesses the significance of the feminine personification of death—the state as represented by the mutilated female body. Benjamin Franklin's famous engraving, *Magna Britannia; Her Colonies Reduc'd* (1765–66), was reproduced widely and syndicated during the American Revolution. In this evocative cartographic corpse (see the book's cover), Britannia's vacant eyes beseech heaven, as her arms and legs—the named colonies—are strewn before her mangled body. More than a rationale for colonial rights, Franklin's engraving made pertinent popular Anglo-American associations of gender with terror; science and satire blend in his ironic depiction of widely understood fears—fears of dissection, social death, and sexual violation.

The French Revolution, symbolized by "Dame Guillotine," adapted the trope of female dismemberment. In the 1790s as two new political parties, the Francophobe Federalists and Francophile Democratic-Republicans, vied for power in the United States, the Medusa head and cadaverous female Fury continued to associate the disturbing female form of death with sexual disorder. Federalist satirists transformed the French Goddess of Liberty into a devouring mother, a female cannibal. Grotesque images of female rage and slaughter became indistinguishable from the death of the public sphere.

In "Immortalizing the Founding Fathers," Andrew Burstein explores a less violently conceived but equally political process of state legitimation. Eulogists deployed hyperbolic prose in their public commemorations of the lives of Benjamin Franklin, George Washington, John Adams, Thomas Jefferson, and Andrew Jackson, for purposes beyond constructing a comforting civil religion: they conceived a national cosmology. Entwining quasi-religious symbolism with a sentimental and millennial vocabulary, practiced eulogists made the dead "great men" epitomize the cause of national unity, as they paternalistically and pantheistically gazed down on their successors from heaven.

Franklin, who died first, in 1790, was eulogized as the radiant "Sun," illuminating America with his creative genius. The disembodied inventor and diplomat was regarded as the nation's spirit. But Washington, who died in 1799, was the one true patriarchal father in this cosmology. Eulogized as transcendent and flawless, the real (flawed) Washington became in death the "savior" and mythic body of the nation. "His deeds are immortal," assured future jurist Joseph Story in 1800. "They live in the heart of his country; and his country lives but to celebrate them."

Adams and Jefferson, by a miraculous double apotheosis—each died on the fiftieth anniversary of independence, July 4, 1826—constituted a different legacy. Cast as mere humans—less than divine—in public speeches and sermons, they announced the end of the Revolutionary age and summoned nostalgic feelings for its disappearance. At his death in 1845, Jackson was domesticated, called a good neighbor, good husband, and solid citizen. Attempts were made to link the controversial ex-president to the worthy Washington; but unlike the case of former rivals Adams and Jefferson, the fiercely partisan personality of Andrew Jackson could not be regenerated to symbolize national harmony, thus demonstrating the trials of the Union in the decades leading to the Civil War.

Satire, eulogy, and the early American novel all manipulated emotions for political ends. In "The Politics of Tears," Julia Stern focuses on the obsession with death and taboo sex that flowed through sentimental fiction produced in the 1790s. A democratic body of mourners paid homage to the heroine of Susanna Rowson's popular novel *Charlotte Temple* (1791/1794). They came to the tomb of "poor Charlotte" on lower Broadway, in New York City, for decades. Seduced, abandoned, dying in childbirth, the fictional Charlotte was given an actual gravesite at Trinity Church, transforming an "imagined community of bereavement" into a real one. Early American readers, Stern claims, "lusted after death" and were drawn to the newly created "fetish" of the perfect female victim. Insofar as men, as well as women, responded to Rowson's novel, they found a means to define national identity through collective sympathy.

Incest was a dominant motif in William Hill Brown's *Power of Sympathy* (1789). Victims die either from "too much feeling" or from unnatural desires. A brother and sister—the upper-class Harrington and orphaned Harriot—unknowingly share the same father. They meet and fall in love. What at first appears to be an egalitarian "love match" later proves deadly; upon learning the truth of their paternity, Harriot falls ill and dies, and Harrington commits suicide, unable to live without his sister-lover. In stark contrast to *Charlotte Temple*, no democratic mourners gather for Harrington. His "transgressive" act of incestuous passion is rebuked; his death becomes a reminder that classes in the new republic remain, as Stern puts it, "relatively impermeable."

Perfect fathers and perfect victims led to the construction of two versions of the body politic. The male founders infused the language of statecraft with a patriotic glow of immortality. The state genealogy, emanating from larger-than-life heroes, inspired awe and nostalgia, and most importantly, a faith in the nation's permanence. Sacralized fathers passed on the "bequest" of democratic rule to their political sons, insuring masculine authority. On the other hand, the social body of the state, constituted by common feelings and shared sympathies, found an odd solace in a collective fascination with dead women. "Stolen innocence" evoked the fear of sexual transgression and the peril faced by unprotected women. Given too much freedom—or too little—women in America were trapped in a suffocating environment, where the act of choosing a husband or lover might be their last. In that sense, political liberty could prove as mortally dangerous as political tyranny.

In contrast, dismemberment represented sheer power devoid of sympathy or grief. As Franklin, in his design of "Magna Britannia," understood, the state or nation could be feminized as a passive object of conquest. Transformed into a mute, immobile, mutilated corpse, the female body fell prey to the aggressiveness of state power and the invasive male gaze. But when women endangered the state by demanding political rights, they became "fiery-Frenchified Dames," in the words of the prolific Federalist editor William Cobbett, promoting factionalism. As "monsters in human shape," devouring mothers and castrating machines (like "Dame Guillotine") threatened the generative principle itself.

The culture of death was visual, emotional, and deeply psychological in all of its political discourses. Disembodied in the sublime prose of eulogists, death was also displaced onto grotesque satirical projections. It wafted uneasily over imaginary communities of bereavement, confusedly celebrated dying Indians, and inspired brutal new possibilities through technological wonders like the guillotine. Mourning was the most visual encounter with death: the deceased were lowered into their graves as tears flowed, and loved ones remembered the dead by visiting cemeteries and reading gravestone inscriptions. Just as the last gaze upon the corpse was a potent memory, dismembered bodies, unrecognized by loved ones, conveyed a powerful image of social disorder. In the political vocabulary of the early republic, tears were the soothing balm for emotional wounds, while memory sutured a fragmented Anglo-American culture. New party divisions threatened the life of a republic conceived and sustained through a language of—to quote from Jefferson's First Inaugural Address—"harmony and affection."

In Part III, "Physical Remains," Michael Meranze, Matthew Dennis, and Douglas R. Egerton address the contested meanings of actual remains: bones, ashes, and the dismembered body parts of rebellious slaves. In "Major André's Exhumation," Meranze elucidates the diplomatic struggle that took place over a forty-year period. In 1780, in the middle of the American Revolution, John André was hanged in New York as a spy, by order of General George Washington. Though liked and respected by his captors, the genteel prisoner submitted to the noose when he might have been shot instead—the way a gentleman met his end in this era. Four decades after this "spectacle of bodily suffering and dishonor," André's remains were reclaimed by the British government; he persisted as a symbol of lost civility— lost once amid the violence of the Revolutionary world and, once again lost, in the minds of the well-bred and exacting English, to the unrefined character of nineteenth-century Americans.

In 1821, the year the British consul in New York exhumed André's body and returned it for reburial at Westminster Abbey, James Fenimore Cooper published his novel *The Spy*, revisiting André's story. Cooper links the fates of General Washington, Major André (as the character Henry Wharton), and Harvey Birch, who represents those responsible for capturing the fated officer behind enemy lines in civilian dress. Cooper makes Birch a model democrat, validating "plebian patriotism." Birch operates clandestinely; he sacrifices his name and endangers his life for the good of his country. With Washington's secret support, he saves Wharton's life several times, figuratively erasing a haunting memory and polishing Washington's tarnished past—the real André was condemned by the real Washington.

In the real world of 1821, the British consul encountered those he termed "noisy" American patriots at the site of André's erstwhile grave in Tappan, New York. Though four decades had elapsed, he could not rid his mind of images of André's original captors, rude democrats all. Elsewhere, the return of André's remains summoned forth tears of international reconciliation. A shared sympathy for the dead bound the hearts of the men and women of worth on both sides of the Atlantic, no longer enemies.

In "Patriotic Remains," Matthew Dennis examines American bones in historical relief: as sacred relics, curious artifacts, and sometimes, worthless trash. He compares the way white settlers viewed Indian mounds with the rather different treatment of the bones of Revolutionary War sailors who ended their days aboard British prison ships in Wallabout Bay, off the coast of New York. In the process, Dennis discovers how the Catholic practice of preserving relics was adapted for democratic political purposes.

The Indian burial mounds of the southern and western Mississippi River watershed provoked an early debate over national origins. Rather than acknowledge the "work of Indians," American investigators of the late eighteenth and early nineteenth centuries transformed these sacred artifacts into evidence of a glorious lost race akin to the ancient Hebrews. As America's classical ruins, the mounds became sacred land, and civilizing white settlers saw themselves as rightful heirs; in this way, the vanishing Indians lost all claim to their land and their past.

At first, the sailors' bones fared no better. Buried in sand off Brooklyn, patriot prisoners' remains washed ashore, causing the poet Philip Freneau to mourn their "mean tombs." His politically charged poem of 1781 did not stir any action until 1799, when Washington's death became a partisan issue in New York. High Federalists hoped to build a grand monument to the fallen leader, and laboring Democratic-Republicans countered with a call to "bury the relicks of our brethren." Nine years later, the Tammany Society organized a fund, orchestrated a grand procession, and built a "tomb for the martyred brave." In time, patriotic feeling for the anonymous sailors waned, and the tomb was forgotten. Like the Indian mounds, Dennis concludes, "these patriotic dead were overrun by the tread of encroaching urban pioneers." Jefferson had famously written that "the earth belongs in usufruct to the living," contesting one generation's legal right to bind another. In at least this sense, Jefferson was right: the dead can be refashioned by each succeeding generation as symbolic battles rage over bones, the landscape, and the power to dictate national memory.

Douglas R. Egerton provides a very different perspective on the legal and spiritual rights to the dead. In "A Peculiar Mark of Infamy," he demonstrates how white southern masters resorted to the "terrifying logic" of judicial dismemberment to discipline the bodies and souls of their slaves. Many kinds of torture were practiced quite commonly in the eighteenth century, including brandings, burning, the amputation of limbs, whippings, and castration. Rebellious slaves who engaged in conspiracy and insurrection posed the greatest challenge. Masters knew that public executions could be turned into displays of defiance. This was case when Denmark Vesey met his fate in 1822. White observers noted that he and his allies faced death "with the heroic fortitude of Martyrs." Slave owners, therefore, sought to use dismemberment as a form of retribution beyond the grave. Already familiar with the English tradition of beheading traitors and aware of certain African religious traditions, they understood that dismemberment was a fate worse than death to slaves: the deceased would be denied an afterlife, unable to protect family left behind, and forced to wander the earth for a ghostly eternity.

The three essays that comprise "Physical Remains" independently demonstrate how ars moriendi, the art of dying, took on a distinctly different quality during times of war or rebellion. Those normally seen as outcasts—prisoners of war, spies, and slaves—could assume a new identity at death; the politically invisible might acquire national significance through heroic martyrdom. In these essays, the language of stoicism is significant, too. Physical grace under extreme pain evidences the power of the human will in facing and conquering the terror of death.

The final section of this book, Part IV, "After Life," explores whether death is the great equalizer in American culture. In "Immortal Messengers," Elizabeth Reis examines the popularity of angels in American religious life. She begins with the Puritans, who seemed to need the devil more than they needed angels. Reis explains why angels rarely appeared to seventeenth-century colonists, especially women. Rejecting the Catholic tradition of female mystics, Cotton Mather confidently asserted in 1696 that, "if ever an Age for Angelical Apparitions shall come, no question but men, and *not women only* will be honoured with their Visage."

In the eighteenth century, the evangelical fervor of the Great Awakening enabled the faithful to employ angelic messengers in spreading the gospel. Less mainstream sects, like the Shakers, found that angel sightings could be used to test the faith of followers. While early nineteenth-century theologians sought to curb the rise of heavenly communications, denying that any biblical evidence existed for female angels, the images associated with divine messengers had already changed: no longer invisible, not necessarily male in form, talking, writing, and touching the living, angels became a permanent fixture in the religious iconography of American culture.

" 'In the Midst of Life we are in Death' " is an examination of ordinary diarists and letter writers in antebellum New York state, tracing their efforts and energies in seeking the comfort of a more sympathetic, sentimentalized religious experience. Nicholas Marshall takes careful note of the disease environment—the growing prospect of early death among a traveling population—and finds that men and women turned to religion to ease their pain, save their relatives, and ensure that they reconstituted their families and friends in heaven "where parting is no more." In the same way that other Americans turned to angels to aid in communicating with dead relatives, Marshall's diarists gave in to comforting visions of heaven. Sectarian divisions ended, too, as many of those seeking comfort routinely attended several denominational churches.

Washington Irving ruminated about death, incorporated death into his most popular stories, and devotedly attended to the establishment of Sleepy Hollow Cemetery. In "The Romantic Landscape," Thomas G. Connors recreates the close connection in Irving's life between romantic legend and a sentimentalized landscape of the dead. After traveling in Europe, visiting medieval ruins and rural cemeteries, Irving returned to New York, where he transformed his Sunnyside home into a pastoral retreat and the Hudson River vista into a shrine to the memory of his family. Integrating architecture and nature, bringing new life to a fictionalized world, he created a sentimental geography all his own. Death, for Irving, was a nostalgic return to the innocence of childhood and to a simpler, uncorrupted American past.

There are obvious, and some not so obvious, connections between chapters. The obvious include Stevens's and Dennis's common interest in the "vanishing Indian" phenomenon in American history, and the recurrence of horrific mutilations and dismemberment themes in the work of Cohen, Isenberg, and Egerton. The well-published Puritan Cotton Mather appears in Stevens, Wells, and Reis; the multifaceted Benjamin Franklin relates to the different themes in the essays of Isenberg, Burstein, and Stern. Meranze and Connors find richness in Washington Irving's New York; Marshall travels a bit farther up the Hudson River to encounter more ordinary folk. Thus the four conceptual sections separating essays do not necessarily preclude the commingling of subjects.

There are other compelling connections. To a remarkable degree, early American culture reinvented some rejected Catholic practices in the service of a Protestant-dominated world. In several of the essays in this collection, Catholicism looms in the background. Stevens shows how Puritan missionaries contrasted their noble ideals to the brutal treatment Indians suffered at the hands of Spanish and Catholic explorers. Cohen proves that a literature of horror, conceived through Puritan propaganda, was used to vilify Irish Catholics and remove a "papist" monarch from the throne of England. Dennis reveals how artifacts became relics, using a Catholic religious tradition to advance a Protestant national heritage. Anti-Catholic sentiment also informed Francophobic satire in the Federalists' response to the French Revolution, and even Washington Irving saw fit to caricature the Irish laborers in his neighborhood. Yet angels and ruins, medieval religious symbols, found their way easily into popular religious culture.

Americans were part of a larger Western tradition, and so death was never a uniformly American experience. As literary sentimentalism in America had English and French roots, so, too, did its powerful corollaries, pleasing melancholy and grisly horror. The controversy over Major André's remains revealed that the British and Americans spoke the same language of sympathy, despite the deep divide excited by war and revolution. The terrifying logic of dismemberment also connected the Old World and the

New; and as Douglas Egerton notes, the dissected corpse of the rebellious slave related back to English fears as well as to African religious belief.

A fascination with death continued throughout the nineteenth century. Victorian Americans preserved the memory of their dead children in photograph albums. During and after the Civil War, soldiers' journals were maintained, recording hopes and fears up to the anguished moment of death. To this day, the mass media manipulates emotions with images of starving children, AIDS victims, and war-torn villages, creating what has been called "compassion fatigue" among the American public. Debates over euthanasia continue to be framed in terms of the "good death," while exotic images of the undead, vampires and zombies, offer a "regression fantasy" of eventual rebirth. The gendering of death persists as well: perfect female victims abound in the news and in movies, and heroic sacrifices are still imagined primarily as a rite of passage for the stoic male.

Honoring the dead continues as a national tradition, as does the gruesome task of recovering human remains and converting them into relics. Three weeks after the World Trade Center tragedy, New York Mayor Rudolph Guiliani announced that victims' families would each receive a specially manufactured, decorative wooden urn containing ashes taken from the sacred site. Despite cultural transitions, old themes are reappropriated; echoes of the American past tell us that in certain ways, though time advances, the human condition changes only very slowly, if at all.

Part I
Mortality for the Masses

Chapter 1
The Christian Origins of the Vanishing Indian

Laura M. Stevens

They are wasting like the morning dew.
—*Eleazar Wheelock (1768)*

The history of the United States is a history of one nation's construction and many native peoples' deaths. Much of American culture is a meditation on this double-edged fact. The fascination with Indians can be seen, then, as a long eulogy, voicing the combined guilt and relief of self-absorbed mourners made wealthy by an unloved relative's death. From James Fenimore Cooper's 1826 novel *Last of the Mohicans* to Kevin Costner's 1990 film *Dances with Wolves*, the nonindigenous peoples of America have remained riveted to the spectacle of indigenous people passing away.[1]

Many of the qualities and images considered essentially "American"— freedom, aggression, virtue, the frontier—have found expression through reference to American Indian deaths. Michael Rogin has argued that "conquering the Indian symbolized and personified the conquest of the American difficulties, the surmounting of the wilderness. . . . Not the Indians alive, then, but their destruction, symbolized the American experience."[2] America, as a territory or a culture, would hardly exist without visions of Indian death.

As the most telling evidence of manifest destiny, dying Indians are also vehicles of affect directed toward varied ideological ends. That is to say, they have been central to nineteenth-century sentimental literature, to Jacksonian politics, and more recently to environmental movements.[3] Suggesting "an uncompromising power they deemed benevolent," Americans catalyzed the process, described by Andrew Burstein, through which "Sentiment and coercive power, long seen in opposition, merged into the attractive combination that sentimental democrats have paraded at home and abroad ever since."[4] The impact of this image has extended beyond the United States, influencing the conflicting emotions of other imperialists. Dying Indians are one manifestation of what Renato Rosaldo has termed imperialist nostalgia, "where people mourn the passing of what they have transformed," so that "putatively static savage societies become a stable reference point for defining (the felicitous progress of) civilized identity."[5] Standing for conquest, images of dying Indians have helped to rationalize aggression, absolving responsibility through sad depictions of inevitable demise.[6]

The link between Indians and death is so fixed that texts of late twentieth-century popular culture have needed only to display Indians to induce melancholy. Consider the "Keep America Beautiful" public service commercials on pollution in the 1970s, which featured the weathered face of Iron Eyes Cody in feathered headdress, shedding a single tear. Consider also the Indian in Oliver Stone's 1994 film *Natural Born Killers*. He is the only person whom the ultraviolent Mickey and Mallory regret murdering. His ghost haunts his killers, creating rare feelings of remorse.[7] Like the house in Steven Spielberg's *Poltergeist* (1982), America is haunted by the Indian burial grounds on which it is built, the same graveyards upon which Philip Freneau, "the Poet of the American Revolution," built much of his literary reputation.[8]

Why have Americans so persistently described the deaths of native peoples? Why this convergence of satisfaction and sorrow, of inevitability and guilt? How is it that carnage comes to be rendered with such affective control? Why are Indians, especially perishing ones, so convenient to the stories and longings of America? While much scholarship has pointed out the role that the vanishing Indian played in assertions of manifest destiny, this provides only an incomplete explanation. In particular, we need to consider the earliest manifestations of concern with Indian mortality, that which is found in missionary writings.[9] Although they were not nearly as successful as their French and Spanish counterparts at converting Indians, English missionaries wrote a great deal about their desire to save the souls of America's natives. They and their supporters, who lived in Britain as well as America, produced large numbers of sermons, journals, letters, and fund-raising tracts in the colonial period. While many of these texts reached only a small group of readers, enough of them enjoyed a broad enough audience—through broadsides, extracts in newspapers, and sermons—to affect the ways the British felt about American Indians.

Missionaries have given us some of our earliest elegies to the vanishing Indian. Thoroughgood Moore, a missionary from the Society for the Propagation of the Gospel in Foreign Parts, wrote of the Iroquois in 1705, "They waste away, and have done ever since our arrival among them (as they say themselves) like snow against the sun, so that very probably forty years hence there will scarce be an Indian seen in our America."[10] Perhaps no commentator has improved upon this simple reflection. Missionaries did more than mourn the Indians' passing, however. They thought themselves in a race to save heathens from a damnation that would be forever sealed by death. In their depictions of dying Indians, the early missionaries dwelt mostly on the loss of unconverted souls, or on the victory of the saved. A preoccupation with the contrasting tropes of waste and conservation guided their descriptions of death, as they set in rhetorical opposition the slaughter of heathens and the hopeful prospects of converted souls. Two genres of writing about death, war narratives and death scenes, adopted the same contrast. The first described horrible carnage in words of sorrow, tinged with angry impotence at the failure to recover lost souls; the second (drawing on the tradition of ars moriendi, or the art of dying) combined a more pleasing melancholy with a sense of evangelical accomplishment.

Missionaries shaped Anglo-Americans' attachment to the vanishing Indian by juxtaposing virtuous Protestant colonists and greedy Catholic ones. They encouraged their readers to think of British colonization as a recuperative enterprise that would compensate for the destructive tendencies of Indians and Catholic colonists alike. They proudly distinguished scenes of blood spilling over the land from bucolic images of English farmers laboring alongside Christian Indians. By developing an extensive catalogue of exemplary Indian deaths to advertise their successes in America, English missionaries further prompted their readers to attach profound meaning (even joy) to a more pleasing construction of Indian death. By the late eighteenth century, however, missionaries had come to defend their failure to convert sufficient numbers of Indians by attributing Indian mortality rates to what they considered to be a depraved existence. The sum of these gestures encouraged readers to transform the destructive impulses of war into the constructive impulses of evangelism, marking the dying Indian as the symbol of both impulses.

This is the beginning of that peculiar portrayal: dying Indians viewed by Anglo-Americans as a phenomenon laden with rich but imprecise significance. It is in these texts that we first see a tension between the desire to save Indians and fascination with their demise. Counterintuitive though this idea may seem, the Europeans most concerned with saving Indians (or at least with saving their souls) taught subsequent generations of Americans to feel a pleasing melancholy at the sight of Indian death. Only missionaries could have performed this complex and largely unintended task. For only Europeans trying to convert the Indians could have brought a particular set of preoccupations to bear on the spectacle of native demise: a wish to make conquest an act of kindness, a need to scrutinize converts for signs of redemption, and a belief in the Christian paradox of eternal life through death. Only Christian missionaries could have taught us to read Indian death as a sign of the benevolent cultivation of America.

It is well known that the idea of Protestant mission helped English colonists claim a higher moral ground over the Spanish, who had been vilified in translations of writings by Bartolomé de Las Casas, the Dominican missionary and early advocate of native rights.[11] Protestant propaganda conveniently cast the English as benevolent foils to the Spanish and provided a rhetoric to alleviate qualms about the violence they perpetrated in the English colonies. The story of Spanish brutality—what came to be called the Black Legend—relied on a contrast between frugality and waste.[12]

By "waste," I mean a general sense of dispersal and unnecessary loss: of objects, lands or people discarded without purpose, thrown away with unused potential left intact.[13] For the English this term described the unenclosed and (to their eyes) uncultivated lands of America. It also referred to the needless loss of life that they identified with Indians and Catholics alike. English writings linked the cruelty of Spanish conquerors to their prodigality and greed. As *Tears of the Indians* (1656), a translation of Las Casas's *Brevissima relacion*, says of Jamaica, "So lavish were the swords of the bloud of these poor souls, scarce two hundred more remaining; the rest perished without the least knowledge of God."[14] The text juxtaposes the Americas' abundant population and agricultural production before the conquest, with the countless deaths directly caused by the Spanish. Mexico was "a pleasant Country, now swarming with multitudes of People, but immediately all depopulated, and drown'd in a Deluge of Bloud." In his preface, the translator quotes from scripture to emphasize the loss of countless souls who could have been saved from Hell:

Never had we so just cause to exclaim in the words of the Prophet *Jeremiah; O that our heads were waters, and our eyes fountains of tears, that we might weep* for the Effusion of so much Innocent Blood . . . by reason of the cruel Slaughters and Butcheries of the Jesuitical Spaniards, perpetrated upon so many Millions of poor innocent Heathens, who having onely the light of Nature, not knowing their Saviour Jesus Christ, were sacrificed to the Politick Interest and Avarice of the wicked Spaniards.

The Spanish were thus cruel and poor managers of colonial wealth. Greedy for gold, they destroyed a fortune in farming revenues, not to mention a rich harvest in souls. The only verifiable product of their venture was an "effusion of . . . innocent blood." The English accordingly met this massacre with a fountain of tears, offering a compensatory outpouring of emotion to the sight of slaughter.

The English were self-promoting, asserting that they did not bear the "lavish swords" of the Spaniards, but rather frugal instruments of husbandry and trade. While it surely damaged America's ecology and indigenous economy, the plantation-style colonialism that the English practiced enabled them to make this claim.[15] Their devotion to Christian mission followed similar logic. Importing the gospel and cultivating converts, even as their exports generated a luxury economy in England, they showed themselves to be caretakers of America. Protecting the Indians from the Spanish, they also preserved Indians from the internecine wars and intemperate appetites that, they felt, would shorten an indigenous existence. They were saving the Indians from themselves.[16]

That Puritan settlers combined their benevolent ideal with a deuteronomic vision of divine retribution, seeing Indians as trials sent by God to his covenanted people, necessarily threatened this easy distinction.[17] While some proponents of mission expanded their rhetoric of husbandry to protest the wartime atrocities of English colonists, others marked violence as divinely ordained. Drawing on the Hebrew Bible, they combined narratives of conquest with descriptions of a promised land. The slaughter of native peoples was detached from English agency and elided with images of a well-tended earth. A strong rationale for Indians' pain and suffering was in place.

While the English caused immense destruction in America, they were able to depict themselves as the remedy to loss. Eventually, native death came to be seen as the sad but inevitable by-product of progress, and Indians were blamed for failing to use their land's resources. In this way, Indian death could occur anonymously, as a result of a commercial economic model. The inscrutable will of God became an invisible hand, granting wealth to what would become the United States. Diseases spread, wars broke out, and Indians simply withered away from poverty, drink, or sadness.

The emphasis on husbandry is a particularly revealing feature of Christian tracts, which provided the English with a rhetoric that accommodated their aggression, converting a deuteronomic vision into an evangelical mandate. *New England's First Fruits* (the title itself marks colonialism as cultivation) expresses both a desire to save Indians and satisfaction at their ultimate demise. The earliest of the "New England Company" or "Eliot" Indian tracts, which raised money in England for efforts to convert local indigenous peoples, *New England's First Fruits* is an obvious attempt to meet divinely willed Indian death with a nurturing evangelical response. Describing missionary projects and the founding of Harvard College while justifying the Pequot war, this tract relies on scriptural precursors to generate a mix of sympathy and aggression.[18]

It begins by advertising New England's, and seeking England's, pity for "those poore *Indians* . . . adoring the *Divell* himselfe for their *GOD*." In desperate need of help, the Indians were said to exist in a state of pain and spiritual exile. Images of souls "swarm[ing]" toward Hell are matched in drama only by descriptions of the colonists' desire to save Indian souls. The tract expresses a powerful purpose: "The Lord . . . hath given us some testimony of his gracious acceptance of our poore endeavours towards them, and of our groanes to himselfe for mercy upon those miserable Soules (the very Ruines of Mankind) there amongst us; our very bowels yerning within us to see them goe downe to Hell by swarmes without remedy." The earnest tone of this passage marks New England as a colony of compassion, emblematized by the "bowels" of feeling that meet the spectacle of damnation. This religious compassion helps the text assert the settlement's peaceful nature: "At our entrance upon the Land, it was not with violence and intrusion, but free and faire, with their consents." Fair treatment had had a positive effect, so that the "humanity of the English towards them doth much gaine upon them." The closing comments of the tract's first part mirror its opening, asking readers "to pitty those poore Heathen that are bleeding to death to eternal death." Wielding their sermons and prayers, the Puritans tended the fields and souls of America. They took what was fallow, and made it fruitful.[19]

In spite of this show of compassion, native death was portrayed as a sign of God's favor. Even the eradication of whole villages through disease and the massacre of the Pequots were seen as acceptable outcomes: "Thus farre hathe the good hand of God favoured our beginnings," the text proclaims,

In sweeping away great multitudes of the Natives by the small Pox a little before we went thither, that he might make room for us there. . . .

[In] that Warre which we made against them Gods hand from heaven was so manifested, that a very few of our men in a short time pursued through the Wildernesse, flew and took prisoners about 1400 of them, even all they could find, to the great terrour and amazement of all the Indians to this day: so that the name of the Pequits (as of Amaleck) is blotted out from under heaven.[20]

The peaceful habitation of America was possible only because God "swe[pt] away great multitudes" of Indians. And when conflict arose with the Pequots, God saw to it that they experienced utter defeat.

Even as the English boasted about their treatment of the Indians, and even as they expressed their desire to save them, they took spiritual comfort from indigenous death. This affective tension is possible because the text places a missionary mandate within a deuteronomic vision of a covenantal relationship with God. It claims that the Puritans have eradicated the Pequots from the Promised Land, just as in Exodus 17:13, Joshua "mowed down the people of Amalek with the edge of his sword." As the historian Alfred A. Cave has observed, "The inner logic of Puritan ideology required that the Saints be beleaguered and besieged in this world, and Indians could play the role of foes of God's own people quite admirably." If Indians were God's punishment for disloyalty, their destruction marked a renewed blessing. Of course, this interpretation exposes the central problem with the English claim to be benevolent colonists. They removed themselves as responsible actors by hiding behind a shield: their adherence to the will of God. Converting Indians was also important for practical reasons: "else these poor Indians will certainly rise up against us." Christian mission was the surest way of saving the English, whether or not it saved the Indians.[21]

As even this one text suggests, the bodies of dying Indians have had an impact on the literary consciousness which is as forceful as it is imprecise. As they elicited pity for heathens, missionaries shaped this pity, investing it (intentionally or not) with political meaning. They detached death from its cause, marking it as an unintended result of a well-meaning enterprise. The bodies of dying Indians by this means perform the function that Elaine Scarry ascribes to the injured bodies of war: legitimation. "Though it lacks interior connection to the issues," she writes, "wounding is able to open up a source of reality that can give the issue force and holding power."[22] The dying Indian comes to signify the predetermined progress of a nation. As in any war, "Injury becomes the extension or continuation of something else that is itself benign."[23] In this case that something is a desire to save souls, expressed through an abhorrence of waste.

The deuteronomic treatment of Indians pervaded many Puritan writings in the colonial period. Cotton Mather's sermon *Humiliations Follow'd with Deliverances* (1697), for example, introduces a victorious captivity narrative within this framework. Mather describes the experience of Hannah Duston, who was captured by Indians after seeing her newborn child killed. One night when the Indians were asleep, Duston, her nurse, and a third captive grabbed some hatchets and slaughtered their captors. Mather compares Duston to Jael, who hammered a tent peg into the head of Sisera, the commander of Israel's enemy forces (Judges 4:17–22):

[T]hey all furnishing themselves with *Hatchets* for the purpose, they struck such Home Blowes, upon the Heads of their *Sleeping Oppressors*, that e're they could any of them struggle into any effectual resistance, *at the Feet* of those poore Prisoners, *They bowed, they fell, they lay down; at their feet they bowed, they fell; where they bowed, there they fell down Dead.*[24]

Rather than obscuring the brutality of this event, Mather revels in the scene's savage excess. The repetition and spondaic heaviness of his retelling invest the act with the momentousness of epic. Mather sounds less like a preacher than a bard describing a battle with Grendel or Goliath. Like many writers of war propaganda, he demonizes the enemy and enjoys its utter extirpation.

This rhetorical brutality makes more sense when we see that it draws upon the parts of Deuteronomy that establish Israel's covenant through the enemy's destruction. Deuteronomy commands that, in most war, Israel should practice restraint to avoid loss: it should enslave survivors, take booty, and preserve the trees of a conquered city (Deut. 20:10–22). When the Israelites invade Canaan, however, Moses commands them to wage total war, purifying the Promised Land by purging it: "You must utterly destroy them . . . and show no mercy. . . . You shall save alive nothing that breathes" (Deut. 7:4; 10:16). Mather's description of the scalping is gratuitous and cruel, but in the excess of the event's retelling lies its discursive necessity. This excess signifies the Indians' eradication, echoing the deuteronomic command. Like Moses (Deut. 8:11–20), Mather uses violence to call for humility and victory: "If we now did Humble our selves throughout the Land, who can say, whether the Revenges on the Enemy, thus Exemplified, would not proceed much rather unto the Quick Extirpation, of those Bloody and Crafty men."[25] As in *New England's First Fruits*, slaughtered Indians suggest God's favor.[26]

Viewing this text alongside Mather's missionary work highlights the complexities of the treatment of Indians. The violence that Mather embellishes in 1697 results in the same loss of Indian life that he, his father Increase Mather, and Nehemiah Walker describe a few years later in a letter to the president of the New England Company: "The number of Indians in this land is not comparable to what it was fifty years ago. The hand of God has very strangely wasted them; and the war which they began upon the English in the year 1675, hastened a strange desolation upon whole nations of them."[27] Having rejoiced at their slaughter, Mather and his coauthors now marvel at their near extinction. The deaths that the English propagate later come to provoke their sadness.

The treatment of death as waste in the Puritan texts foreshadows later missionaries' depictions of vanishing Indians. In 1766 the evangelical minister Eleazar Wheelock, who had founded an Indian charity school in the 1740s and who later founded Dartmouth College, juxtaposed conversion and destruction. He wrote, "It looks to me more & more as though God designs to make a Short work with the Natives, that they will soon be christianised, or destroyed. If they will not embrace the Gospel it is likely in a few Generations more, there will be no more an Opportunity to Shew our Charity towards their naked Starving Bodies or perishing Souls."[28] Yet, even as he urged his readers in 1771 to fund more missionaries, in order to "save the poor savages from that temporal and eternal destruction which is so evidently just at their door," Wheelock explained that he was redirecting his attention to the education of English students. This change had become necessary in order to "perpetuate the usefulness of [Dartmouth] when there shall be no Indians left upon the continent to partake of the [school's] benefit, if that should ever be the case."[29] His anticipatory mourning does not reflect a desire to improve the Indians' chance for survival, so much as to seize an opportunity to exert Christian charity before that opportunity disappears.

As their writings suggest, and as historians have shown, Cotton Mather and Eleazar Wheelock were not selfless in their expressions of sorrow for dying Indians. Their responses masked interests in the security of their communities and, at least in Wheelock's case, financial gain. These descriptions of vanishing Indians are part reality but also part wish fulfillment in that they displace English aggression onto Catholic, Indian, or divine agents. Not all missionaries deflected responsibility for Indian deaths from the English, however. John Eliot and Daniel Gookin, who oversaw the Praying Indians of Puritan New England, risked the wrath of their fellow colonists when they protested the Indians' treatment during King Philip's War.[30] Moravians such as John Heckewelder also publicly condemned the violence that their Indian converts suffered. "Here they were now murdered!" he wrote in 1820 in his *Narrative of the Mission of the United Brethren,* "Together with the Children!—whose tender years—innocent countenances, and Tears, made no impression on these pretended White Christians: were all butchered with the rest."[31] Heckewelder exposed the gratuitous brutality of settlers who would slaughter pacifist Delawares.

Even those missionaries who protested English atrocities, however, unwittingly furthered the trope of the vanishing Indian and the aggression it legitimated. Throughout the colonial period they devoted much of their energy to recording the deaths of the Indians to whom they ministered. Texts such as John Eliot's *Dying Speeches of Several Indians* (1685), John Cripps's *True Account of the Dying Words of Ockanickon, an Indian King* (1682), and Experience Mayhew's *Indian Converts: or, some Account of the Lives and Dying Speeches of a Considerable Number of the Christianized Indians of Martha's Vineyard, in New-England* (1727), deal specifically with American Indian death.[32] They also share a great deal with the accounts that Catholic missionaries, especially the Jesuits, wrote of Christian Indians' deaths. Through their calm demeanor and pious speech, these Indians provided readers with a collection of exemplary deaths to complement a European tradition of dying speeches, hagiographies, funeral sermons, and advice manuals outlining the importance of a "good" death.[33] Texts of the ars moriendi, or the art of dying, encouraged readers to see death as a final test for which they must prepare themselves, and to understand others' deaths as scenes that should be read for signs of that person's salvation or damnation.

Erik Seeman has observed that in the majority of the missionaries' accounts, the dying Indian is almost indistinguishable from a European Christian. Seeman has divided these deathbed accounts into "model" ones, which exemplify the European conventions of a good death, and "unorthodox" ones, disrupting European conventions with indigenous elements.[34] As the preponderance of "model" deaths suggests, most missionaries sought to integrate their Indian converts into a Christian paradigm. One of the many texts that Experience Mayhew described in *Indian Converts* was that of the minister Wunnanauhkomun:

[H]e called them all to [his wife and children], and took his Leave of them with Words of Comfort and Counsel; at the same time laying his Hands on each of his Children, and blessing them. Having done this, he immediately began another Prayer, wherein he expressed to *God* his Willingness to leave this World and go to him, which he declared his Hopes that he should, whenever his frail Life ended. And thus resigning up his Spirit to *God* that gave it, he immediately dy'd when his Prayer ended.[35]

Wunnanauhkomun's death reads like an example from an ars moriendi manual. He prepared himself with a life of virtue and charity. Exemplifying the advice given in *The Rules and Exercises of Holy Dying*, he was "careful that he d[id] not admit of any doubt concerning that which he beleeved." "Mingl[ing] the recital of his Creed together with his devotions," he was "especially active about the promises of grace, and the excellent things of the gospel." Rather then expressing regret at being separated from his family, he "intreated the Lord, that the Everlasting Covenant of his Grace might be established with his Wife and Children." He "willingly submitted to [God's] good will," blessed his family, and ended his life with a prayer.[36]

English hegemony was never far from the center of discourse. Missionaries wrote of conversion as a way to save Indians from damnation, but also as a path to survival in their conquerors' world. They wished to mourn them according to Christian traditions and to prove that Indians were as worthy of salvation as any European. They also inspired the English to fund missionary work. Resisting a deuteronomic vision, they used accounts of good deaths to show that the colonization of America could involve benevolence rather than bloodshed. But if conversion projects sought to minimize carnage, they also contributed to a developing sentimental discourse of imperial ownership, which only advanced as Indians died in greater numbers.[37]

The hegemonic implications of the Indian deathbed scene are easy to see in a text such as *New England's First Fruits*, which is littered with Indian corpses as trophies of war. Interspersed with these accounts of vanquished savages are references to one Indian, who "could never be gotten from the English, nor from seeking for their God, [and] . . . died amongst them, leaving some good hopes in their hearts that his soule went to rest." This Indian was Wequash, a Pequot who had defected to the Narragansetts and had played an important role in the Narragansett-English alliance against the Pequots.[38] Supposedly poisoned by other Indians, Wequash not only died in an exemplary state of calm, but he also refused the ministrations of a native powwow and expressed his acquiescence to Christ's will. Finally, "Before he dyed, he did bequeath his Child to the godly care of the English for education and instruction and so yielded up his soule into Christ his hands." The death of Wequash delegitimized the violence of war as it allowed the authors of this text to assert the benevolence of their colonizing project.[39]

Even when scenes of Indian death did not link Christian mission so obviously to conquest, accounts of Indians' good deaths still reinforced a discourse of benevolent domination. The progression from Christian benevolence to overdeterminative imperialist grief offers a striking parallel to the changing modes of criminal punishment Michel Foucault studied in *Discipline and Punish*. During the eighteenth century, he observed, "The body as the major target of penal repression disappeared."[40] As reformers pushed for more merciful forms of execution, the representation of pun-

ishment altered, to strengthen its deterrent goal. This resulted in an ab-
straction of power, the reinforcement of which was grounded in the individual's self-regulation. The symbol of governmental legitimacy was no
longer the body of the condemned, but rather his or her interior. Once
representation of power became more diffuse, it became harder to resist.
Ironically, it was a growing societal desire to alleviate suffering that caused
these changes. Such a shift in emphasis, from damaging the criminal body
to reforming the criminal self, could have emerged only from benevolent
motives, or from a distaste for state-sanctioned slaughter.

A similar process took place in missionaries' treatment of Christian Indians' deaths. An emphasis on its evidentiary value led missionaries to see
death as an emotionally evocative text that should be read for spiritual
signs. The Protestant Reformation had introduced the notion that the moment of death was a template, an event offering diagnostic possibilities for
enhanced understanding. Protestants scoffed at deathbed conversions, but
they remained wary of assuming salvation until the moment of death.[41]
A good death, following a good life, offered the best assurance of preservation from a descent into hell. This function was particularly important for Indians, whose convictions the English had to evaluate in spite of
linguistic and cultural gaps in understanding. In this way, even model accounts of Indian decease differed from good European deaths. Always
worried that their converts might backslide into pagan beliefs, missionaries
tended to view such deaths with relief, as the safe delivery of a soul. As a
result, they encouraged their readers to see the good deaths of Indians as
accomplishments.

Thus when Experience Mayhew published *Indian Converts* to celebrate
the lives of the Wampanoags his family had converted, he prompted his
readers to experience pleasure at the sight of a dying Indian.[42] The ency-
clopedic format in which he presented these deaths, sorting them by gender, age, and vocation, added to the effect by suggesting an inventory of
spiritual products. Mayhew's book borrowed much from Protestant hagiographies and martyrologies, such as Foxe's *Book of Martyrs*.[43] The colonial framework of the text, however, along with its overriding concern with
proving conversion, gives it an added sense of epistemological mastery.
Mayhew proves the heathens' conversions by rendering them transparent
to an English gaze. This is one of the reasons why Mayhew makes the
reader privy to the most intimate information about the Wampanoags,
ranging from details about their bodies to gossip about their marriages.
Besides asserting his reliability, he makes us feel that we have complete access to the Indians: James Nashompait "came in and laid himself on his
Bed; and then turning his Face to the side of the House, and calling on
his God, immediately resigned up his Spirit to him."[44] As they empty themselves to God they also empty themselves to us. This allows for a more complete sense of cultural ownership than violence ever could afford. Granting

his readers an intimate, if formulaic, knowledge of the Indians, Mayhew claims that the English are worthy stewards of America.

Perhaps this is why we sometimes see images of the Christian dying Indian drawn in contrast to the carnage of war. In 1757, Timothy Horsfield, justice of the peace in the Moravian town of Bethlehem, interrupted his usual reports of Indian raids on Pennsylvania's frontier to inform Governor Denny that "the Indian Man John Smalling has deceased." Horsfield's letters were often rushed, as he coped with the urgent circumstances of the Seven Years' War, but he paused to deliver a detailed, if clichéd, account of an Indian convert's good death from smallpox:

Some time before his death he desired one of the Brethren to visit him & speak something to him of our Saviour, he said he Remembered, he had been Baptized by the Brethren, and wished he could feel so in his Heart as he did at that Time, the Brother that visited him Informed me, that he was a real Penitant, and that shortly before his Departure he spoke with much Confidence that he should soon go to Rest. He instructed his wife, his Mother, and Father in Law Geo: Hoys, to leave off the Indian ways, and to hear what the Brethren would tell them of our Saviour.[45]

The authenticity of Horsfield's feeling for the Indian man "Smalling" is easy to sense, given the connections between the Moravian community he oversaw and the Delawares they had converted. But for him to communicate this death in such detail to Pennsylvania's governor, and in a separate letter to Benjamin Franklin and other members of the Pennsylvania Assembly, is quite remarkable.[46]

Most likely, Horsfield disseminated Smalling's deathbed speech as evidence of the loyalty of the Moravian Indians, who already had been accused by panicky colonists of supporting enemy Indians' attacks. But the intense emotional component in his communication projects something more. As he speaks out against the carnage of war, Horsfield is asking the governor to share in his mourning for the dying Indian. Denny and Franklin are drawn into this moment of cheerful mourning, asked to commemorate the Christian death of one Indian even as they offer bounties for the scalps of countless others.[47] If those overseeing the defense of Pennsylvania's frontier outposts took consolation in an Indian ally's Christian death, it can hardly come as a surprise that the broader Anglo-American culture would soon do the same.

The link between Christian Indians' deaths and the carnage of war is more emotional than logical, but it is not weaker for this fact. Whether authentic or corrupt, missionary sentiment made possible the complex emotions with which Anglo-American readers met the sight of Indian death. Confronted elsewhere with blood and violence, Horsfield and his readers took refuge in the poignancy of a solitary event. In response to the meaninglessness and waste of war, there appeared a vision of peaceful cohabitation and spiritual productivity. Such desirable goals had somehow crystallized in the death of an Indian.

The influence of missionary writings on broader treatments of Indians has been a subtle but palpable one. We do not often find the writers of "dying Indian" poems directly quoting missionaries, nor do we see many soldiers expressing regret that they have not saved more Indian souls. What we do see, however, are texts ranging from the literary to the political that comment on Indian death in ways developed by missionaries. We perceive an apparently self-contradictory logic that gathers its validation from the Christian paradox of life gained through death, as well as from the claim that British colonialism, combined with conversion, could be an act of benevolent recuperation. We also find the tendency to turn the scene of Indian death into a sentimental spectacle, and to meet that spectacle with intense but ineffectual emotion. Missionaries were the ones who assembled the economic and emotional framework that made this possible: the simultaneous sense of loss and gain, and the paired feelings of pleasure and sadness that Anglo-American audiences have so long expressed at the sight of a dying Indian. Even as it manifests a fascination with waste, Indian death produces moral achievement and conveys narrative closure. Death amounts to emotional and spiritual production, associating English settlement with cultivation and care.

This immersion in a missionary vision was pervasive enough that elements of it are present in texts by antireligious writers. Philip Freneau ridiculed both Indians and their missionaries in "The Indian Convert," but in his treatment of Indian death he reveals the influence of missionary writings. *The Rising Glory of America,* first written with his Princeton classmate Hugh Henry Brackenridge in 1771, is instructive:

But why, to prompt your tears, should we resume,
The tale of *Cortez,* furious chief, ordained
With Indian blood to dye the sands, and choak,
Famed Mexico, thy streams with dead? . . .
Better these northern realms demand our song,
Designed by nature for the rural reign,
For agriculture's toil.—No blood we shed
For metals buried in a rocky waste.—[48]

Brackenridge and Freneau display sadness at the carnage accompanying colonialism, aligning indigenous Americans and Spanish invaders with waste. *The Rising Glory of America* begins by averting the reader's eye from Mexico, a land where blood flows from corpse-filled streams, staining the barren land. Tears flow in response to this river of blood, but the poet stems both streams by turning our attention to the "northern realms" of America. This is a land of abundance set against the southern "rocky waste" of Spanish greed. It is a place of conservation, a nation where no blood is shed. It is, most of all, a country ordained by nature, not violated and ruined by an invader. Indians—or, more accurately, their bodies— signify these differences and validate the British. The Indians of British America are just as dead as those of Mexico. But instead of bleeding over the earth, they are neatly buried (as if dead only from natural causes) within the "rural reign" of America.

Brackenridge and Freneau implement a missionary logic, transforming native death so that it signifies first waste and then productivity, changing a symbol of loss into one of conservation. The dying Indian is a vehicle for sentiment and a symbol of manifest destiny. Indian deaths occurring under English colonial rule are clean and supportive of the land's continued fertility. The missionary logic responds to converts' deaths with an outpouring of emotion. In texts, it converts loss into literary gain. Though Freneau, a well-known deist, profited little from Christian faith, he and Brackenridge imitated and extended the earlier missionaries' project, so that death songs supercede death, and Indians perish into poetry.

Fifteen years after cowriting this poem, Freneau published a revision of it. As Julie Ellison has noted, most of his revisions substituted new visions of a Pax Americana for a pre-Revolutionary conception of English liberty.[49] The poem's deployment of Indian death, however, remained the same. That the dying Indian could legitimate Freneau's America as easily as it did the young Freneau's and Brackenridge's Britain, proves something else: Indian death is about stoicism and inevitable loss, but it is just as much about the efficient management of wealth. Describing Indian death, it seems, has always been the way to own America.

Chapter 2
Blood Will Out:
Sensationalism, Horror, and the Roots of American Crime Literature

Daniel A. Cohen

> *Horror and fatality have been stalking abroad in all ages.*
> *Why then give a date to this story I have to tell?*
>
> —Edgar Allan Poe, *"Metzengerstein" (1832)*

In a culture preoccupied with the proximity of death, early American readers were particularly fascinated by murders and public executions. Although publications on crime and punishment were consistently popular, they changed dramatically in form and content between the late seventeenth and mid-nineteenth centuries. Most of the earliest publications were Puritan execution sermons, religious works that focused not on the sordid details of crimes and trials but on universal issues of sin and salvation. By the first half of the nineteenth century, however, American crime literature became far more secular, legalistic, and sensationalistic. Coinciding with an upsurge of crime coverage in newspapers, murder publications of this latter period most often took the form of trial reports and criminal biographies or autobiographies. Whether in newspapers or in separate books and pamphlets, treatments of crimes and trials tended to focus far more attention than the earlier sermons on the specific, sometimes shocking, physical details of individual homicides and on the lives and motivations of individual killers.[1]

In *Murder Most Foul: The Killer and the American Gothic Imagination* (1998), cultural historian Karen Halttunen particularly focuses on the latter period. She characterizes the new configuration of murder literature in the early republic as "Gothic," linking it to a mode of fiction popularized during the second half of the eighteenth century, and she argues that these publications were an ironic "response" or "indispensable corollary" to "the modern liberal view of human nature introduced by the Enlightenment"

and to a "revolution" in "humanitarian sensibility." According to Halttunen, the new "Gothic" narratives tended to focus on particular types of
homicides such as mass murders, domestic murders, sex-related murders,
and murders involving claims of insanity. These texts also generally emphasized certain details or motifs, such as the personality and motive of the
killer, the sequence of events leading up to the crime, the precise time and
setting of the murder, the weapon used and specific injuries inflicted, the
pain suffered by the victim, the disposition of the corpse (especially in
cases of mutilation or dismemberment), the execution of the criminal, and
"the reader's role as voyeur to the crime."[2]

Halttunen organizes her "Gothic" themes and motifs into two main categories: "the cult of horror" and "the construction of murder as mystery"
(or, more briefly, "horror" and "mystery"). She claims, in one of her most
provocative formulations, that these "Gothic" elements coalesced into a
new "pornography of violence." Above all, Halttunen emphasizes the
"Gothic" construction of the murderer as an "unnatural" or "subhuman"
monster, a phenomenon she attributes to the ultimate failure of Enlightenment thought to comprehend human evil. "The most important cultural
work performed by the Gothic narrative of murder," she writes, "was its reconstruction of the criminal transgressor from common sinner with whom
the larger community of sinners were urged to identify" into a "moral
monster from whom readers were instructed to shrink with a sense of *horror"* and *"mystery."*[3]

There may be, however, a fatal chronological flaw in Halttunen's characterization of the early nineteenth-century configuration of American
murder literature as a "response" or "corollary" to the "humanitarian" Enlightenment (or to related cultural movements of the late seventeenth and
eighteenth centuries). Most of the major themes and specific motifs that
she describes as constituting a *new* pattern of literature were not only present, but prominent, in popular English murder publications of the early to
mid-seventeenth century—and virtually all of the other elements she describes had appeared by the end of that century. It is difficult to see how
themes and motifs whose popularization largely *predated* the Enlightenment and the humanitarian revolution can be explained as responses or
corollaries to them.[4]

To understand the transformation of American crime literature, it is crucial to recognize the remarkable similarities that exist between seventeenth-
century English murder publications and the pattern of writing and
reporting that emerged in the United States by the early nineteenth century. In light of these similarities, crime literature of the early republic cannot be explained as the ironic by-product of a new "Enlightenment" or
"humanitarian" world view. Rather, the new literary pattern resulted from a
gradual breakdown of exceptional Puritan cultural controls in New England (where almost all of the older execution sermons had appeared)

and a gradual proliferation of American crime publications outside that region. These trends allowed for the emergence, over the course of the eighteenth and early nineteenth centuries, of an alternately moralistic, legalistic, and sensationalistic literature of crime and punishment. However, despite some new elements, American crime publications of the early national and antebellum periods were in many respects strikingly reminiscent of the popular murder publications that had long shocked, entertained, and edified earlier generations of English readers.[5]

As in colonial America, readers in early modern England were endlessly engrossed by murders and other serious crimes. Between 1550 and 1700, English authors and printers produced literally hundreds of publications dealing with capital cases, especially homicides. The literature included pamphlet crime accounts, trial reports (synopses or summaries of judicial proceedings), plays based on real-life criminal cases ("docudramas," to borrow the modern designation), and broadside ballads (short narrative verses printed on a single sheet of paper). This literature varied not only in genre and format, but also in tone and content, including pious, moralistic, legalistic, and sensationalistic elements, often interwoven in individual texts.

A remarkable number of these publications dealt with murders of the types that Halttunen particularly associates with the "Gothic" mode, especially domestic homicides and sex-related killings. That pattern is amply documented in Joseph H. Marshburn's annotated bibliography of early modern crime publications, *Murder and Witchcraft in England, 1550–1640 As Recounted in Pamphlets, Ballads, Broadsides, and Plays* (1971).[6] Of the forty or so murder cases that Marshburn treats in detail, over half were either domestic homicides, sex-related homicides, or both. More specifically, seven featured wives implicated in the murders or attempted murders of their husbands (most acting in collaboration with illicit lovers); four involved husbands who murdered their wives; two featured servants who murdered their masters; and individual cases involved a prostitute who murdered her own infant, a father who killed his two young daughters, a young man who murdered his mother and brother, a father and stepmother who unknowingly murdered the man's long-lost son, a disabled beggar who murdered his lover, a woman who helped murder a man who interfered with her marital plans, an apprentice who murdered his uncle at the behest of a manipulative "strumpet," a prostitute and a male partner who robbed and murdered a series of men by luring them—with the promise of sex—to secluded locations, and a man who hanged himself in romantic despair.[7]

Not only did late sixteenth- and seventeenth-century English crime publications deal with homicide cases of the general types identified by Halttunen with the later "Gothic" mode, but the specific contents of early modern murder pamphlets focused on precisely the sorts of details, motifs, and images that she associates with the later cults of horror and mystery. Such publications (to borrow Halttunen's terminology) often included "detailed attention to the events leading up to a murder"; designation of "the precise date and hour of the crime"; descriptions of the murderer's "personality traits" and "motive"; "precise" descriptions of "the weapons used" or "illustrations of the weapon"; "specific details about the state and fate of the victim's corpse" (especially in cases of dismemberment); descriptions or illustrations of the "crime scene"; positioning of the reader "as voyeur to the crime"; and attention to "the judicial death of convicted murderers." These elements were not only frequently emphasized in the texts of the early modern murder pamphlets, but were also dramatized in lurid woodcuts that most commonly appeared as frontispieces or on title pages. A pamphlet published in 1607, for example, described two cases of husbands who murdered their wives. The title page was dominated by two large woodcuts placed side by side: the first depicted one of the murderers suffocating his sickly wife by jamming a napkin into her mouth; the adjoining image pictured the second malefactor resolutely watching as flames incinerated his murdered wife's corpse in a fireplace (Figures 2.1a).[8]

Subsequent murder pamphlets included even more horribly graphic descriptions of mutilated, dismembered, or decomposing corpses. Perhaps the most gruesome of all was contained in a 1623 account of the murder of Mr. Trat, a country curate, in a dispute over control of his parsonage. After stabbing him to death on the road, the killers took him back to his own home, where they "did cut up his carkeise, unbowell and quarter it; then they did burne his head and privey members, parboile his flesh and salt it up; that so the sodaine stincke and putrefactions being hindered, the murtherers might the longer be free from discoverie." When the stench eventually led authorities to break into the house fifteen days later, they found the victim's arms, legs, thighs, and bowels "powdred up into two earthen steenes or pots" downstairs, with most of the trunk of his dismembered corpse stashed in a tub upstairs. Another horrific crime, first described in a pamphlet of 1633, was Enoch ap Evans's murder of two close relatives. After beheading his brother and his mother with a sharp hatchet—as the narrator delicately put it, "hee divided" his mother's "head from that breast, and those paps which gave suck unto him"—the young man then drenched the severed heads in water to wash off the blood, and wrapped them tightly into a cloth bundle. Reportedly a fanatical religious dissenter, Evans then walked to the home of a nearby kinsman, where he sat down and read a Bible. Perhaps owing to its usefulness in exposing the dangers of religious nonconformity, this revolting story was recounted in at least four separate pamphlets by 1650.[9]

Other early seventeenth-century murder pamphlets may not have been quite as gory as those on Trat and Evans, but they did feature many of the other motifs that Halttunen attributes to the later "Gothic" mode. In 1635, Henry Goodcole, a preacher who ministered to condemned criminals at Newgate Prison in London, produced a lurid pamphlet that focused on the last of several murders committed by a "Strumpet" and her male accomplice, nicknamed "Canberry-Besse" and "Countrey-Tom," respectively. The pair evidently had developed a cruel but lucrative modus operandi: the woman would spot an intoxicated, wealthy-looking male target at a public venue such as a playhouse or tavern, flirt with the man, and then lure him to a secluded outdoor location with the promise of sexual favors; there she and her partner would rob and murder their victim. The frontispiece of Goodcole's pamphlet was a collage that included, in the foreground, a view of the crime scene, showing one of the murderers stripping the victim's corpse. Matching cuts of Tom and Besse, each hanging from the gallows, framed the collage on left and right. A somewhat ambiguous image in the background probably depicted Tom accosting someone with a club. Running horizontally along the bottom of the page was a separate large cut of the "short Trunchin, or Bastinado," evidently made of wood but studded with iron nails, with which Tom assaulted his victims. This threatening—and suggestively phallic—image of the murder weapon was repeated in the margin of an interior page of text, alongside a description of the pair's last homicide. The lurid pamphlet also included sections identifying the specific neighborhoods of London frequented by prostitutes and describing various stratagems used by courtesans to entrap their victims. The account of "Canberry-Besse" and "Countrey-Tom" may thus be seen as an early forerunner of the "urban exposés" or "urban mysteries" that engaged so many American readers of the mid-nineteenth century.[10]

In 1637, Henry Goodcole shifted his focus from public to domestic depravity, producing a pamphlet that depicted several horrifying instances of familial violence. This tract featured the cases of two women who murdered their own children, a female servant who poisoned her master and mistress, and a man who raped his ten-year-old daughter. A woodcut on the title page shows Goodcole's main subject, a widow named Elizabeth Barnes, kneeling on the ground over the body of her daughter as she slits the young girl's throat with a large knife (Figure 2.2). The accompanying text describes how, early on the morning of March 24, 1637, Barnes took her daughter on a long excursion, purportedly to place the child with a relative. To insure that the child went willingly, her mother brought along "an Apple Pye, a Herring Pye, Raisins . . . and other fruits." Such sweets, Goodcole noted, were just the sort of "baits, used by loving Parents, to quiet and still their children." That evening Barnes took her daughter into the woods, some four miles from their residence, and there, as they sat down to rest, the mother took the treats from her basket for the girl to eat. Later that night, at "about the houres of xi. and xii.," she "drew out of her sheath a knife, and with that knife barbarously did cut the throat of the

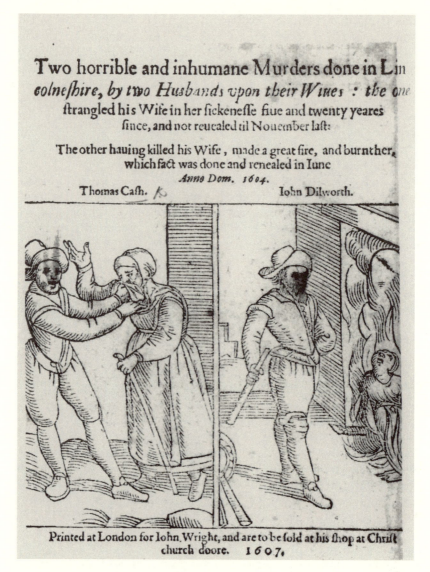

Two horrible and inhumane Murders done in Lincolneſhire, by two Husbands vpon their Wiues : the one ſtrangled his Wiſe in her ſickeneſſe fiue and twenty yeares ſince, and not reuealed til Nouember laſt:

The other hauing killed his Wiſe , made a great fire, and burnt her, which fact was done and reuealed in Iune
Anno Dom. 1604.

Thomas Caſh.   Iohn Dilworth.

Printed at London for Iohn Wright, and are to be ſold at his ſhop at Chriſt church doore.   1607,

Figure 2.1a. Title page of *Two horrible and inhumane Murders done in Lincolnshire* (London, 1607). By permission of The British Library.

child." Goodcole's murder pamphlets featured many of the elements identified with the later American "Gothic" mode: a preference for domestic murders or murders involving sexually depraved women; detailed accounts of the events leading up to the murder; specificity concerning the date and even the hour of the crime; and detailed descriptions or illustrations of the

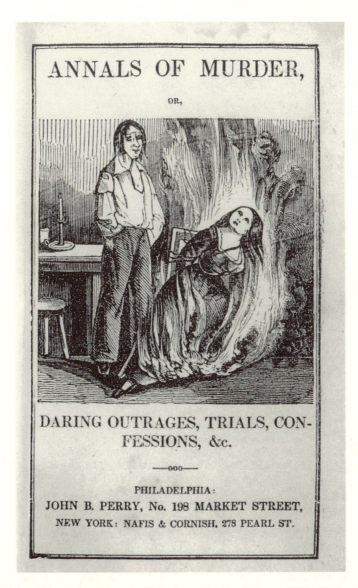

Figure 2.1b. Title page of *Annals of Murder, or, Daring Outrages, Trials, Confessions, &c* (Philadelphia and New York, 1845). Note the strikingly similar, equally sensationalistic, images of spousal incineration in the early seventeenth-century, pre-Enlightenment English murder pamphlet and the nineteenth-century, post-Enlightenment American murder compilation.

homicide itself, the scene of the crime, the murder weapon, and the execution of the malefactor.[11]

Natures
Cruell Step-Dames:

OR,

Matchlesse Monsters of the Female

Sex; *Elizabeth Barnes*, and *Anne Willis*.

Who were executed the 26. day of *April*,

1637. at Tyburne, for the unnaturall murthe-
ring of their owne Children,

Also, herein is contained their severall Confessions,
and the Courts just proceedings against other notorious
Malefactors, with their severall offences
this Sessions.

Further, a Relation of the wicked Life and

impenitent Death of *Iohn Flood*, who raped
his own Childe.

Printed at London for *Francis Coules*, dwelling in
the Old-Baily. 1637.

Figure 2.2. Title page of Henry Goodcole's *Natures Cruell Step-Dames: or, Matchlesse Monsters of the Female Sex; Elizabeth Barnes, and Anne Willis* (London, 1637). By permission of the Folger Shakespeare Library. Note the characterization of the murderers as "Monsters," the description of their crimes as "unnaturall," and the graphic illustration of a familial homicide.

Given the frequently horrific nature of the homicides featured in seventeenth-century crime pamphlets, it is not surprising that their authors often characterized the killers as unnatural or subhuman "monsters"—that is, in terms virtually identical to those linked by Halttunen to the American "Gothic" of the late eighteenth and early nineteenth centuries. The very titles of the publications reveal the pattern. One pamphlet about a father who murdered two of his own children was entitled *The Unnatural Father* (1621), and four broadside ballads concerning cases of familial violence were called *The Monstrous Mother* (1633), *Two Unnaturall Mothers* (1637), *The Unnatural Husband* (1639/40), and *The Unnaturall Mother that Buried Her Child Alive* (1639/40). A pamphlet that recounted the cases of two murderers—a beggar who strangled his "betrothed wife" and a "lascivious young Damsell" who killed her own infant—was entitled *Deeds Against Nature, and Monsters by Kinde* (1614). One of Goodcole's sensationalistic titles fits this pattern: *Natures Cruell Step-Dames: Or, Matchlesse Monsters of the Female Sex.* Such hostile characterizations are also scattered throughout the texts. Goodcole describes "Canberry-Besse" and "Countrey-Tom" as "Monsters" and Elizabeth Barnes as a "ravenous Wolfe."[12]

In their efforts to dehumanize murderers and exploit an ideologically useful "pornography of violence," some accounts of atrocities linked to the broader political and religious strife of the seventeenth century were even more extreme than ordinary murder pamphlets. Such was certainly the case with *The Teares of Ireland* (1642), a fierce propaganda tract depicting the horrific atrocities allegedly committed by Irish Catholics against civilians in a military uprising against the ruling Protestants. Generally attributed to an English Presbyterian divine named James Cranford, the pamphlet depicted an appalling series of sadistic tortures, gang rapes, and mass murders, including several cases in which individual members of households were raped, killed, and mutilated in the presence of loved ones.

In Cranford's work, textual descriptions of atrocities were accompanied by engravings that graphically depicted the carnage. Some of these gruesome illustrations were at least as pornographic and elaborately voyeuristic as the images featured in many later American murder pamphlets. One image showed the "Papistes" cutting open a pregnant woman's womb and tossing the fetus into a fire. Another depicted the rebels cutting or tearing off the arms, legs, ears, nose, cheeks, and tongue of a prominent Protestant—after having, according to the accompanying text, raped his wife before his eyes and murdered his children and servants (Figure 2.3a). A third image depicted a Catholic bashing the brains of Protestant children against a wall, as their parents watched weeping. A fourth invited readers to gaze at a domestic scene in which a mother, tied to a chair, threw an anguished glance toward her husband, also tied to a chair, as he stared directly at their two seven-year-old children, who were roasting on spits in a

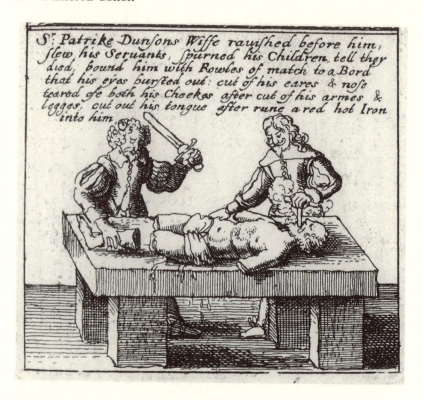

Figure 2.3a. Dismemberment and mutilation of a Protestant gentleman by Irish Catholic rebels in *The Teares of Ireland* (London, 1642).

blazing fireplace just a few feet away (Figure 2.4a). Cranford variously described the Catholic perpetrators of the alleged atrocities as "bloud-thirstie Monsters," "bloudy Tigres and Vultures," "Monsters of nature," "brutish creatures," "savage beasts," "bloudy wolves," "cruell beasts," and "barbarous Monsters." Such dehumanizing epithets matched the most extreme characterizations of murderers found in American crime pamphlets of the early republic.[13]

Fictional romances that purported to depict real-life crimes represented another seventeenth-century variant of the popular murder pamphlets. In 1621, John Reynolds, a "merchant of Exeter," published the first installment of a lengthy collection of violent and prurient romances thinly disguised as a theological treatise on divine judgments against murderers. Generally entitled *The Triumphs of Gods Revenge Against the Crying and Execrable Sinne of (Wilful and Premeditated) Murther* (5th edition, 1670), Reynolds's compilation featured ostensibly historical accounts of sexual intrigue and intimate homicide, set in foreign countries (Figures 2.5a and b). While some con-

Figure 2.3b. Similar engraving of the dismemberment of a homicide victim by his murderers on the title page of *An Account of the Apprehension, Trial, Conviction, and Condemnation of Manuel Philip Garcia and Jose Demas Garcia Castilano . . . for a Most Horrid Murder and Butchery, Committed on Peter Lagoardette . . .* (Norfolk, Va., 1821). Courtesy American Antiquarian Society.

temporary readers evidently believed Reynolds's lurid tales to be translations of French or Italian romances, the author himself insisted that they were true accounts of cases that he had learned about during his travels abroad. His "histories" involved intricately intertwined cases of adultery, incest, spousal or filial betrayal, and familial homicide, all culminating in gruesome judicial punishments.[14]

Although most of Reynolds's stories were probably pure fiction, at least one edition of his compilation, published in 1661, also appended accounts of several real-life English murder cases that had already been treated in shorter pamphlets and ballads. The verisimilitude—and sensationalism—of editions published during the mid-seventeenth century and thereafter was commonly enhanced by the addition of elaborate, multiscene "action" engravings for every case, placed together sequentially at the outset

Mr Dauenant and his Wife bound in
their Chaires, Striped the 2 Eldeſt Child
ren of 7 years old roſted them upon
Spittes before their Parents faces, Cutt
heir throte and after murdrd him,

Michael McGarvey beating his Wife to death.

Figure 2.4a *(top)*. A bound woman looks in anguish at her husband, who in turn
stares at their two children being roasted on spits, while another man, probably a
Catholic rebel, watches, in *The Teares of Ireland* (London, 1642). Such violent images were as elaborately voyeuristic as American murder illustrations produced two
centuries later. Figure 2.4b *(bottom)*. A man whips his wife to death as another
woman watches from a doorway, in *Tragedies on the Land, Containing an Authentic Account of the Most Awful Murders* (Philadelphia, 1853). Courtesy American Antiquarian Society.

of each history in horizontal rows like modern comic strips. The illustrations focused on each story's sexual intrigues, treacherous murders, and grisly punishments, adding still further to the voyeuristic quality of the romances (Figure 2.5b). As in contemporary murder pamphlets, the villains in Reynolds's lurid "histories" were occasionally labeled with such dehumanizing epithets as "unnatural and bloody Monsters," "Tygers and Monsters" or "Monsters of Nature." Monstrous though they may have been, Reynolds's lascivious murderers proved to be enduringly profitable as literary commodities. New editions continued to appear well into the eighteenth century, with one updated version issued as late as 1778.[15]

It is important to note that many of the sensationalistic crime publications of the seventeenth century also included substantial religious and moralistic content. Recall that Henry Goodcole was a clergyman who ministered to condemned malefactors at Newgate Prison, and that John Reynolds's prurient compilation of murder cases was thinly disguised as a treatise on God's punishment of murderers. Indeed, seventeenth-century English crime publications often featured short theological discussions (sometimes in a Calvinist vein), harsh warnings against sin, and prescriptions for salvation little different from those contained in early New England execution sermons. Thus one of Goodcole's first crime pamphlets was explicitly presented to readers as a criminal conversion narrative, depicting the "happy Conversion, contrition, and Christian preparation" of a condemned malefactor. In general, the spiritual content of English murder pamphlets became more prominent during the second half of the century; as that happened, the crude sensationalism of the genre was somewhat attenuated. Yet far from being expressions of inconsistent or opposing world views, the motifs of piety and sensationalism were intricately intertwined in seventeenth-century murder pamphlets. The precise balance between those two literary strands varied depending on the specific author and the particular criminal case—and, over time, in response to broader social or cultural trends—but most seventeenth-century English murder publications incorporated elements of both.[16]

While not as pervasive as "horror," constructions of murder as "mystery" also occasionally appeared in seventeenth-century English crime pamphlets. In *Murder Most Foul*, Halttunen appropriately links the emergence of "murder as mystery" to the popularization of the trial-report genre in the United States after about 1790. Many trial reports were published in England during the seventeenth century; but the courtroom proceedings that they summarized differed greatly from the competitive, lawyer-dominated, adversarial criminal trials that would emerge in America by the end of the eighteenth century.

Most seventeenth-century English criminal trials—even capital cases—were

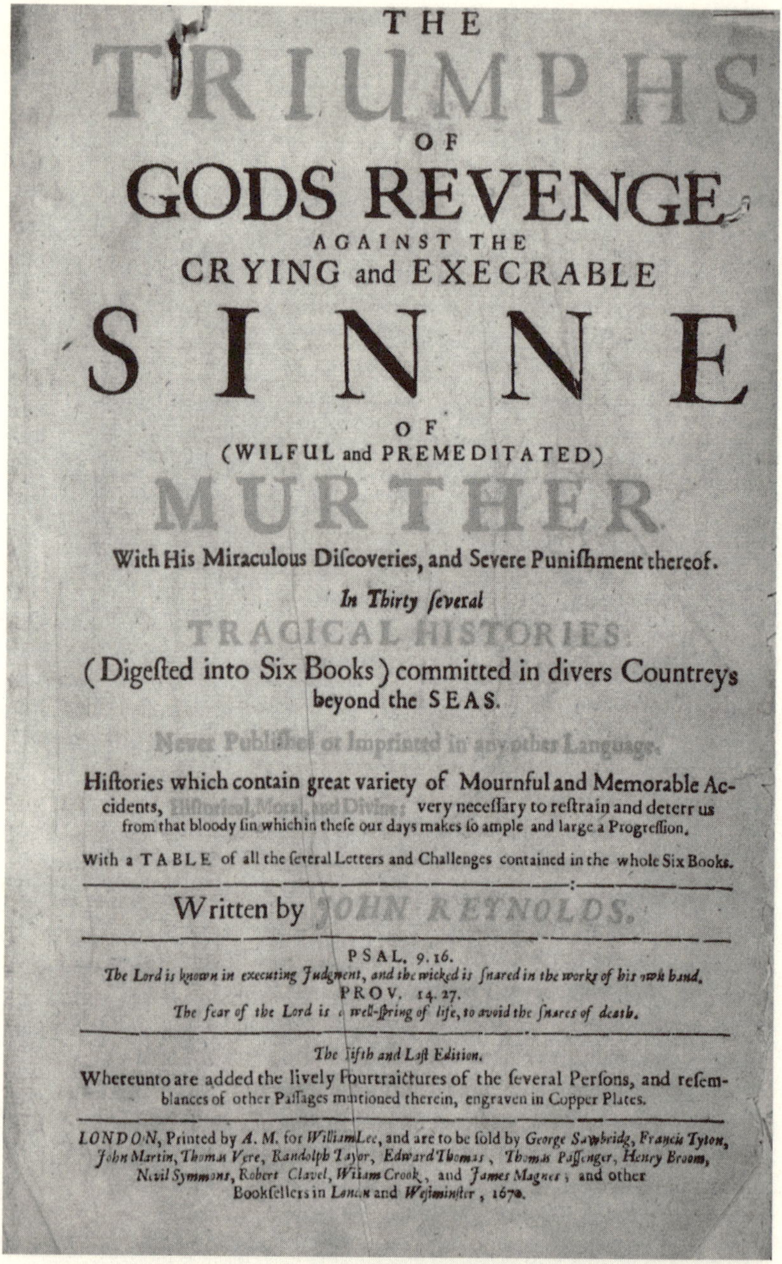

THE
TRIUMPHS
OF
GODS REVENGE
AGAINST THE
CRYING and EXECRABLE
SINNE
OF
(WILFUL and PREMEDITATED)
MURTHER
With His Miraculous Difcoveries, and Severe Punifhment thereof.
In Thirty feveral
TRAGICAL HISTORIES:
(Digefted into Six Books) committed in divers Countreys beyond the SEAS.
Never Publifhed or Imprinted in any other Language.
Hiftories which contain great variety of Mournful and Memorable Accidents, Hiftorical, Moral, and Divine; very neceffary to reftrain and deterr us from that bloody fin which in thefe our days makes fo ample and large a Progreffion.
With a TABLE of all the feveral Letters and Challenges contained in the whole Six Books.

Written by JOHN REYNOLDS.

PSAL. 9.16.
The Lord is known in executing Judgment, and the wicked is fnared in the works of his own hand.
PROV. 14.27.
The fear of the Lord is a well-fpring of life, to avoid the fnares of death.

The fifth and Laft Edition.
Whereunto are added the lively Pourtraictures of the feveral Perfons, and refemblances of other Paffages mentioned therein, engraven in Copper Plates.

LONDON, Printed by *A. M.* for *WilliamLee*, and are to be fold by *George Sawbridg*, *Francis Tyton*, *John Martin*, *Thomas Vere*, *Randolph Taylor*, *Edward Thomas*, *Thomas Paffenger*, *Henry Broom*, *Nevil Symmons*, *Robert Clavel*, *William Crook*, and *James Magnes*; and other Bookfellers in *London* and *Weftminfter*, 1670.

Figures 2.5a and 2.5b. Title page *(left)* and interior page *(right)* of John Reynolds's *The Triumphs of Gods Revenge Against the Crying and Execrable Sinne of (Wilful and Premeditated) Murther*, 5th ed. (London, 1670). This popular collection of romances was thinly disguised as a religious treatise on murder. As on the interior page shown

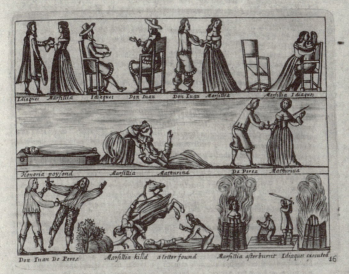

Idiaques Marsillia   Idiaques   Don Juan   Don Juan Marsillia   Marsillia Idiaques

Honoria poyson'd   Marsillia   Mathurina   De Perez   Mathurina

Don Juan De Perez   Marsillia kill'd   a traitor found   Marsillia after burnt   Idiaques executed

GOD's Revenge against the Crying and Execrable Sin of Murther.

HISTORY XVI.

Idiaques causeth his Son Don Juan to marry Marsillia, and then commits Adultery and Incest with her. She makes her Father in Law Idiaques to poyson his own old wife Honoria ; and likewise makes her own brother De Perez to kill her Chamber-maid Mathurina : Don Juan afterwards kill De Perez in a Duel : Marsillia hath her brains dasht out by a horse, and her body is afterward condemned to be burnt : Idiaques is beheaded, his body likewise consumed to ashes, and thrown into the air.

LET Malice be never so secretly contrived, and the shedding of Innocent blood never so wretchedly perpetrated, yet as our Conscience is to us a thousand witnesses, so God is to us a thousand Consciences, first to bring it to light, and then their Authors to deserved punishments for the same, when they least dream or think thereof. For as there is no peace to the wicked, so they shall find no peace or tranquillity here on earth, either with God or his creatures, because if they would conceal it, yet the very Fowles of the air, yea, the stones and timbers of their chambers will detect it : For the Earth or Air will give them no breath nor being, but they shall hang between both, because, by these their foul and deplorable facts, they have made themselves unworthy of either. A powerful example, and a pitiful precedent whereof we shall behold in this ensuing Historie, where some wretched miscreants and graceless creatures making themselves guilty of those bloody crimes (by the immediate Revenge and Justice of God) received exemplary, and condign punishments for the same. May we read it to Gods glory, to the comfort of our hearts, and the instruction of our souls.

In the City of *Santarem*, which (by tract of time, and corruption of speech) some term *Saint Aren*, and which (after *Lisbon*) is one of the richest and best people of *Portugal* ; there

here, many editions of Reynolds's collection featured strips of engravings at the beginning of each chapter, graphically depicting sexual intrigues, family betrayals, intimate homicides, and gruesome punishments.

very brief, relatively informal, judge-dominated proceedings. They were governed by few strict rules of evidence, without elaborate opening and closing arguments, and with neither prosecution nor defense typically represented by professional attorneys. In fact, according to legal historian John H. Langbein, defendants accused of capital crimes other than treason were generally prohibited from employing lawyers to defend themselves at their trials until the 1730s. Even then, defense attorneys were not always permitted to cross-examine prosecution witnesses, and they were not allowed to address juries directly until that practice was permitted by statute in 1836. Hampered by such restrictions, the accused in early modern English murder cases were rarely able to mount elaborate defenses that could raise doubts about prosecution evidence or construct alternative theories of the crime. In short, there was nothing very "mysterious" about most seventeenth-century English capital trials. Rather, they tended to be short, predictable proceedings (often lasting less than an hour) that rarely hinged on intricate detective work, clever cross-examinations, or imagination reconstructions of disputed events.[17]

Nevertheless, despite the perfunctory nature of most early English homicide trials, at least a few seventeenth-century crime publications prefigured the later American construction of murder as mystery. One such work was produced by Robert ("the Plotter") Ferguson, a wily Protestant clergyman and propagandist who schemed against England's Stuart monarchs, helped contrive the Rye House Plot of 1682, and later supported the seizure of power by William of Orange in the Glorious Revolution. In 1684, Ferguson published a pamphlet in response to the alleged suicide of Arthur Capel, the earl of Essex, in the Tower of London, following Capel's arrest on charges of plotting against Charles II. *An Enquiry Into, and Detection of the Barbarous Murther of the Late Earl of Essex* (1684) asserts that Essex did not cut his own throat, as officially reported, but rather had been assassinated on orders of the king's "Popish" brother, James, Duke of York (later King James II). Fortunately for the cause of English Protestantism, the author piously noted, "the over-ruling Providence of God" would not "suffer a crime so hateful to Heaven" to be committed "without leaving some prints and footsteps" by which it could be "traced and detected."[18]

In this lengthy pamphlet, Ferguson mustered many arguments and much evidence to solve the "Hellish Mystery" of Essex's violent death and to expose the "monsters of humane [*sic*] Nature" who had betrayed the Protestant patriot. First, he cited the testimony of a thirteen-year-old boy, among others, who saw the "bloody Razor" (presumably used to kill Essex) thrown out of a Tower window at about the time of his death. Clearly, Essex could not possibly have tossed the weapon out the window *after* cutting his own throat—hence the murderer must have disposed of the weapon. Second, Ferguson described the intimidation and persecution of several witnesses who could contradict the suicide theory. He even claimed that two such witnesses, a sentinel and a warder at the Tower of London, had been murdered in order to silence them. Third, he claimed that Essex's long and deep neck wound, running through both jugular veins, could not possibly have been self-inflicted using the "small French Razor" that he had allegedly employed. Fourth, there were several damning contradictions in the testimony of key witnesses, particularly relating to issues of timing and to the discovery of Essex's corpse in a "closet." Fifth, suspicious tampering at the scene of the crime eliminated clues that otherwise might have been gleaned "from an observation of the site and posture wherein the Body is found." Sixth, witnesses had seen the *"print of a bloody foot"* on one of Essex's stockings, presumably left by one of the assassins. Seventh, the earl's cravat had been cut to pieces, demonstrating that it had not been removed before his throat was cut. Surely, Ferguson argued, it was implausible to think that Essex would have removed his wig—so that it would not interfere with the stroke of his razor—and yet have left his cravat in place, wrapped three times around his neck. Eighth, the reluctant and irregular "behaviour" of the coroner's jury suggested "that there was a secret and hidden Villainy" in Essex's death, "which some of them were either forbidden or afraid to ravel into." Ninth, the gate leading to the earl's apartment, generally left open, was kept shut on the morning of Essex's death. Tenth, the duke of York (whom Ferguson accused of ordering the assassination) was spotted that morning, with several others, heading toward an alley near the Tower gate.[19]

Again and again in his pamphlet, Ferguson deployed the language of "mystery" and the methods of criminal "detection" to vindicate the earl of Essex and cast suspicion on the duke of York. He repeatedly referred to the death of Essex as a "mystery," a "Hellish Mystery," or a "villanous mystery." His impressive array of physical and circumstantial evidence and logical arguments and deductions all foreshadowed strategies pursued by prosecutors and defense lawyers in American trials of the early national period. They are also strikingly similar to the clichéd clues that came to pervade detective fiction and murder mysteries as those genres developed over the course of the nineteenth and twentieth centuries. In all, Ferguson assembled an astonishingly elaborate and evocative catalog of plot devices: the bloody razor tossed out the window, the brutally silenced witnesses, the mysterious discrepancies at the crime scene, the bloody footprint on the victim's clothes, the mutilated cravat, and so on. Whether or not the author's painstaking effort actually proved that a murder had been committed, it surely confirmed that Robert Ferguson was a master "plotter" in more ways than one.[20]

Another mysterious case, this one presented to English readers in the form of a trial report, even more closely prefigured American crime publications of the early republic. In 1699, four gentlemen from the town of Hertford were charged with having murdered a wealthy, young, unmarried

Quaker woman, Sarah Stout, by strangling her and throwing her corpse into a local river. Because one of the accused men, Spencer Cowper, was himself a lawyer, the procedural restrictions that normally would have prevented English criminal defendants from employing the services of legal counsel were effectively nullified. As one of the accused, Cowper was able to construct the sort of aggressive, elaborate defense that he would never have been allowed to mount in an English courtroom of the period on behalf of a defendant other than himself. In fact, the evidence and arguments that he presented, as documented in the published report, show remarkable similarities to the defenses regularly constructed by criminal attorneys in highly publicized American capital cases of the early nineteenth century.[21]

The case against the four men was entirely circumstantial. The dead woman's servant had last seen her mistress with Spencer Cowper in Stout's home at about eleven o'clock on the night of her death. Cowper was there, in part, on legal or financial business, but evidence presented by the defense suggested that Stout was pursuing the married man romantically. After the servant went upstairs to warm a bed for Cowper, she heard the outside door slam shut, and when she came downstairs again, she found both Cowper and her mistress gone. The household waited all night for Stout, only to learn the following morning that her corpse had been found floating in the river. Witnesses testified that the other three defendants had been talking among themselves at a nearby lodging house near the time Stout left her house with Cowper. Having been jilted by Stout, one of the men said, "she cast me off, but I reckon by this time a Friend of mine has done her business." And when one suggested that "*Sarah Stout's* courting days are over," another replied, "I will spend all the Mony I have, for joy the business is done." The prosecution also introduced evidence that Stout, whose body was found floating in the river, had swallowed very little water. The king's attorney called several physicians and sailors to attest that the absence of ingested water proved that Stout had been killed *before* being dumped into the river. When people drowned, these expert witnesses insisted, they swallowed large quantities of water and sank. This graphic forensic testimony, which included descriptions of an autopsy performed on the victim, closely resembled the kind of medical evidence that would later be presented in American trial reports.[22]

For the defense, Cowper argued that Sarah Stout had committed suicide and that he was being framed by his personal and political enemies. To strengthen his claim that she had committed suicide, Cowper called several medical experts who contradicted the prosecution's forensic testimony concerning drowned bodies. He produced other witnesses who claimed that Stout's corpse was not actually floating when it was discovered. Most significantly, Cowper employed what were to become the standard tactics of defense lawyers in similar American cases after 1800: casting aspersions on the mental health and moral character of the victim. He called several witnesses who testified that Sarah Stout had seemed "very melancholy" during the months leading up to her death, allowing Cowper to suggest that she had probably drowned herself in a "Love-fit." He also introduced into evidence several aggressively flirtatious letters, allegedly written by the deceased to Cowper and to another man. One defense witness testified that the unmarried woman occasionally sneaked out at night without her mother's knowledge and "entertain[ed] her Friends in the Summer-house, now and then, with a Bottle of Wine." After a half-hearted charge by the judge that favored the defendants, the jury returned "in about half an hour" with verdicts of "not guilty" for all of the accused men.[23]

Judging by the late seventeenth-century cases of the earl of Essex and Spencer Cowper, the construction of murder as mystery did not presuppose a new Enlightenment view of human nature, a revolution in humanitarian sensibility, or the rise of Gothic fiction. Rather, it required (1) an appropriately ambiguous death; (2) an effectively adversarial trial system; and/or (3) a sufficiently conflicted social or political setting—all to provide motive and opportunity for the imaginative elaboration of competing theories of an alleged crime.

It was not until the end of the eighteenth century that the sensationalistic motifs found in earlier English murder publications came to dominate American crime literature. One of the first cases to mark that transition was a highly publicized murder mystery, eerily similar to the Stout-Cowper case of 1699, that took place in New York almost exactly one hundred years later. On the evening of December 22, 1799, a young, unmarried Quaker woman named Elma Sands was last observed waiting at home to be picked up by a man she considered her fiancé, the well-connected Levi Weeks, who boarded in the same house. Another member of the household reported admitting Weeks to the house and hearing Elma's familiar footsteps coming down the stairs, followed by the sound of the front door opening and closing. Weeks returned to the house alone around ten o'clock that night, appearing "pale and much agitated." Elma's corpse was found about ten days later, floating in a well.[24]

As in the Stout-Cowper case of 1699, the resulting trial of the young man hinged on graphic—and sharply conflicting—forensic testimony concerning the state of the young woman's corpse and on conflicting portrayals of the victim's moral character. Weeks's high-powered defense team, led by Aaron Burr, Alexander Hamilton, and Brockholst Livingston, presented evidence that Elma Sands frequently went out evenings, was sometimes "melancholy," and had likely drowned herself in a "love fit." With conflicting medical testimony and an imperfect circumstantial case, the judge's charge essentially directed a verdict of "not guilty," which the jury returned "in about five minutes." The controversial case of Levi Weeks, with its striking parallels to that of Spencer Cowper, elicited three different published trial reports of varying lengths, making it one of the very first in a long series of highly publicized courtship- or sex-related murder trials in the early republic.[25]

Some of the elements of horror and mystery which became prominent in the Weeks-Sands case and in other murder cases after 1800 can actually be traced to American crime publications of a century or more earlier. These same motifs appeared in two rare pamphlets involving homicide cases outside of Puritan New England (where most of the earliest American crime pamphlets originated). In 1678, Thomas Hellier, an English immigrant servant working on a tobacco plantation in Virginia, slaughtered his master, mistress, and a household maid with an ax. An anonymous author, probably an Anglican clergyman named Paul Williams then living in Virginia, produced an account of the domestic multiple homicide—based largely on interviews with the condemned murderer—that was then sent across the Atlantic to London, where it was published in 1680.

In his prologue, the author praised John Reynolds's popular compilation on God's revenge against murder. He disputed those who dismissed the work as "a queintly contriv'd Romance," implicitly invoking it as a model for his own pamphlet. Although the minister's pamphlet on the Virginia homicides had substantial religious content and was not nearly as lurid as the tales told by Reynolds, it did feature many of the elements attributed by Halttunen to the later "cult of horror," including details concerning the life and character of the murderer, the killer's motive, the chain of events leading up to the carnage, and the murders themselves, with specific references as to weapon, date, and time. Hellier's case also anticipated the later American fascination with mass murders and domestic homicides.[26]

About a dozen years later, in 1692, a printer in Philadelphia published an account of the murder of a merchant named John Clark in West Jersey. The legalistic pamphlet, *Blood Will Out, or, An Example of Justice in the Tryal, Condemnation, Confession and Execution of Thomas Lutherland* (1692), consisted primarily of a trial report, followed by the murderer's detailed posttrial confession. As in many nineteenth-century murder pamphlets, the published confession included a brief account of Lutherland's prior life and character, a description of his motive (robbery), "detailed attention to the events leading up" to the murder, and a somewhat gruesome firstperson account of the homicide itself, in which Lutherland slowly strangled Clark with a rope, as the dying man begged for mercy. Although he admitted to robbing the merchant, Lutherland pleaded "not guilty" of murder at his trial. And like many early nineteenth-century homicide cases, Clark's killing was a mystery solved largely by circumstantial evidence. The title of the pamphlet, *Blood Will Out,* referred to the ancient belief—at times incorporated into early modern legal practice—that a murder victim's corpse would bleed afresh when touched by its killer. The experiment had evidently been tried without success in Lutherland's case, but in his confession, the murderer acknowledged that the test had terrified him: "When I touched the murthered Corps of *John Clark,* I was afraid the Blood would have flown in my face."[27]

The publications concerning the cases of Thomas Hellier and Thomas Lutherland serve to underscore the almost exclusively *regional* character of the execution sermon, the first dominant American crime genre. As a free-standing literary form, the execution sermon seems to have been an innovation of the New England Puritans. Although sermons were frequently delivered to condemned criminals (or at their funerals) in seventeenth-century Britain, and were sometimes synopsized in other crime publications, they were rarely, if ever, published there as separate books or pamphlets. Furthermore, no gallows sermons were published in North America during the seventeenth century outside of New England, and only a very few appeared elsewhere in America during the eighteenth century.

The dominance of the execution sermon genre was an essentially regional phenomenon—and of limited duration. For several decades, through formal censorship, less formal pressure or influence, and the temporary absence of effective competition, New England's Puritan ministers were able to control the region's popular print culture more effectively than their counterparts in Britain. Yet their monopoly on regional crime publications was breached by 1704, just thirty years after it began, and the regional dominance of the execution sermon genre arguably ended by the 1730s.[28]

Not even Puritan clergymen were immune to the lure of sensationalism. Before the end of the seventeenth century, New England ministers and printers started tinkering with the religious literature of crime, evidently trying to strengthen its message and broaden its appeal. They began to attach various supplementary materials to the published sermons, including crime and execution accounts, dying confessions of the criminals, and transcripts of jailhouse dialogues between condemned malefactors and Puritan clergymen. Some of these supplementary materials were intended to reinforce or amplify the pastoral messages of the ministers, but others reflected—and probably stimulated—a growing interest among New England readers in the worldly details of criminal cases. Now, sensationalistic elements that had long characterized early modern English murder pamphlets began to seep into the volumes of execution sermons. Puritan ministers such as Cotton Mather seem to have been willing collaborators in the process of literary transformation, evidently hoping that more readers would be willing to consume their sermons if they were sweetened by a dollop or two of sensationalism. This trend was sometimes marked by changes in title-page typography, as the emphasis shifted from the sermons

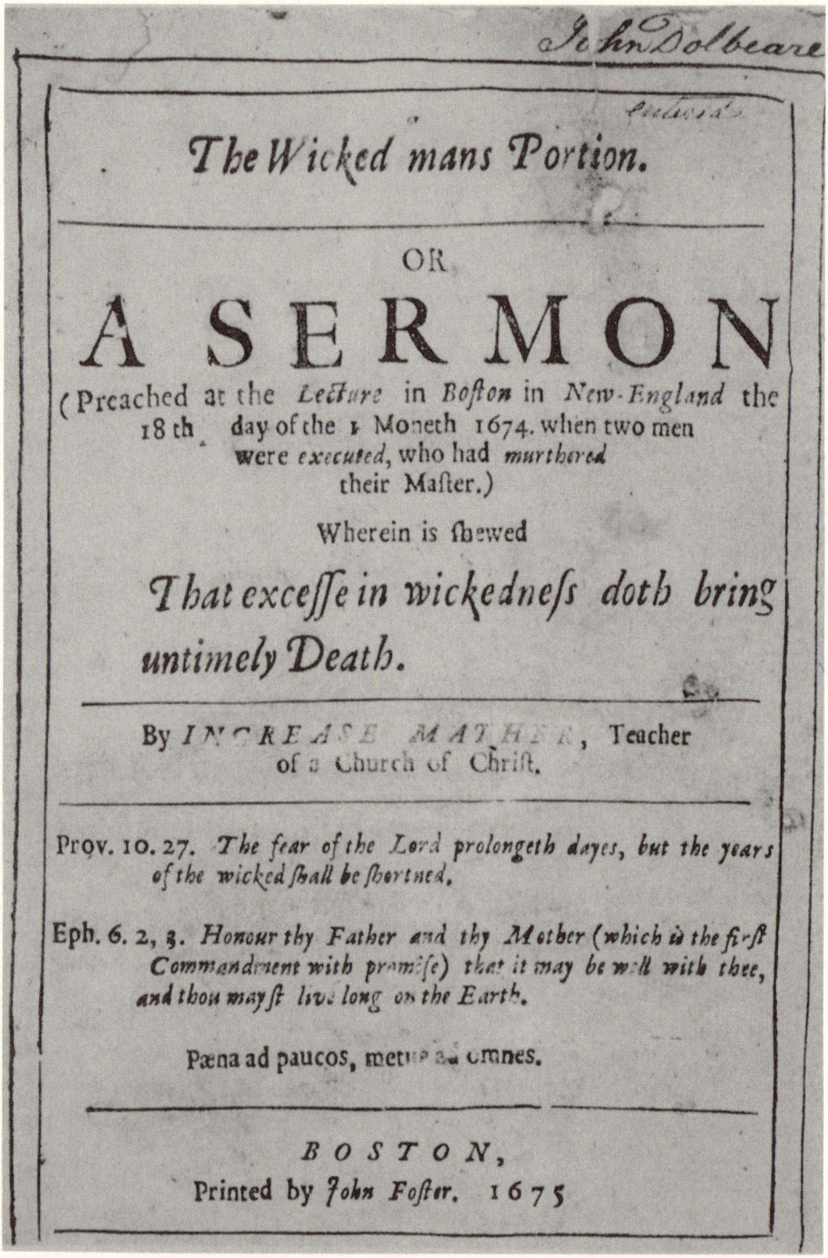

John Dolbeare

The Wicked mans Portion.

OR,

A SERMON

(Preached at the *Lecture* in *Boston* in *New-England* the
18 th day of the 1 Moneth 1674. when two men
were *executed*, who had *murthered*
their Master.)

Wherein is shewed

That excesse in wickednesse doth bring
untimely Death.

By *INCREASE MATHER*, Teacher
of a Church of Christ.

Prov. 10. 27. *The fear of the Lord prolongeth dayes, but the years*
of the wicked shall be shortned,

Eph. 6. 2, 3. *Honour thy Father and thy Mother (which is the first*
Commandment with promise) that it may be well with thee,
and thou mayst live long on the Earth.

Pæna ad paucos, metus ad omnes.

B O S T O N,
Printed by *John Foster.* 1675

Figures 2.6a and 2.6b. Title pages of two early volumes of New England execution sermons, Increase Mather's *The Wicked mans Portion* (Boston, 1675) and Cotton Mather's *The Sad Effects of Sin* (Boston, 1713). Both illustrations courtesy American Antiquarian Society. In the first *(left)*, the word "SERMON" appears in large typeface

The Sad Effects of Sin.

A True Relation of the

Murder

Committed by

DAVID WALLIS,

On his Companion

Benjamin Stolwood:

On *Saturday* Night, the first of *August*, 1713. With his Carriage after Condemnation ; His Confession and Dying Speech at the Place of Execution, &c.

To which are added, The Sermons Preached at the Lecture in *Boston*, in his Hearing, after his Condemnation ; And on the Day of his Execution, being *Sept.* 24. 1713.

Boston, N. E. Printed by *John Allen*, for *Nicholas Boone*, at the Sign of the BIBLE in *Cornhil.* 1713.

and the names of the two murderers do not appear on the title page at all; in the second *(right)*, "Murder" and the murderer's name are emphasized, while "Sermons" appears only in small print toward the end of the subtitle.

themselves to the details of crimes, criminals, and executions (compare Figures 2.6a and b). By the 1720s, printed execution sermons were sometimes accompanied by detailed crime accounts, with such sensationalistic lines as, "D——n you, you dog, if you stir hand or foot, or speak a word, I'll blow your brains out."[29]

Between 1700 and 1730, New England printers and booksellers gradually became less dependent on the patronage of Puritan ministers. During those years, they occasionally ventured beyond the sermon format and produced a smattering of other crime genres, largely derived from England: criminal conversion narratives, execution accounts, trial reports, newspaper stories, and even crime ballads. By the 1730s, two types of execution broadsides—"last speeches" and "dying verses"—emerged as popular alternatives to execution sermons. While the earliest gallows broadsides tended to be quite pious and moralistic, later "last speeches" became increasingly secular in tone and biographical in content, packed with sometimes picaresque details concerning the lives and misdeeds of condemned malefactors. Between the 1730s and 1790s, both types of execution broadsides, along with a small but growing number of longer crime accounts and criminal autobiographies, vied for readers with the dozens of execution sermons that continued to appear. The result was a distinctly hybrid eighteenth-century configuration of regional crime literature.[30]

After 1800, however, a dramatically different popular literature of crime and punishment rapidly emerged in New England and elsewhere in the United States. Publishers discarded two of the dominant genres of the eighteenth century: execution sermons and "last speech" broadsides. The "last speeches" disappeared quite suddenly after the turn of the century, while gallows sermons petered out more gradually, vanishing entirely after the mid-1820s. Meanwhile, three new elements were added to the literary mix. First, trial reports, never very popular in New England during the eighteenth century, quickly emerged after 1800 as a dominant crime genre. Second, criminal biographies and autobiographies—typically much longer and more elaborate than the old "last speeches"—began to appear in large numbers. Many of these new biographies (both of criminals and of their victims) incorporated language and motifs derived from the several types of fiction—sentimental, Gothic, and romantic—that were revolutionizing American literary culture during the early national period. Third, newspaper editors dramatically increased their coverage of crimes and trials; this was particularly the case after the rise of the urban "penny press" during the 1830s.[31]

It should be emphasized that American murder publications of the early republic were by no means *identical* to the seventeenth-century English literature. In that regard, Halttunen skillfully delineates a number of specific motifs, such as a particular conception of "horror" as a "shutting down of the sensory faculties," and a new fascination with underground or concealed places. These do appear to have been carried into murder pamphlets of the early republic from contemporary Gothic fiction. Halttunen also relates new themes in nineteenth-century murder pamphlets to the rise of the "modern sentimental family" and changing conceptions of mental illness. In addition, as I demonstrate in *Pillars of Salt, Monuments of Grace,* other important innovations in early republican crime literature were influenced by contemporary sentimental literature, new courtship patterns, the development of a modern consumer culture, and the emergence—by the end of the eighteenth century—of a highly competitive, lawyer-dominated, adversarial trial system in the United States.[32]

Beyond these specific influences, the transformation of American crime literature, which had actually begun by the dawn of the eighteenth century, was less a "response" or "corollary" to the Enlightenment, or the humanitarian revolution, than a result of the gradual breakdown of a temporary and highly exceptional pattern of Puritan-dominated print culture in early New England.[33] The breakdown of that exceptional pattern, along with the proliferation of crime publications in other regions of North America (where Puritan influence had never been dominant), allowed for the reemergence of sensationalistic elements in Anglo-American murder publications that had long flourished in Old England's "pre-Enlightenment" crime literature.

That process was well under way by the early eighteenth century, and it continued during the decades that followed. After 1800, with the rapid popularization of the trial report, the sudden disappearance of the "last speech," and the more gradual demise of the execution sermon, a new pattern of legalistic and sensationalistic crime literature became dominant in New England and elsewhere in the United States. When authors, journalists, and publishers of the nineteenth century "touched" the corpses of American murder victims, it was as it had been in England two centuries earlier: the wounds would often flow afresh. Despite the early and exceptional efforts of New England's Puritan ministers to staunch the literary sensationalism of crime, the old adage ultimately held true: blood will out.

Chapter 3
A Tale of Two Cities:
Epidemics and the Rituals of Death in Eighteenth-Century Boston and Philadelphia

Robert V. Wells

> *What occurrence [is] so common as death?*
> —*Elizabeth Drinker (February 25, 1798)*

In a meditation written in seventeenth-century England, John Donne observed, "No man is an island, entire of itself; every man is a piece of the continent, a part of the main. If a clod be washed away by the sea, Europe is the less. . . . Any man's death diminishes me because I am involved in all mankind; and therefore never send to know for whom the bell tolls; it tolls for thee."[1] These words remind us of the importance of the social aspects of death rituals, that indeed, no man or woman is an island when it comes time to confront the last great passage. Historically, as well as today, rituals have provided both direction and comfort for the dying and their survivors, setting forth a script to be acted out with clearly defined roles and dialogue. Moreover, commonly accepted rituals link bereaved family and friends at a time when isolation is likely to be the least desirable of conditions.[2]

However clear and useful the rituals of death may be under normal circumstances, authors as varied as Thucydides, Edgar Allan Poe, and Albert Camus have reminded readers that during epidemics, rituals may become distorted or abandoned in the face of fears induced by unfamiliar and often loathsome forms of death.[3] Although the rituals of death in early America were well defined, epidemics occurred which not only undermined the power of rituals to comfort and direct, but even forced their temporary abandonment.[4] Two individuals who lived through such terrifying episodes were Puritan minister Cotton Mather, whose experiences with measles in 1713 and smallpox in 1721 illuminate tensions in his community, and Elizabeth Drinker, the wife of a Quaker merchant, who suffered through social collapse during the yellow fever epidemic in Philadelphia in 1793.[5]

Before observing how epidemics distorted the rituals of death, we must establish some sense of what normal practice involved. In his survey of colonial American culture patterns, David H. Fischer argues for the existence of four culturally and regionally distinct "deathways."[6] Here I will emphasize instead three broad sets of rituals, encompassing common expectations and their social contexts—because differences in the response to death were as often the result of personal circumstances as regional culture.[7]

The first set of rituals began at the moment when death was imminent, when one prepared to die—preferably with resignation to God's will. While obviously a personal if not spiritual exercise, preparation for death was most often accomplished amid family and friends. The second set of rituals involved separation beginning with the moment of actual death, extending through the preparing of the body and ultimately its interment. The deceased was literally and symbolically transferred from the world of the living to that of the dead, while survivors were consoled by various acquaintances. The final set of rituals emphasized the restoration of grieving survivors to a normal place in society and efforts to preserve the memory of the deceased.

The diary of Elizabeth Drinker (discussed at greater length below) goes far in helping us establish a sense of the normal rituals of death. An old friend and neighbor, Rebecca Waln, died in April 1798, after suffering a relapse for having "ventured out too soon after her late illness." During Waln's last days, Drinker and her sister attended this old friend, who had grown "insensible to light and noise." As Drinker prepared for a follow-up visit, Waln's servant girl arrived in tears with news that Elizabeth's old friend had died. Drinker "went over and stayed with the afflicted children 'till their other friends and relations arrived." She remained until a woman arrived to lay Waln out, at which time Drinker left, not wanting to be present when "that awful business commenced." Two days later, on the morning of the funeral, she went back "to take a last look at my old friend." Waln's family had prepared two rooms for company, but an ill-timed rainstorm kept many away. Only a handful accompanied the corpse to the burial ground. Although Drinker herself did not go, she almost shuddered when she wrote that this was "one of the longest days I have known."[8]

One of the most poignant episodes in Drinker's diary is her reaction to the death of her first-born child, Sally Drinker Downing, who died in September 1807, at the age of forty-six. Despite the mother's evident grief and personal loss, she was demonstrably appreciative of the support provided by a wide circle of acquaintances. While Sally lay ill for a number of days in September, her mother and family members remained at her side. On the twenty-fourth, Drinker alluded to her declining hopes for her daughter, and acknowledged her own weariness. Although Sally died around dawn on the twenty-fifth, Drinker did not write again until the twenty-eighth, noting only that she could not "recollect" the intervening days "in any order." When she was able to resume writing, Sally was "already in her grave." By then, Drinker was able to take pleasure in the fact that Sally had died well, "very quiet . . . without any struggle, sigh, or groan." Her body had been kept "till an apparent change took place"—assurance that the deceased was not merely in a coma. Elizabeth judged that such caution "always should be the case." She and two of her other children were the only ones "of our house" who accompanied the body to "the place of fixedness." Family and friends joined the procession, one of whom gave "a short testimony at the grave" regarding "a sense of well-being of the deceased." After the funeral, Drinker reported "great numbers" calling on the family, though she admitted a willingness to see but a few. Two days later she gratefully noted that an obituary had appeared in one of the local papers.[9]

One more example from Drinker's diary will suffice to familarize us with the details of ordinary death rituals. Dolly Salter, a friend of the family, had died outside of town, but was to be buried in Philadelphia. The Drinkers offered their house as a staging area from which the funeral would commence. On the morning of April 28, 1781, the body arrived and was transferred into a coffin obtained that day. The top was immediately screwed down, according to the family's wishes. Drinker admitted not seeing the body, commenting that her sister had, and thought that Dolly "appeared much like herself, considering what she had suffered." Family and friends arrived over the course of that day, perhaps in response to direct invitation, as was often the case in the Drinkers' world. At 6 P.M., the body was brought to the burying ground. After the interment, fifteen to twenty members of the funeral party returned to the Drinkers' for tea.[10]

From Drinker's extended comments, we see both the rituals of death at various stages—from preparation through separation to restoration—and the central role that family and friends played in insuring that neither the dying nor survivors faced this momentous passage alone. It is the collapse of this network of social support that becomes strikingly apparent in the distorted state of affairs brought on during epidemics.

It takes only a brief perusal of the diaries of Cotton Mather to realize how central death was to the life of this Puritan pastor. He was, of course, deeply concerned with the state of his own soul and how he might best prepare for death. His family was large and subject to the unhealthy conditions all faced in the American colonies. By the time Mather died in 1728, he had outlived two of his three wives and all but three of his fifteen children. His pastoral duties frequently required that he deliver comfort, counsel, and consolation as death approached, followed regularly by direct participation in funerary rituals. As he contemplated ways to improve on the management of death, Mather devised useful lessons which he conveyed in his funeral sermons; these in turn offered him opportunities to publish his ideas for the benefit of the community.

Our focus is on his responses to two different epidemics. The first was an outbreak of measles in the fall of 1713, during which he lost his second wife, newborn twins, a two-year-old daughter, and a maidservant. Despite his personal catastrophe, he remained cognizant of his pastoral duties to console those who suffered and provide an example of proper behavior in the face of imminent death. His ties to the community were never broken. The second epidemic was quite different. In 1721, Boston was visited by smallpox, a killer justly feared because of both fatality rates and disfiguring symptoms. Mather had recently become aware that inoculation was used in Africa and Turkey to inhibit the worst effects of the disease, and he vigorously proposed its adoption in Boston. Because inoculation meant deliberately giving a healthy person a live dose of smallpox and Mather had little proof that this treatment would work, many Bostonians attacked him, both in body and in reputation, as a threat to public safety.[11]

The first mention of the 1713 measles epidemic brought forth Mather's pastoral instincts. On October 18, he observed, "The measles coming into the town, it is likely to be a time of sickness, and much trouble in the families of the neighborhood. I would, by my public sermons and prayers, endeavor to prepare the neighbors for the trouble which their families are likely to meet withal." But the next day, his concern shifted to protecting his own family. On that day he expressed "apprehension of a very deep share, that my family may expect in the common calamity of the spreading measles." His strategy for prevention at home included augmenting "expressions of piety, in the daily sacrifices of my family," as well as awakening "piety, and preparation for Death, in the souls of the children."[12]

Within a week, his fears had been realized. On October 24, his son Increase was taken with what "appeared to be the measles." Three days later, a "desirable daughter," Nibby, was afflicted. But it was not until the thirtieth that he revealed one of his deepest fears. On that day, his wife delivered twins early, in an unexpected labor. He admitted "much distress" over her attendance on their sick children, believing that measles was almost universally fatal to pregnant women. But her safe delivery left him sensible to the "numberless favors of God." Even witnessing another child contract measles did not depress him.[13]

Amid growing concerns for his own family, Mather nevertheless was mindful of the community and his own almost Mosaic responsibility for its safety. On the twenty-seventh, he believed the presence of a "very sensible calamity" in the town required him to prepare a lecture on how all might succeed in "getting the blood of the great Passover sprinkled on our houses." Over the next two days, he reflected on how the epidemic was bound to intensify the kind of misery that winter ordinarily inflicted on his poverty-stricken New England neighbors. He vowed that he should act to "animate . . . charity . . . and . . . compassion." On November 4, he considered publishing a "little sheet" of advice for the sick and their families, but worried that he might not find the time.[14]

This was, of course, understandable. His wife, three more children, and his maid were all afflicted with measles. On November 7, uncertain over what "cup" God might ask him to drink, and struggling for a "patient submission unto the will of God," Mather decided to undertake a personal fast, humbling and sacrificing himself before God, so that "His wrath may be turned away from me, and from my family; and that the Destroyer might not have a commission to inflict any deadly stroke upon us." The next day, the Sabbath, Mather instructed his flock of the need for "patient submission to what ever cup our Heavenly Father shall order for us." He must have struggled with these words, for his wife just then had "the surprising symptoms of death upon her," a calamity he had feared since first hearing of the "venomous measles invading the country." The burden he assumed in trying to protect both family and flock was no doubt oppressive.[15]

Over the next two weeks, Mather grieved. His wife died on the ninth, and while Mather was pleased that God had "extinguished in her the fear of death," his own acceptance of loss was more difficult. Despite several desperately sick children, Mather arranged for publication of the sermon he preached at his wife's burial: "What Should be the Behavior of a Christian at a Funeral." He also contemplated a newspaper article recommending care for the sick. On the fourteenth, the epidemic proved stronger than the regimen of health he practiced at home, as his maidservant succumbed. Mather paused, and digressed in his personal journal, and seized on the consolation that this "wild, vain, airy girl" had become disposed to "serious religion" under his care.[16]

The minister's trial continued. While contemplating the need to prepare for his own death, and reflecting on "how a family visited with so much death, may become an example of uncommon piety," he was called upon to resign himself to the loss of his three youngest children. When the twins died one after the other, on November 18 and 20, Mather had little to say; they had been in his life a scarce three weeks. But the loss of Jerusha (aged two years, seven months) was another matter. On the day of the second twin's death, he "begged that such a bitter cup, as the death of that lovely child" might elude him. But as soon as he had buried the twins, he was forced to accept God's will "with the most submissive resignation" he could muster. From her deathbed, Jerusha roused long enough to ask her father to pray with her and expressed confidence that she "would go to Jesus Christ." Despite the toddler's optimism, Mather despairingly wrote: "Lord I am oppressed; undertake for me!"[17]

His resiliency in the face of so much personal tragedy is remarkable. On November 22, the day after Jerusha died, his pastoral instincts revived, as he observed: "It will be a great service unto my flock, for me to exemplify a patient submission to the will of God." Mindful that his family now had no living child under the age of seven, Mather turned his thoughts to how he might "with most exquisite contrivance and all the assiduity imaginable . . . cultivate my children, with a most excellent education." He calculated that the best thing he could do for his afflicted town was to provide "an example of bearing adversity after a suitable manner," believing the "eyes of the people are much upon me." He resolved that the best solution to his own anguish was to "die daily, and become a man dead unto this world; crucified unto all worldly enjoyments and impressions." Mather became so enamored of this daily preparation for death as a means of dealing with separation and loss, but still so attached to the world and mindful of his role in it, that he proposed to publish a sermon on the topic for the edification of his neighbors.[18]

As the epidemic subsided, and Mather recovered from "a month which devoured" his family, his thoughts stayed more regularly on how he and the town might benefit from such affliction. He resumed his common practice of fasting and prayer, still faulting himself for "the sins that have procured such a desolation . . . such as exhibits me to all the country, for an example of suffering affliction."[19] Calm acceptance of God's will, he believed, would both protect his family in the future and induce his neighbors to behave with a similar sense of humility. He found satisfaction on December 17, the public day of prayer in Boston, when a "liberal collection" for the poor and hungry was conducted. And by the twenty-third, he prepared a letter for circulation to the countryside on managing the measles. Local doctors had already declined his request to prepare such a document, and so, while anticipating "some invectives," he performed what he thought a necessary service. Thereafter, he was silent on the measles, although his diary ends with a list of the names of his children, with the note "Of 15, Dead 9, Living 6."[20]

If Mather anticipated "some invectives" for publishing recommendations on how to treat the measles, he perhaps should not have been surprised at the public reaction to his suggestion that smallpox might best be countered by deliberately infecting the well with this loathsome disease. Whereas he never lost sight of his connection to the people of Boston in 1713, the 1721 smallpox epidemic reduced the controversial minister to an island in a sea of angry neighbors.

At the time smallpox was first mentioned in the Boston public records, May 12, 1721, Mather was preparing a pamphlet advising women who were facing their "hour of travail" (childbirth) to prepare for death. And he was offering counsel to a black man scheduled for execution. There was also, at that moment, a tone of disaffection among certain members of his congregation, and he was losing parishioners. When Mather first noted in his diary on May 26 that "The grievous calamity of the small pox has now entered the town," he was already acquainted with the practice of inoculation, and wondered "how many lives might be saved by it." He decided to "lay the matter before the local physicians."[21]

Over the next nine months, the diarist wrote about many aspects of the epidemic, though he began his ruminations with a typical sense of self-importance by reminding himself of the need for humility lest God punish him for vanity. He recalled a sermon he had preached some months before warning Boston of the "speedy approach of the destroying Angel." Once again juggling his concern for the safety of his own children with the dictum that he must submit to God's will, Mather resolved to take action. Preparation and resignation, in his view, were not the same as fatalism. He was keenly aware, too, that his own life would be in danger, because his pastoral duties required exposure to the "horrid venom of the sick chambers."[22]

He prepared a history of inoculation for the local doctors on June 6, although he thought his essay on "the new discovery" might "save the lives . . . and the souls of many people," he expressed uncertainty about submitting it to the booksellers, "waiting for Direction." In spite of these words, he did not delay before sending a letter to doctors urging inoculation. His pastoral instincts surfaced, as he recognized the need to attend to "miserables neglected and perishing in sickness."[23]

The tone of Mather's discussion of smallpox changed dramatically in mid July, when he admitted that many citizens of Boston were angry over his proposed plan to infect the healthy to prevent death. He reassured himself that he was right to take "unspeakable consolation" in advancing methods that would "infallibly" save lives. The people, however, were unconvinced. As Dr. Zabdiel Bolyston began to follow Mather's advice and inoculate, the minister was surprised and obviously felt betrayed by the public's "furious obloquies and invectives." The depth of his anger is evident: "They rave, they rail, they blaspheme; they talk not only like idiots but also like fanatics." To Mather, "The Destroyer, being enraged at the proposal of anything that may rescue the lives of our poor people from him, has taken a strange possession of the people on this occasion."[24]

His confidence in the propriety of his actions was unshaken, though he was alarmed for his family. On July 18, he admitted that "the cursed clamor of a people strangely and fiercely possessed of the devil, will probably prevent my saving the lives of my two children" by inoculation. The contradiction is intriguing: he harbored no doubts as to the efficacy of inoculation, and wished to set an example for all of Boston; yet he recorded at this moment that his family's safety depended *solely* on prayer. Perhaps he was less sure of inoculation than he admitted, or perhaps he feared physical attacks on his children. In any case, the minister delayed until August 15 before inoculating his son Samuel.[25]

Between July 16 and September 4, Mather explicitly recorded Boston's hostility toward him a total of eleven times. He claimed that the town was engaged in a "monstrous and crying wickedness," in "epidemical follies," and revealingly referred to himself as one who was being "crucified." On August 22, when Samuel exhibited an unexpectedly severe reaction to his inoculation, Mather worried that if the son died, the father might "suffer a prodigious clamor and hatred from an infuriated mob." Two days later, as Samuel was recovering, Mather angrily observed, "The town is become almost an Hell upon earth, a city full of lies, and murders, and blasphemies." He felt that "Satan seems to have taken a strange possession of it, in the epidemic rage, against the notable and powerful and successful way of saving the lives of the people." After one last reference on September 4 to "a rage of wickedness among us," amidst "the arrows of Death," Mather abandoned his critique of the town.[26]

One reason for ignoring Boston may have concerned, once again, the suffering in his own family. In early September, he had reason to fear for the life of his daughter Nancy, who eventually recovered. But on the nineteenth of that month, daughter Abigail, who had recently given birth, went into decline, though not from smallpox. On the twenty-fourth, when Mather expected to baptize his new grandchild—to be named Resigned—he learned after morning service that the child had died. Mother followed daughter into the arms of death only two days later, but not before Mather had lamented, "To strengthen a dear child in the agonies of death is a sad work." Faced with this double loss, he reverted to his old familiar rituals, reminding himself of the need to serve as an example to his flock and to humble himself before his God.[27]

What is remarkable, given the antagonisms of the summer, is that Mather seems to have been gradually reunited with the community in October. He regularly noted the increasing demands on him to deliver prayers for the sick. As the epidemic proceeded, Bostonians began to post notices to this effect at the Old North Church. There were 202 such requests on October 7, and 322 on the fifteenth, all of which left him "exceedingly tired." Still, he resolved to make his prayers "as pertinent and pathetic as ever I can." He recognized that an epidemic was no time to fall short in the requisite rituals, no matter how great the demand on his time and energy. On October 28, recovering from a brief bout of illness himself, Mather commented, "Still objects of compassion enough."[28]

The peace between minister and town was soon to be broken. At the end of October, several relatives approached Mather, asking for assistance in warding off the pox as Dr. Boylston undertook more extensive inoculation.[29] Whether it was this that elicited renewed public criticism of Mather is unclear, but on October 29 he once again referred to attacks by "absurd and wicked people," confessing that he had not always preserved a proper "meekness" in his remarks on "the folly and baseness" around him. He did not let up in ministering to the numerous ill and needy, yet feeling "this abominable town treats me in a most malicious and murderous manner."[30]

This last metaphor proved something more, when just before dawn on November 14, an unknown person "threw a fired granado into the chamber" of his home, where a recently inoculated relative slept. Fortunately, for Mather and company, the fuse was knocked out as the bomb came through the window. A paper attached to the bomb read, "Cotton Mather, you dog, damn you: I'll inoculate you with this, with a pox to you." It is hard to imagine a more powerful message expressing the community's anger over his experiments in the face of death. Yet Mather did not want to admit this publicly: when he wrote a news account of the bomb-throwing incident several days later, he suggested that the offender was simply a disaffected member of his congregation.[31]

Nor was Mather intimidated by this attack. On November 19, he wrote in his diary, at some length, that all he was guilty of was "communicat[ing] a never-failing and a most allowable method of preventing death." He espoused "unutterable joy at the prospect of my approaching martyrdom." The depth of his passion and conviction is further evident in his elaboration: "when I think on my suffering Death for saving the lives of dying people, it ravishes me with a joy unspeakable and full of glory." In this instance, his powerful sense of righteousness is truly exceptional.[32]

Mather continued to promote inoculation, but he never approached martyrdom again. He prepared pamphlets and circulated them to the uninformed in Boston, across Massachusetts, and as far as Europe.[33] He reminded himself of the need to control "any tendency toward the least wish of evil" toward his opponents, finding a moment on December 6 to pray for the person who threw the bomb. At the same time, however, he bitterly promised "warnings . . . to be given unto the wicked printer" whom he blamed for fomenting community hostility toward him.[34]

As the epidemic wound down, Mather found himself ministering only to those who had accepted inoculation and were recovering from their mild cases. So strong was his attachment to his supporters that he referred to them as "my patients," adding that he would even "consider them as my relatives" whose piety and favor with God he would thus seek to improve. When time came for a ritual thanksgiving, he invited only those of his flock "who have had the benefit of the smallpox inoculated," gathering them at his home and not at the church.[35]

Seven decades later, Elizabeth Drinker chronicled the collapse of the rituals of death in Philadelphia in the yellow fever epidemic of 1793. Yellow fever is frequently a relatively mild infection with high rates of recovery, but when it is fatal it produces not only a yellowish tinge in many of its victims, but also external and internal hemorrhages. The latter produces the "black vomit," which led to its popular name.

Yellow fever had been present intermittently in Philadelphia from 1699 to 1762 before disappearing for thirty years.[36] In 1762, Drinker made brief note of "a sickly time in Philadelphia [with] many persons taken down with something very like the yellow fever."[37] But having moved out of town for the summer, occupied with a new husband and even newer baby (Sally), she expressed little interest and no concern over what was happening. Her reactions thirty years later were greatly different. Over the summer and fall of 1793, perhaps as many as five thousand perished in the epidemic, while half of the fifty thousand inhabitants fled to the surrounding countryside. Despite the presence of many other deadly killers, including tuberculosis (which probably killed more Philadelphians in the 1790s than yellow fever), this particular form of death proved especially alarming because of its unfamiliarity in 1793 and its disagreeable manifestation.[38]

On July 8, 1793, Drinker and her family made their annual escape from the heat and smells of a Philadelphia summer, taking up residence in nearby Germantown. As she began a new volume of her diary, she did not realize that this particular summer was to be so exceptionally fatal that she would later add "Book of Mortality" to the cover.[39]

During a fairly uneventful month in Germantown, Drinker peppered her diary with references to everyday concerns over health, and she rather laconically observed on August 16, " 'tis a sickly time now in Philadelphia, and there has been an unusual number of funerals lately here." Thereafter, she found the epidemic unavoidable, a constant theme until the end of November. Her initial offhand reference was soon succeeded by an anxious and even despairing attention to the general disaster. Two days later she noted the first of over four hundred deaths that she would record, naming either the victim or his or her family connections. Faced with an almost unimaginable scale of mortality, and gradually aware that several thousands of her fellow Philadelphians had died, Drinker may have recorded the many names both as an act of memory and to give a human dimension to what was a social catastrophe.[40]

After speculating on the causes of the epidemic, Drinker began to report evidence of the breakdown of social order in Philadelphia.[41] On September 1, she mentioned that a man was found dead in the road and that the body had been left several days. This was the first of many instances in which normal expectations of aid and comfort were denied. On September 4, she recorded the "sad story" of a young woman who had been serving as a nurse, but when she herself took sick, neighbors sent her off. Eventually a magistrate arranged for a cart to take her to the hospital, and there she was denied admittance, only to be found dead in the cart the next morning. The story of Robert Broker was further evidence of social disarray. The night Broker died of yellow fever, his wife went into labor. She called out her window for help, but no one responded until the following morning, when she, too, was found dead, though the newborn was alive. Given Drinker's own eagerness to care for her family and friends, this violation of social duty must have appalled her.[42]

Early in September, the Pennsylvania assembly resolved to abandon its business. Drinker's Philadelphia neighborhood was by now nearly "depopulated by death and flight," prompted by reports of several hundred Irish immigrants arriving with the fever. Most spectacular were the rumors: that several hundred French soldiers were marching on Philadelphia from New York, and that "5 Negroes" had been "taken up for poisoning the pumps." Drinker wisely judged these stories to be "flying reports, and most likely to be false." In late September, she heard of efforts in New York to cut off communication with Philadelphia.[43]

Perhaps most shocking of all was the mounting evidence that long familiar death rituals were being abandoned in the fevered yellow face of the "King of Terrors." Among the first rituals to go were funeral processions. On September 4, Drinker observed, " 'tis said many are buried after night, and taken in carts to their graves." Two days later she reported, "the doors of houses where the infection is are ordered to be marked to prevent any but those absolutely necessary from entering." Moreover, "the ringing of Bells for the dead" was already forbidden. The normal pattern of laying out bodies and keeping them at home for several days was also abandoned. Josiah Elfrith was "buried as many others are in 2 or 3 hours after his departure." And again, "the dead are put in their coffins just as they die without changing their clothes or laying out, are buried in an hour or two after their disease [decease?]." Owing to the frequency and suddenness of death, "graves are dug before they are spoke for, to be ready." But the degree to which rituals were distorted by fear may have reached its worst when "two or three dead bodies were thrown into Friends burying ground over the wall." By the end of the month, reports came from the city that "coffins were kept in ready piles" and trenches were dug in the potter's field for the poor.[44]

The custom of family and friends' participation in death rituals was abandoned during the epidemic. When a woman who had acquired yellow fever in Philadelphia died in Germantown on September 23, Drinker duly noted that no one but her husband and children were with her when she died. The next day, Drinker lamented that no one would assist the husband, who was therefore "under the necessity of putting her in the coffin and that into the hearse." He was fortunate to find a man to carry the coffin to the grave, though without any escort of family or friends. On September 28, Michael Pragers, a Philadelphia merchant who also died in Germantown, had to be buried in an orchard when he was refused a spot in the local cemetery. Bodies were found in houses days after death, and funerals were sometimes so secret that neighbors were unaware of nearby deaths.[45]

Drinker was normally a very sociable woman, but as the epidemic progressed, she expressed significant discomfort when faced with visitors recently arrived from Philadelphia. On September 30, she remarked that

Josiah Lions "was by no means an acceptable visitor" owing to his companionship with a recent victim.[46] Her own son Henry found himself sick from smoking a cigar while taking a walk on October 5, and quickly dashed into an orchard to "discharge" his stomach. He was alarmed lest he be thought ill of "the prevailing disorder." On October 17, Drinker commented on the curious case of Samuel Shoemaker, thought by his attendant to be dead. On returning with a coffin, the attendant found his charge sitting on the side of the bed, "endeavoring to put on his shoes." That Shoemaker actually died an hour later did not reassure Drinker, who observed that he came very close to being "screwed in his coffin" alive.[47]

Although Drinker was familiar with the accepted rituals of her time, she only once resorted, like Mather, to the standard litany, observing on October 9, "The gloom continues in our city, the awful disease by no means lessened—may we endeavor for preparation and resignation." Preparation and calm resignation were certainly not characteristic of Drinker or her fellow Philadelphians during this epidemic. Once the epidemic had subsided in November, Drinker was careful to note the return of traditionally conducted funerals.[48] But she was also aware that the fever had left numerous widows and orphans in need of assistance. Soon, she and her husband became active in raising money for relief, not just out of a conventional sense of obligation, but as a means, too, of reestablishing community and social bonds that had been so severely damaged by the epidemic.[49]

The rituals of death under average circumstances in eighteenth-century America were clearly established. They involved extensive community support for the dying and their families. But in times of epidemics, when faced with often fearsome, and occasionally unfamiliar causes of death, community solidarity could easily deteriorate. When the rituals of death were so distorted, if not abandoned altogether, men and women were left, however temporarily, as islands in a sea of disease.

Part II
The Politics of Death

Chapter 4

Death and Satire:
Dismembering the Body Politic

Nancy Isenberg

> *I embraced her, but as I imprinted the first kiss on her lips,*
> *they became livid with the hue of death; her features appeared*
> *to change, and I thought that I held the corpse of my dear mother*
> *in my arms . . . . I started from my sleep with horror . . . I beheld*
> *the wretch—the miserable monster that I had created.*
>
> —*Mary Shelley,* Frankenstein *(1818)*

Death and the state have something in common: both have been personified as a woman. Satire, too, acquired the metaphorical physique of a female. In his highly influential periodical, *The Spectator,* Joseph Addison dressed Satire in a feminine guise, writing in 1711: "*Satyr* had Smiles in her Look, and a Dagger under her Garment."[1] During the volatile years of America's War for Independence, through the French Revolution and the birth of the American party system in the 1790s, death was inextricably linked with gendered images of state power. In British and American political caricature alike, death loomed large.

In a strange, if not perverse, way, the visual "birth" of American republicanism and democracy in the world of satirical prints came not with a whimper or bang, but with the far more potent symbol of dismemberment. Beginning with the Stamp Act protest in 1765 and appearing consistently throughout the American Revolution, engravers rendered both crude and sophisticated caricatures that employed female figures, animals, and men whose bodies were torn, maimed, and mutilated. By the 1790s, as national parties formed, Federalist satirists published depictions of the French Revolution that offered "Dame Guillotine" serving up severed heads, while the plebian *sans-culottes,* based on accounts of the counterrevolutionaries, rapaciously mangled and devoured body parts.

Historically, the genre of satire and artistic representations of death have both utilized the elements of irony. Both have been meant to shock or in some way scandalize viewers or readers, while ultimately reflecting seriously on issues of philosophic import in human affairs. And both play into basic fears associated with annihilation. It was believed that both satire and death possessed the power to destroy an individual's identity. Death is the Other—unknown, dark, savage, and incomprehensible. If death suggests the absence of life (figuratively imagined as disappearance—or the absence of a reflected image), satire represents the grotesque, suggesting a perverted or distorted mirror image of the person. As a device of propaganda, moreover, both satire and death could be used to illustrate the symbolic decay of the nation-state, to inflict mortal wounds on legislation, and to viciously attack a public figure by putting a rhetorical dagger in his or her back.

Sex and violence have remained staple themes in satire, concentrating on ludicrous or grotesque images of human folly. According to Addison, scathing satirical wit taunts readers like a female smile, while its revelations can kill like a hidden dagger. Death in art similarly has had a long history of engagement with sadistic themes. In *Death and the Maiden* (1517), Swiss satirist and artist Niklaus Manuel captured the macabre eroticism of death. Portrayed as a decomposing skeleton, Death steals a kiss (the "kiss of death") and much more: he reaches under the skirt of his female victim as she invites his eternal conquest of her body and soul. The "transi" figures of the Middle Ages were the first to depict rotting flesh; skeletons and piles of corpses added to the nameless and faceless reminders that death steals or wipes out a person's identity. Not even a beautiful young woman is immune: she will turn pale, her hair will fall out, and her tempting flesh will become, in the unabashed words of one art historian, "a rotten heap of muck."[2] The common denominator in Addison and Manuel is their reliance on ironic contradiction. Nothing is quite so vivid as Manuel's scandalous contrast between physical lust (embodied by the maiden) and its most feared antithesis: death as the definitive cessation of bodily desire.

The politics of building an empire, of conquering and colonizing continents, led to the adoption of feminized imagery for the new imperial landscape. As early as 1575, the "New World" or "America" found expression in European art as the Indian Queen. The queen often appeared regal and warlike in bearing, Amazonian in size, "tawney" in hue—a primitive power contained in a voluptuous female body.[3] Flemish artist Jan van der Straet's classic rendering of *America* centered on a languid and seductive nude woman who lies in a hammock gazing up at the arriving explorer, Amerigo Vespucci.[4]

Illustrations of exploration and conquest generally depended on contrasting visions of America. On the one hand, the New World conjured images of a primitive, pastoral utopia, replete with alluring treasures and endless wealth. On the other hand, in the minds of European artists, this same exotic paradise could be a living hell, marked by frightening discoveries such as the Indians' ritual cannibalism. In the background of van der Straet's view of the New World, several naked women sit around a fire, in which male body parts are being roasted and, presumably, are to be eaten.[5]

During the same period, scientists and philosophers readily appropriated geographical metaphors to explain the interior of the human body. They associated the new "science" of the body, introduced through human dissection, with the thrill of "discovery." With the publication of Vesalius's *Humani Corporis Fabrica* in 1543, the interior of the body was mapped out in detailed illustrations. Like seafarers Columbus and Vespucci, discoverers laid claim to bodily organs and systems, labeling each with their names, just like place names on maps. From the sixteenth to the eighteenth century, scientists considered themselves colonizers of the terra incognita of the human body. As a result, the visual territory of the body was now regarded both as an object of domination and as property. The dissected body was feminized and eroticized, for a woman's body best symbolized medicine's proprietary claims. On the title page of *Fabrica*, Vesalius had himself pictured with his right hand on a dissected female body, a gesture that aptly pointed to his mastery of anatomy and life itself: the dissected woman exposed "an open womb."[6]

The principal allegorical image of Great Britain, "Britannia," made her pictorial debut a century later.[7] By the eve of the American Revolution, this classically attired female became a stock figure in most political caricatures. She resembled Athena (or Minerva), carrying a spear and holding up a shield emblazoned with the Union Jack. Often called "mistress of the sea," she was increasingly identified with Britain's worldwide commercial and colonial dominion, accompanied in many prints with icons such as globes, maps, and ships. She grew in popularity alongside the ballad character of the Warrior Woman, a cross-dressing military heroine—a working-class Joan of Arc—who followed her lover into battle.[8]

Eighteenth-century political caricature drew on all of these powerful iconic traditions. Benjamin Franklin's frequently reproduced design, *Magna Britannia; her Colonies Reduc'd* (1765 or 1766), brings together several crucial images: the empire as woman and as map, mutilation and dissection, and macabre sexual humor used explicitly for political purposes (Figure 4.1). There is little doubt that Franklin was one of the most prolific propagandists of the Revolutionary period. He first published the image during the Stamp Act crisis, selecting a design primarily intended to convince members of Parliament to repeal the new tax. Living in London while acting as Pennsylvania's colonial agent, he watched the controversy unfold within an English political context. He participated anonymously in public debate by sending letters to the newspapers, and he testified before Parliament on the injustice of the new taxation system. He hired an engraver to print the emblematic caricature on cards which were subsequently

Figure 4.1. Benjamin Franklin's *Magna Britannia; her Colonies Reduc'd* (1765–66). Courtesy The Library Company of Philadelphia.

distributed to members of Parliament. The cartoon, along with his lengthy interview before the House of Commons on February 13, 1766, were then published and distributed in the colonies.[9]

Although several scholars have assessed Franklin's emblematic design, they have ignored the gendered meaning of dismemberment in his cartoon. One reason for this oversight is that *Magna Britannia* was not Franklin's first design based on dismemberment. His earlier "cartographic caricature," as Karen Cook has termed the snake emblem of 1754, was intended to encourage colonial assemblies to support the Albany Plan, an intercolonial defense scheme. Each severed section of the snake represented a colony, and Franklin made the underlying message clear by appending the motto "Join or Die." If united, the English colonies would survive. If not, as Franklin explained in the *Pennsylvania Gazette* alongside the cartoon, they would find themselves easy prey for their French and Indian enemies; the latter were well known for their inclination to "murder and scalp our farmers, with their wives and children," so as to destroy British America.[10] Disunity, physical mutilation, and "ruin" were common themes in Franklin's two cartoons.

Nevertheless, a snake is not a woman. When it came to his Stamp Act design, Franklin understood that a human subject—a female figure—was necessary. His print played off the surgical trope, then in vogue, used to define the political status of the colonies.[11] The theme of political dissection had found expression in a 1749 caricature, which Franklin was most likely mimicking directly. It was entitled *The Conduct, of the two B[utche]rs* and featured two prominent English officials, posed as quack surgeons. This print has much in common with the last panel of William Hogarth's *Four Stages of Cruelty* (1751), in which a criminal is grossly mangled on the dissection table.[12] *The Conduct, of two B[utche]rs* is a cartographic caricature of Britannia, identifying body parts as territories; the scalpel cuts loose land like discarded limbs.[13]

Dissection is a crucial subtext in Franklin's cartoon, just as public dissections were routinely performed in England and made their way to the colonies in the 1760s. Given that William Hunter and William Hewson were among his close friends, it is probable that Franklin himself witnessed a public dissection.[14] Hewson operated an extremely popular anatomy theater, and Hunter was a principal advocate of "hands-on" dissection. In 1765, Hunter requested government patronage for a plan to open a medical school and anatomy museum. His anatomy collection contained human and animal body parts, heads, limbs, organs and bones, dried, pickled, and jarred for display—13,000 specimens in all.[15]

An uncanny similarity exists between Franklin's *Magna Britannia* and Hunter's early engraving *The Anatomy of the Human Gravid Uterus* (Figure 4.2). Hunter based his image on a dissection of a pregnant corpse that he performed in 1750, commissioning his first engraving two years later. By 1765, he had acquired fifteen plates, which he distributed to some scientists and displayed to others. In both Franklin's and Hunter's images, a female subject is in the seated position, amputated legs resembling chunks of meat, with the bone in the middle visible. These drawings eerily preserve the moment of death, purified like specimens, with neither signs of decay nor evidence of blood. As L. J. Jordanova has argued, Hunter's effect of "realism and butchery" was typical of medical representations of the period. Franklin would have felt completely comfortable mixing science and satire.[16]

In Britain and her colonies, dissection was commonly identified with "mangled corpses," "butchery," and "willful mutilation," in part because the victims of dissection were cut up beyond recognition. Dissection constituted a form of social death legally sanctioned for use against those convicted of capital crimes such as murder, rape, and infanticide.[17] Those executed were denied a proper burial and the possibility of resurrection, and their fragmented bodies reduced them to indistinguishable parts, devoid of spiritual integrity or even a human identity. In the last panel of the *Four Stages of Cruelty*, Hogarth best captured this indignity in his portrait of the dissecting chamber: an attendant drags the victim's intestines across the table to a large pail, a receptacle for body parts; the heart has also been thrown out and a dog is about to eat it. The body is now mere pieces of meat, or simply waste.[18]

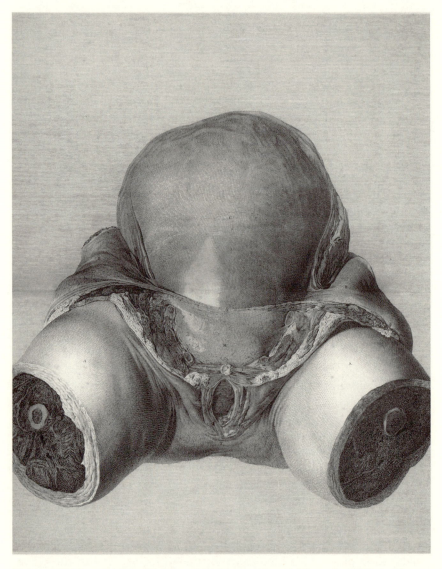

Figure 4.2. Plate IV, *The Anatomy of the Human Gravid Uterus,* by William Hunter (c. 1750–74; rpt. 1851). Illustration by J. V. Rynsdyk.

Reduction is a key theme for Franklin in his Stamp Act emblem as well. Reduction implied not merely the loss of territory, or diminution in size, but the loss of visible status as well—the divestment of public stature and economic standing. The cartoon's motto, *"Date Obolum Bellisario,"* or "Give a Penny to Belisarius," is particularly revealing. Belisarius was a famous Roman general reduced to penury and blindness. Stripped of title and power, and then disfigured, he was transformed from a bold warrior into a weakling, a complete mockery of his former self. Less than a man, perhaps even womanish, he was socially invisible.[19]

Curiously, an earlier Franklin print featured a similar allusion. The frontispiece of the 1747 pamphlet, *Plain Truth,* contained the Latin motto *Non votes, neque suppliciis mulebribus, auxiliary deorum parantur* ("Divine assistance and protection are not to be obtained by timorous prayers, and womanish supplications.") Not surprisingly, in the Stamp Act design, Britannia herself embodies "womanish supplications." Her eyes look heavenward, as if petitioning God for relief from misery. By the time Franklin's Stamp Act print became a broadside, published in Philadelphia between 1766 and 1769, the meaning of the emblem was no longer left to chance. Belisarius was described as "barbarously" having had his eyes "pulled out," and Britannia's physiognomy was interpreted thus: "View the Countenance of Great Britain . . . nothing but abject dependency; Her Eyes, and the Stumps of her mangled Arms raised toward Heaven in Vain."[20]

After the repeal of the Stamp Act, Franklin sent printed cards of his cartoon to friends and family in America. It was meant, as he told his fellow printer David Hall, to "show the Mischiefs of reducing Colonies by Force of Arms." To his sister Jane Mecom, in Boston, he added, "The Moral is, that the Colonies might be ruined, but that Britain would be maimed."[21] Franklin's pun is deviously simple: How can armless Britannia subdue the colonies by "force of arms"? Britain's use of force would reduce her arms to mangled stumps.

Reduction and ruin had a sexual meaning as well. In another letter, signed "Homespun" and published in England and the colonies in 1766 and 1767, Franklin attacked John Bull for a lack of "manners" toward his family members—England's colonies. Conquest and family affection must be at odds. It is in the same context that Franklin employs the political analogy of rape. As to English aggression, he cajoles, "Remember, you courted Scotland for one hundred years, and would fain have had your *wicked will* of her. She virtuously resisted all your importunities, but at length kindly consented to become your wife."[22] To Franklin, political force—force of arms—is figuratively rape.

To equate maiming and ravishment was not unique to Franklin. According to Johnson's *Dictionary,* the words *rape* and *maim* are remarkably similar: both involve privation, the act of taking away by violence, in the case of *rape* or *ravishment*; by reduction of a necessary part, in the case of *maim.* If a woman loses her beauty and grace when violated and deflowered, the maimed victim is disfigured and defective. Both are viewed socially as damaged and defiled.[23]

Neither does it appear coincidental that Franklin's design shares several features with an older Flemish print on war and camp life: Urs Graf's *A*

Casualty of War (1514). Here an armless young woman, with a wooden leg stands beside a lakeside village. Her breast is deeply wounded (in Franklin's print Britannia's spear is pointed at her own, possibly missing, breast).[24] The Flemish figure appears to be partly blind. The military, as one scholar writes, has been "sadistically in her and at her."[25] Rape and maiming are intertwined in this disturbing portrait of women and war.

Later variations of *Magna Britannia* stress the theme of sexual violation even more. In 1768, the print was published in *The Political Register*, a London magazine, accompanied by another caricature of Britannia being poked in the eye by a French figure. Lord Bute (leading minister and America's antagonist) stabs her in the back and lifts her skirts, saying, "Now I show you her Weakness you may strike home," while Spain indelicately thrusts his sword into her buttocks.[26] Two later prints, one published by M. Darly in England, entitled *Britannia Mutilated* (1774), and a similar Dutch version (1780), dramatically embellish Franklin's original design (Figure 4.3). Now Britannia is completely naked, chained to what appears to be a rock or a tree—the British oak in Franklin's original. The Dutch adaptation adds bloody stumps and color, making her dismemberment more gory and sensational.[27] Adding chains, and removing her clothes and spear, converts Britannia from the maimed warrior into a colonial fantasy of female captivity. Like the classical story of Andromeda, whose parents had her chained to a rock, Britannia represents (far more explicitly) the ideals of female helplessness, daughter sacrifice, and an erotically charged image of sexual submission.[28]

Images of dismemberment persisted throughout the Revolutionary War. Paul Revere engraved *America in Distress* (1775) featuring a seated female figure surrounded by male physicians. One doctor has an ax in his hand, another a knife, and a third, holding chains, says, "She is Mad & must be chained!" Threatening to chop, slice, stab, and restrain, the British state physicians are ready to kill, if not dissect, their most unwilling patient.[29]

Rape and ruin were equally important themes. Francis Hopkinson, one of the foremost American satirists of the Revolution, played off *Magna Britannia* when he published a poem in 1778, entitled *"Date Oblolum Belisario."* His Britannia had become an old woman dressed in rags. America is cast as the orphan child whom she had formerly taken under her care. Sexual molestation remains a subplot, but here the villain is Britannia's son King George III: he "beheld the maid" and "With fierce lascivious eye, / To ravish her plan he laid, / And she was forc'd to flee."[30]

By the end of the war, dismemberment came to symbolize territorial disputes, as in English artist James Gillray's *Britannia's Assassination* (1782). In this print, Britannia is pictured as a decapitated statue, seated on a globe. In the background, a male Indian (representing America) flees. Under one arm he carries the arm of Britannia, who is holding an olive branch; under the other, he carries her head. A similar theme was used in another

BRITTANNIA   MUTILATED.
or the Horrid (but true) Picture of Great Brittain, when Deprived of her Limbs, BY HER ENEMIES

Figure 4.3. *Britannia Mutilated. or the Horrid (but true) Picture of Great Brittain when Deprived of her Limbs by her Enemies,* published by M. Darly, November 29, 1774. Courtesy The Library Company of Philadelphia.

pro-British engraving entitled *The Belligerant Plenipo's* (1782), which anticipated the outcome of the Paris peace negotiations (Figure 4.4). France, Holland, and Spain, whose plenipotentiary envoys are identified as male figures, are missing either legs or arms; the amputated parts are lost colonial possessions, scattered at the feet of George III. Only America, portrayed as an Indian princess, wears a smile, saying, "I have got all I wanted Empire!" Her pleasure comes from the fact that the half of George III's crown that does not sit upon his head adorns one of her breasts.[31]

The half-crown that adorns the breast is significant. Why is the crown placed there rather than on her head? To the English, America is painted as a young woman who covets wealth, and who employs her feminine wiles to seduce Britain into giving her half the kingdom. Much like Franklin's satirical editorials, the treaty negotiations are a family affair, a divorce settlement or an inheritance dispute. While George III makes concessions, his greedy female relative America (it could be wife, sister, or daughter) secures for herself a political fortune. She proudly wears the crown over her breast. Consequently, pro-English satirical prints emphasized America's criminal theft

Figure 4.4. *The Belligerant Plenipo's*, published by W. Richardson, December 6, 1782. Courtesy Colonial Williamsburg Foundation, Abby Aldrich Rockefeller Folk Art Museum, Williamsburg, Virginia.

and greed, comparing the rebellious colonies to an ungrateful relative. In contrast, those who supported the Revolution, such as Franklin, Revere, and Hopkinson, underscored English aggression and America's desire to flee from sexual persecution and political ruin.

In another significant way, Hopkinson's poem and Revere's caricature allude to an unspoken assumption present in Franklin's earlier print: the commingling of birth and death imagery. If the state was metaphorically female, then civil unrest and revolutions, while capable of giving birth to new nations, could also physically drain the mother country and leave her life in ruins (or leave her dead). Losing a body part is akin to losing a child, when the amputee is a woman. Paul Revere's 1775 engraving *America in Distress* depicts a live woman surrounded by physicians armed with cutting tools and weapons (further conflating the act of giving birth with the threat of death). The doctors are preparing for an operation that resembles a caesarean birth or induced abortion. Or might they be prematurely rushing their patient to the dissecting table? Given that Franklin's model was Hunter's *Gravid Uterus* (based on dissections of pregnant corpses), which was published in 1774, the keenly focused

Revere must have appreciated the connection between pregnancy and dissection.[32]

There would be no depictions of virgin births or ordinary live births of America in political satire. In Hopkinson's poem, for example, Britannia loses her biological connection to America; she is recognized as merely the temporary legal guardian of an orphaned nation. Revere's engraving most likely reveals that the English physicians are interested in aborting what they see as an unnatural birth of "liberty" by a mad woman. As in Franklin's *Magna Britannia*, there is no prospect of birth. Delivery had one meaning and one destiny—death.

So, on both sides of the Atlantic, the creative act of political separation was not once analogized to a natural birth. From Franklin to Hopkinson, the mother country was either driven by a death wish, wherein mother and child were both killed, or else the natural parentage of Britannia was denied. The symbolic act of cutting the umbilical cord was displaced by images of death and disownment. At best, the nourishing mother country could merely postpone death or separation, because, as Franklin suggested, her masculine alter ego desired world domination. The aggressive impulse of the empire-building John Bull or George III threatened to incite a premature and unnatural demise of the state.

While Franklin praised the natural fecundity of colonial America, he likewise acknowledged that dismemberment was the ultimate symbol of tyranny and the miscarriage of justice.[33] Inspired by Hunter's engravings, Franklin envisioned Magna Britannia as a fertile, nourishing mother turned corpse; now mute and immobile, she is denied the capacity to give and sustain life. Nation-states set in motion their own deaths, arresting their natural increase by placing the need for absolute power above survival. And what better way to convey this disturbing truth than to mutilate the female body, representing waste and ruin through the imperiled corpse of Magna Britannia.

If *The Belligerant Plenipo's* projected the image of an uneasy reconciliation between Great Britain and the United States in 1782, diplomatic relations remained tense for decades. Although allies during the Revolution, France and America would also clash, engaging in a limited conflict known as the Quasi-War from 1797 to 1801. During the first decade under the federal constitution, American politics gave birth to a party system, dividing the nation into two distinct factions. Diplomatic struggle and party identity were intertwined because each party identified the other as the puppet of a foreign power. The ruling Federalists berated "Frenchified" Democratic-Republicans, who in turn saw the party in power as slavish Anglophiles, afraid to challenge Britain's naval supremacy.

Amid partisan bickering, English émigré William Cobbett became the most widely read journalist in the nation, as well as the foremost defender of Tory and Federalist political views. Settling in Philadelphia in 1794 and writing as "Peter Porcupine," he published fifteen pamphlets within five years, and edited the most popular newspaper at the time. Although, by employing an American pseudonym, he tried to disguise his Englishness, his British roots explain his vitriolic rejection of the French Revolution.[34] Cobbett flayed democratic supporters with his sharply shaved quill pen, transforming everything associated with the French Revolution into a bloody burlesque. He had ample friends and ample enemies, for as First Lady Abigail Adams noted, his "shafts are always tipt with wit."[35]

By 1798, at the peak of Cobbett's popularity, several political issues converged, all of which seemed to legitimate his conspiratorial portrait of the French. In April of that year, President Adams publicly announced that the French government had offended three American envoys sent to Paris. In the so-called XYZ Affair, the French had tried to bribe the envoys, supporting the claims of Cobbett and the Federalists that French republicanism was bottomed on corruption. The XYZ Affair led to severe repercussions in the United States when Congress passed the Alien and Sedition Acts, threatening expulsion of the French from America and gagging journalists critical of the administration. War fever swept the country. Cobbett gladly stoked the flames, stigmatizing all Francophiles by labeling them as potential traitors. If the French invaded, he wrote in *Porcupine's Gazette*, then anyone "who is for the enemy, is the enemy of his country," and should be shot.[36]

Cobbett placed satire at the center of every major political controversy and provided pungent invectives which, in turn, supplied American caricaturists with humorous material. Two popular prints, *The Times: A Political Portrait* (1798) and *Cinque-Tetes; or the Paris Monster* (1798), deserve particular attention, because they show the persistence of dismemberment as a political and sexual trope. These prints also reveal how much the iconography had changed: one references the guillotine, the other a ritualization of revolutionary violence. The ironic detachment of Franklin's satire was being replaced with graphically visual examples of corporeal taboos to convey the horror of the Revolution. Three allegorical images dominated: monstrosity, savagery, and cannibalism. Cobbett's writings were suffused with these same allusions. His satire staged the Revolution as a farce, as a failed theatrical production and, in the words of Edmund Burke, a "monstrous tragic-comedy."[37]

In *The Times: A Political Portrait*, Cobbett's fear of a French invasion materialized (Figure 4.5a).[38] A military figure rides in a "Chariot," representing the federal government, but he is delayed from moving forward by democrats, led by Thomas Jefferson and his ally, the Swiss-born Pennsylvania Congressman Albert Gallatin. The verse beneath their feet, "Stop de wheels of de geuvernement," mocks Gallatin's heavy accent.[39] While George Washington would be expected to assume the role of the military

Figure 4.5a *(above)*. *The Times: A Political Portrait* (1798). Courtesy Collection of The New-York Historical Society, negative accession number 2737. Figure 4.5b *(below)*. Detail from *The Times: A Political Portrait*. In the background, standing before the ship, is a female figure, most likely the Goddess of Liberty, who is endowed with large, ominous breasts. On shore, a ghostly figure with a skull for a head (perhaps Death itself) carries a head on a pike.

leader in this print, the figure does not resemble him in build or features—features that would be easily recognized by all Americans. A closer look reveals the countenance of John Adams, the sitting president in 1798; this is odd because Adams was rarely identified in military dress. But the symbolism remains relevant: in May 1798, Adams appeared in military uniform and wore a sword when addressing the twelve hundred young men who marched to his home to offer their services in a prospective war with France.[40]

Cobbett's arch enemy, Francophile editor Benjamin Franklin Bache, also appears in this print. His role is central to the plot of the caricature: he is trampled under foot by the team of soldiers who pull Adams's carriage. A page of his Philadelphia newspaper, the *Aurora*, lies just beyond the reach of his hands, and a dog simultaneously reads it and urinates on it. In the background, dark clouds are forming, marking the arrival of the French on shore. These *sans-culottes* immediately start decapitating heads, and one darkened, deathlike figure dances gleefully with a bloody trophy on a pike held in the air. On the ocean there appears a buxom female figure, the French Goddess of Liberty. The inscription under the invaders' feet makes the allegorical image perfectly obvious: "The Cannibals are landing" (Figure 4.5b).

The most fascinating aspect of this print is the message it conveys about the Alien and Sedition Acts. Cobbett had constantly attacked Bache and other democrats as "howling *sans-culottes*," equating their political prose with "savage speech."[41] Like the Sedition Act, Adams's troops and carriage crush Bache's treasonous paper, while the dog—symbolizing his generally devoted readership—expresses its unprecedented contempt for his libelous defamation of the government.[42]

The allusion to Bache's "savage speech" is directly connected to the gruesome acts of the French invaders. Cannibalism, perhaps the most disturbing taboo, equated the French with savages. Their transgression, action without speech, prefigures the demise of the public sphere.[43] Cobbett had implied that savage speech devours civility and the last remnant of rational public discussion. Nothing more aptly conveys this anxiety than cannibalism because eating human flesh is an action beyond conscience or sympathy, invoking an uncivilized world where words have no value.

In Europe and America alike, cannibalism was a persistent motif during the French Revolution, a dark, unsettling family secret: the desire of a country to "devour its own children."[44] Rhetorically and graphically, in the writings and prints of the Revolution's critics, cannibalism conflated the savage consumption of body parts with sexual deviance; the image of bodily mutilation was infused with a perverse, even pornographic, meaning. Cobbett picked up on these sexual connotations in his writings. To emphasize sexual disorder he made the French Revolutionaries a monstrous breed capable of unthinkable transgressions against the human body. In Cobbett's writing such as *The Bloody Buoy* (1796 and 1797), bodies are subject to "overkill"; they are literally ripped apart, sexually mutilated, and parts are eaten.[45]

The Bloody Buoy is a tedious catalogue of graphically disturbing tales. In one account, a woman about to be married is raped and her breasts are "torn off"; in another, a female victim has her "embryo" ripped from her womb and put on a pike. The revolutionaries are "assassins," in Cobbett's words, turning their country into a blood fest, "hacking [women and priests] to pieces, tearing out their bowels," or "biting their hearts." Elsewhere he identifies a town square that had become a public morgue, filled with "naked female dead bodies."[46]

Such unnatural acts made the Revolution "monstrous." Its desire for blood could never be quenched, while its penchant for theatricality unleashed social disorder. The Goddess Liberty, the French republic's symbol of freedom, had transmogrified into a devouring mother.[47] Liberty became a "many-headed Hydra," who consumed her children, unable to distinguish her enemies from her own flesh and blood.[48] Massachusetts Federalist Fisher Ames described the French Jacobins in his own country in similar terms. The Democratic-Republicans were a "female monster" and were compared to an ancient fury "with eyes that flash wild fire"; "she speaks, and an epidemic fury seizes the nation."[49]

Cobbett constantly ridiculed the perversion of sexual and familial roles—another sign of the unnatural consequences of the French Revolution. American democrats, he feared, were gamely putting on French airs, in a burlesque imitation that was upsetting the natural order of society. Those American democrats who dressed à la tricolor when they organized civic feasts were, to him, contemptible buffoons. Cobbett's acerbic wit emerges as he accuses these men of taking the French idea of fraternity too far, reducing their democratic clubs into scenes of foppery and homosexuality, with abundant "ganderfrolicks, and their squeezing, and hugging and kissing one another."[50] Likewise, American women who dared admire those "terrible termagants," the "heroines of Paris," and who spouted the doctrine of sexual equality were "fiery Frenchified Dames," "monsters in human shape, a bully in petticoats." He found such women "completely odious."[51]

In Cobbett's vocabulary, French women fell into three categories: monsters, passive objects of grotesque mutilation, and horrified spectators. The feminized gaze was developed in the execution literature of the Revolution. A helpless spectator watched parents, spouses, or loved ones being murdered or decapitated. Such treatment of the feminized gaze reflected a unique erotic sensibility, suggesting a kind of necrophilia while evoking the terror of watching the murderous Revolution unfold.[52] Cobbett achieved the same effect when he described "republican marriages" as the collective drowning of naked men and women "tied together face to face."[53] In two separate accounts, he mercilessly places the reader in positions of impotence. One story told of a father "put to death before the eyes of [his] child," a ten-year-old boy, "whom they besmeared his face with his blood."[54] An equally gruesome dual murder concerned a French official's failed escape to America, in which the decapitated head of the father was "pressed against his lips," while the son's own heart was "torn from his body."[55]

The dominant plot of American stories of this genre continued to focus on women's anguished vision. A tale appearing in the *Philadelphia Minerva*, in 1796, told of a young woman who asked a soldier to spare her father's life; but, as she turned to him, all she beheld was a "headless trunk."[56] An article in a New Hampshire literary magazine underscored the cruel slaughter of husbands whose wives were then subject to the indignity of looking at the bodies. Here, "a woman dared to ask one of those monsters of liberation" the fate of her husband. He replied: "[Tomorrow] you will see his head on one-side of the guillotine, and his body on the other." And, as the writer pointedly concluded, "He was as good as his word."[57]

This genre may have derived from the famous story of King Louis XVI of France, who tried to shield the queen from seeing the violent dismemberment of her best friend, the Princess de Lambelle. His act of chivalry came too late, for she had seen it all and fainted.[58] For the American reading audience, such stories duplicated the effect of visual torture, a pain twice felt by the spectators: once in seeing the victim die, and again in internalizing the horror. The Revolution did more than execute the king and destroy the social compact; it tore apart the moral covenant of social memory. Memory of the dead was permanently violated; they would always be remembered not as the good husband or loving father, but as a mangled carcass, a "headless trunk."

It was a machine that produced this horror, for the guillotine heightened the highly visual, highly staged performance of death. Ironically it was designed by a doctor to offer a more rational and painless death; this technological wonder, however, soon generated its own sexual slang and black humor. Nicknames such as "Dame Guillotine" or the "widow" feminized the machine. Popular French songs compared the embrace of the blade to a lusty wench, and jokes crudely equated decapitation with castration—associating, in the words of one scholar, "the loss of one capital member with that of another."[59]

In the United States, curious readers learned how the machine worked—or what it looked like—from the *National Gazette* and the *Massachusetts Magazine*.[60] As early as 1794, Philadelphians were able to view a guillotine in action. Patrons paid promoters to see the blade fall and the effigy's head severed, dropping ceremoniously into the waiting basket.[61] At the Tammany Museum in New York City, a guillotine was displayed using

Figure 4.6. *Cinque-Tetes, or the Paris Monster* (1798). Reproduced by permission of The Huntington Library, San Marino, California.

wax figures. One who witnessed the New York machine in action wrote that the display was a "very Natural—but most frightful—awful sight that can be imagined."[62] Guillotine humor found its way to America, when statues were beheaded as student pranks, and the figurehead of the *Queen of France* tavern was decapitated and bloodied.[63]

The second print, *Cinque-Tetes, or the Paris Monster*, applied these ghoulish allusions to the XYZ Affair (Figure 4.6).[64] Three American gentlemen, envoys sent to France, look askance at a Hydra-headed monster that represents the ruling French Directory. Wielding a dagger in its hand, threatening the envoys, the Hydra demands "Money, Money, Money!" The inscription underneath the Hydra likens diplomatic relations to prostitution: the French are scoffing at America's "close hugging," with "smiles and innocence," as they require payment before the French will welcome their "embraces." The cartoon compares France to a "Whore," as Cobbett does. In the same print, a civil feast takes place, in which the guests are a free black, two foppish-looking *sans-culottes*, and the Devil.

While unpalatable to modern tastes, the cartoon accurately captured how French demands for a bribe had tainted diplomatic relations. The new minister of foreign relations, Charles Maurice de Talleyrand-Périgord, sent three private agents to meet with the U.S. envoys. Unless they paid "a great deal of money," one agent insisted, the French refused to negotiate. One of Talleyrand's agents was a woman, Madame de Villette, the niece, adopted daughter, and rumored mistress of Voltaire. Two of the envoys, South Carolinian Charles Cotesworth Pinckney and Virginian John Marshall, had taken rooms at Villette's boarding house. Marshall, the youngest member of the diplomatic team, became enamored of the thirty-two-year-old widow. Thus, the warm "embraces" of the French had a literal meaning, and the missing figure in XYZ was "W"—a real woman, who appeared to be prostituting herself in service to the nation.[65]

The most interesting figure in *Cinque-Tetes*, however, is a woman sitting beside the guillotine, where a man has just been decapitated. The man's head cannot be seen—he is no more than a "headless trunk." Her head is not her own: it has been replaced by a Medusa's head, with snakes for hair.[66] Her abject ugliness and her wrinkled, cadaverous flesh, suggest the devouring fury of "Dame Guillotine."[67] Indeed, she resembles another female fury-like creature (snakes for hair, emaciated, sagging breasts) used in a 1795 print entitled *Goddess Faction* (Figure 4.7).[68] The Medusa head is thus rather significant.[69] With her glance she kills whomever she sees and whoever returns her gaze, making her a powerful reminder of the visual terror of the French Revolution.

While the Federalists fashioned the plot of the XYZ Affair, and gave the story its sexual overtones, the Democratic-Republicans responded with their own sordid account. John Wood's controversial 1802 publication, *The Suppressed History of the Administration of John Adams*, repeats another scandalous rumor; Marshall had not been seduced by the French, rather *he* (along with fellow envoy Pinckney) had seduced a young female "of a respectable family in Paris," promising her safe passage to the United States. Abandoned by her family and her seducers, she still made her way to America's shores, only to be arrested as a spy. What happened to "the unfortunate lady"? Wood does not know. He surmises that she was driven by necessity to work "for her own support and that of a helpless infant." In this retelling, it is the Federalists who engage in dishonorable "embraces." Their adulterous behavior unveils the hypocrisy of their party and the perverse motives behind their unrelenting satirical attacks.[70]

The final irony in this is that Cobbett, the master satirist who so vocally supported the Alien and Sedition Act of 1798, was to find himself forced to leave the country. Philadelphia physician Benjamin Rush brought a libel suit against Cobbett in 1797. Rush not only won the suit, but secured a "ruinous" fine of $5,000 in 1799. Cobbett fled to his native England the following year.[71] But before he left, Cobbett found himself dissected by one of Rush's supporters in a brutal satire that laid out the moral ge-

Figure 4.7. "Goddess Faction," from *Remarks on the Jacobiniad* (1795). Courtesy American Antiquarian Society.

ography of Cobbett's body. As the dissection proceeded, "intolerable" smells were released and "unnatural organs" were discovered—such as a single intestine which tellingly connected the anus and the mouth. The tongue of this reconstructed Cobbett was "bifurcated" like that of a snake, and his lungs were of "enormous size," emitting a "vapour" which "benumbed the faculty of bystanders." After so effectively dismembering his enemies in print, William Cobbett suffered a rather unpleasant mock-death himself.[72]

Over the years, monstrous women replaced the passive and mute symbol evoked by the dismembered corpse of Magna Britannia. Her anguished gaze and compassionate appeal to heaven had yielded to the deadly stare of a Medusa whose looks could kill. Sexual slander and innuendo had become the favorite weapon of partisans. As James Madison concluded in the *Federalist* (no. 10), faction implied "dangerous vice." Nothing expressed rampant vice with such repugnance as the furious woman—a perversion of the female sex—who like a vulture, armed with claws, figuratively fed on the dying remains of the public sphere. This is the ultimate effect of the print "Goddess Faction."

Political ideologies have routinely used women to personify the state. Like the later iconic image of America, the Statue of Liberty, feminized national symbols have generally represented disembodied ideals. Yet as victims and mutilated corpses, women's bodies have far more effectively evoked a collective sense of horror, and to some degree, voyeuristic sadistic pleasure. Sexual violation and female helplessness can be seductive and revolting at the same time.

For the Revolutionary generation, the female corpse was a crucial image in depicting the pains and trials associated with the birth of representative democracy. Fears of upheavals in a shifting social order seemed to demand symbols that captured the fundamental instability of patriarchal presumptions. Sex and violence, virtue and vice, dependency and dangerous liberties, were in this way combined in a society that feared—and was fascinated with—sudden, catastrophic death.

Political satirists rallied the reading public to war and quasi-war with two abnormal symbols: mutilated female flesh and flesh-eating females devouring the state. The death of the state was played out viscerally in terms of the female body. Whether portrayed as mute or mad, passive or furious, victim or perpetrator, the archetypal mother always reminded one of life and death. Dead women embodied the birth of a nation and the inauguration of the political party system. Dead women helped power-wielding men to make each other feel helpless.

Chapter 5
Immortalizing the Founding Fathers: The Excesses of Public Eulogy

Andrew Burstein

> *In a word, he was one of those perfect prodigies of Nature, of whom very few have been produced since the foundations of the earth were laid; and of him it may be said, as truly as any one that ever existed:—"He was a man, take him for all in all* / We ne'er shall look upon his like again."
>
> —*William Wirt, on Patrick Henry, adapting a verse from* Hamlet *(1817)*

To this day, few Americans would wish to dispute the view that the hallowed moment of the nation's birth was effected by an uncommon collective intelligence—a genius of such singularity that it has never been repeated since 1776. Our ethicopolitical history is as pampered and polished as the marble statues that inhabit the pillared public buildings of Washington, D.C. It has long demanded universal acceptance of the purity of a comprehensive idea, once called "liberty" and now called "democracy."[1]

The founders' immortality was certified by the grateful children of America's Revolutionaries and to a certain extent by the Revolutionaries themselves, who required a metaphorical foundation for a house that would withstand internal conflict. They enshrined, as a national value, a harmony that transcended everyday partisanship. Quasi-religious rituals were performed by the social elite, who, dressed in Masonic aprons, lay the cornerstones of significant buildings. Since then, public holidays like the Fourth of July (widely celebrated from 1783 on) have supplemented statues, paintings, patriotic texts, and equally bloated oratory, in which the founding bequest is repeated again and again, and citizens offer up signs of devotion. In the same way that the faded parchments of the Declaration of Independence and the Constitution are displayed at the National Archives for visitors to gaze upon in awe, the moral power of oft-rekindled depoliticized memories insures the continuation of belief—a belief that began as the founders died.[2]

There is something inherently untruthful about most forms of patriotic devotion, and yet the comfort supplied by nostalgia is made to seem an acceptable excuse for it. When William Wirt began his highly influential biography of Patrick Henry in 1805, six years after his subject's death, the author ignored Thomas Jefferson's direct caution—that the real Henry was intellectually lazy, "avaritious & rotten hearted," a crass man who scarcely read a book, who ignorantly opposed the Virginia statute for religious freedom, and who did everything in his career for financial gain. Instead, Wirt made Henry's theatrical statement, "Give me liberty, or give me death," the core value of his life; it is the one thing modern Americans "know" about Patrick Henry.

According to Wirt, no doubt existed among the founders that it was the humbly born Henry who had accelerated America's noble destiny. He had imparted the "revolutionary impulse" to milder men, who had gone on to enact Independence in the Continental Congress. Never mind that Henry left Philadelphia before the instrumental work began. "His language of passion was perfect," his biographer exulted; "It had almost all the stillness of solitary thinking. It was a sweet revery, a delicious trance." Relying on Wirt, one would have to believe that the Revolution occurred hypnotically. In Henry's later years, Wirt reported, young and old came by his home to hear stories, "to behold and admire, with swimming eyes the champion of other days, and to look with a sigh of generous regret, upon that height of glory which they could never hope to reach."[3]

Wirt would not heed even his correspondent John Adams, who, like Jefferson, pointed out the biographer's excesses. Wirt defended himself to the indomitable New Englander: "The present and future generations of our country can never be better employed than in studying the models set before them by the fathers of the Revolution." Nostalgia had greater value to the Revolutionaries' successors than historical accuracy. Wirt and many others among his contemporaries retrospectively portrayed the Revolution as a world historical event ordained by God.[4]

While Patrick Henry has served posterity by becoming an oversimplified symbol of courage and patriotic fervor, it is important to note that the early leaders themselves, including Adams and Jefferson, hallowed the Revolutionary moment and in this sense did not publicly resist the process of their collective immortalization. Certainly they knew how fallible their "genius" was, and among themselves they could be quite explicit. The most outstanding subject of the founders' self-examination was the meritorious, ever-virtuous "Father of His Country," George Washington, whose intellectual limitations were obvious to those who knew him but whose moral weaknesses were lost in the swirl of patriotic devotion needed to sustain a fragile young republic.

As to the "real" Washington, those who interacted with him observed that his pride was easily wounded, that he had an explosive temper, and that during the Revolutionary War he briskly took steps to counter the claims of officers who contested a decision or suggested that their orders were imperfect. As the astute Washington biographer John Ferling puts it, the so-called "First of Men" was "unable to take responsibility for failure." Rival American general Charles Lee called him a "puffed up charlatan"; his last secretary of state, Timothy Pickering, described him as "vain and weak and ignorant"; and Dr. Benjamin Rush, a signer of the Declaration, insisted that at no time after 1777 did he believe Washington "first in war." Pennsylvania senator William Maclay described a bumbling Washington unable to coordinate words with hand gestures in speaking at his inauguration. When a small number of financially strapped "Whiskey Rebels" tried to resist payment of a tax in 1794, the personally offended President Washington overreacted and sent a federal army against them. His vice president, John Adams, avowed that proud Washington did not seek a third term because he sensed his popularity waning and suspected he would face opposition. Upon Washington's retirement, Philadelphia newspaper editor Benjamin Franklin Bache called for a "period of rejoicing"; he had earlier highlighted Washington's limitations by comparing him to various tradesmen, saying that "an able carpenter may be a blundering taylor; and that a good General may be a most miserable politician." To Bache, Washington's presidential legacy served only to "legalize corruption."[5]

In spite of Bache's implication, Washington did resist monarchical corruption which would have seduced most men in his position. Sober and aloof, he lived off the profits of his plantation and a series of shrewd land deals, and he refused a salary, making possible all the subsequent homage he received as a man of the strictest rectitude. Having performed selfless public services made him, somehow, the recipient of a pure light of inspiration. This was the kind of glorification that would attach to Washington in death.

The process of the immortalization of the "Founding Fathers" began even before the death of Washington. It began, most conspicuously, in April 1790, just a year after Washington took the oath of office, when Benjamin Franklin died at the age of eighty-four. The American Philosophical Society, founded by Franklin in 1743, resolved that William Smith, provost of the College of Philadelphia, would prepare a eulogy. Assisted in his effort by distinguished colleagues in the Society—Secretary of State Thomas Jefferson, astronomer David Rittenhouse, and physician/educator Benjamin Rush—Smith delivered his eulogy before President Washington and the members of Congress. It was then "submitted to the Public Candor" in printed form.[6]

"Assembled Fathers of America!" Smith addressed his hearers, cognizant both of the historic import of his lamentation and the implication of his terminology. The "Fathers," as he dubbed his audience, comprised a new and self-fashioned patriarchy of genius, having cast off a patriarchy of inherited rank by revolutionary means. Among the "Fathers," Franklin loomed as their "Citizen, super-eminent in council," on whom Smith and the others modeled their inviolable new order. This first Father was an enlightening "Sun of Science," a "venerable *Sage*," "*Patriot* and *Patriarch* of *America*," and he was now being "consecrated to deathless Fame."[7]

Franklin's "vast and comprehensive mind" had set a paternal example. He had taught "the arts of industry and virtue, to shew [Americans] the happiness which lay within their reach, to teach them to dare, and to bear, and to improve success." In near-biblical cadences, Smith projected the American Genesis: Franklin "conceived the mighty *Idea* of *American Empire* and *Glory*." The workman-creator of the age of Enlightenment had, by his life, defined greatness under the new order.[8]

To the founders' eulogists, who would shape the national historic memory over the next half century, the new nation required a superhuman fabrication. And so, not surprisingly, after their decease, the defining characters of the republic continued to "speak" paternalistically, or pantheistically, urging citizens to understand the nation as something sacred, diffusive, and enduring. This, too, began with Franklin. He "felt and believed himself *immortal!*" exclaimed Smith. "His vast and capacious Soul was ever stretching beyond the narrow sphere of Things, and grasping an *Eternity!* Hear himself, 'altho dead, yet speaking.' " The departed continued to speak, in the guise of a "*Guardian-Genius,* still present and presiding" through the nation's memory. This constituted the very definition of "deathless Fame."[9]

No figure more dramatically symbolized the ascent to supernatural guardianship than George Washington. Franklin's death had occurred at the beginning of the Federalist decade, and Washington's at the very end, on December 14, 1799. Twenty-year-old future jurist Joseph Story drew the link from Franklin in his eulogy of Washington, noting that under the first president's guidance, the nation had risen materially and culturally: "Her arts, self-taught, like her own FRANKLIN, have drawn the lightning from heaven, untwisted the colors of day, and blazoned with the pencil of truth her gallant achievements." In taming the heavens in pursuit of truth, the venerable scientist Franklin had, in this sense, provided a foundation for the inspired governance of Washington. If Franklin was the American Adam, Washington, in some constructions, was its Jesus. No one could equal Washington's bestowal: "His deeds are immortal," Story assured. "They live in the heart of his country; and his country lives but to celebrate them." He had contributed his inner worth to the nation "as if inspired with prophetic enthusiasm." In death, he loomed as his country's "savior," retrospectively appearing to have always possessed something beyond the corporeal—"something, that all felt, but could not describe." Congressman Fisher Ames intoned: "two Washingtons come not in one age."[10]

Henry Holcombe, a Georgia Baptist, represented Washington's graces as providentially instilled. While humble in his formal scholarship, "he possessed an universal knowledge of things." He comprehended with "a singular felicity of perception." His purity was reinforced in his speech—"divine and immortal principles preserved his tongue from every species of profanity"; and in his behavior—"He ruled his appetites and passions in scenes of the greatest trial and temptation." Accordingly, "to draw his true portrait is more than mortal hands can do!" No living being could fully grasp Washington's sublime character: " *'It merits a divine.'* " The comparison to Jesus was inevitable: "O Death! never hadst thou, but in one astonishing instance, such a prisoner before!" (Figure 5.1).[11]

Well into the Jacksonian period, the messianic Washington image remained an option for patriot worship. In 1830, a cohort of more than five hundred Masonic brethren appeared at Washington's Mount Vernon gravesite, having just consecrated a new Methodist church. As a sign of pure faith, the parishioners stood in a "Cordon around the Grave" to scatter sprigs of evergreen symbolic of the Resurrection. Andrew Jackson himself attested that Washington's memory was no better maintained than by the honors which "Religion and Masonry" accorded it.[12]

When American Freemasons eulogized Washington in early 1800, they were mourning the loss of one of their own. Master of the Alexandria, Virginia lodge, Washington had participated in noteworthy Masonic observances during the Revolution in such places as Boston, Philadelphia, and West Point. He presided over Lafayette's induction as an American Mason during the Valley Forge winter and performed Masonic rituals at the laying of the U.S. Capitol's cornerstone in 1793.[13]

To the Masons, a good number of whom are counted among the founders, collaborative, patriarchal nation-building was their self-defining duty.[14] In mourning master, brother, father, and friend all at once, Masonry emphasized the "united sympathy" of its members, self-selected guardians of the public trust. The Masonic Washington was given godly attributes: "in thy hands, the meanest implement of a farmer was more graceful and imposing than the sceptre of a monarch"; "the lustre of thy character was intrinsic, unchangeable"; "his countenance addressed us in a language more than human; in a language, by the tongue, unutterable." He could not belong to America, or to any polity: "Earth, he was not thine! He was the offspring of Virtue, the favourite of Heaven; to Heaven he has ascended."[15]

The Puritans had imagined North America as a holy refuge and pastoral garden. From the time of the Revolutionary crisis, newspapers and pamphlets carried forward a millennial promise: in American history God's moral ends would be realized. Yale's Ezra Stiles found ecstatic language in 1783 as the Treaty of Paris secured peace and independence: "God's American Israel," he said, belonged *"high above all nations which he hath made."* Washington's destiny as well was insured in Stiles's exultation: "O

Figure 5.1. *Apotheosis of Washington* (c. 1800), by David Edwin (1776–1841). Courtesy National Portrait Gallery, Smithsonian Institution.

WASHINGTON! How do I love thy name! How have I often adored and blessed thy GOD, for creating and forming thee the greatest ornament of human kind!"[16]

Thus seventeen years before Washington's death, Stiles had accurately projected a common theme among his eulogists: the notion that the Almighty had intentionally fashioned the moral soldier to fulfill His purposes. "God was about to make another nation in the world," preached Titus Barton, in Tewksbury, Massachusetts, in 1800, "and for materials, he chose the British Colonies in America, the then most weak, and as to the arts of war most unexperienced." When the righteous war occurred, "God who is all and in all, was about to give birth to, perhaps, the most important nation on earth, and he had his instrument prepared. He had his General made and furnished with every talent." Wise Washington lay prostrate "the pride of haughty Britain" and the Pharoah-like king. "Americans," the pastor exhorted a second time, "this was the work of God." Physician and historian David Ramsay of Charleston, South Carolina, joined in the refrain, that Washington was "the chosen instrument of Heaven."[17]

Josiah Bartlett identified Washington's farewell address of 1796 as his "PARENTAL LEGACY," by which he "bequeathed with prophetic reference to future generations" a prescription for peace and contentment. To see the farewell address as a bequest is a curious element in the process of immortalizing the father. The literary scholar Albert Furtwangler has described this text as a "rite of passage" in which Washington conveys his own sense of impending death. In yielding up power, he transcends, helping the mourning public to produce for itself a vision of his pure progression from earthbound exemplar to heaven-sent valedictory.[18]

Major General Henry Lee gave the official eulogy of Washington at the behest of Congress. This was the text that enshrined the words "First in war, first in peace, and first in the hearts of his countrymen." Mourning a national loss that was incomparable, Lee referred to Washington alternately as "the best of men," the "purest mind," and a naturally superior being "combining the physical and moral force of all within his sphere." Signs of immortality were deeply sensed: "An end, did I say? His fame survives! bounded only by the limits of the earth, and by the extent of the human mind." Civic life and national salvation had become one story.[19]

The undisguised objective of the public orator in this age was to command the hearts of his hearers. John Adams composed these lines for a London newspaper near the close of the Revolution: "Men are governed by Words. Their passions are inflamed by Words." William Wirt, famed courtroom pleader as well as the biographer of Patrick Henry, wrote of speechmaking, "The *hearts* of the audience will refuse all commerce except with the *heart* of the speaker."[20] When the eulogist of the great wished to startle his audience, elocution sometimes demanded excess. And so Lee added a course of enthusiasm to his preternatural feast of words: "When our monuments shall be done away; when nations now existing shall be no more; when even our young and far-spreading empire shall have perished; still will our WASHINGTON's glory unfaded shine, and die not, until love of virtue cease on earth, or earth itself sinks into chaos!"[21]

Lee concluded his eulogy with some well-crafted theatrics, momentously affecting that he himself was the recipient of a heaven-born message from the departed patriarch to his collective children. "Methinks," said Lee, "I see his august image, and hear, falling from his venerable lips, these deep sinking words: CEASE, Sons of AMERICA, lamenting our separation. Go on. . . . " The immortal spirit of Washington continued, in Lee's impassioned fabrication, to urge unity, religion, learning, peace, and self-reliance as the means to achieve a different kind of immortality—the political: "Be American in thought and deed. Thus will you give immortality to that union, which was the constant object of my terrestrial labours." Heavenly virtues and the prudent management of terrestrial affairs united in the first president's bequest.[22]

The same literary conceit was employed in succeeding years, wherein Washington "spoke" from the grave. A communication in the newspaper *American Citizen*, in 1804, signed "WASHINGTON," was addressed to "My once beloved Countrymen." Its tone remained self-sacrificial, while exhorting patriots to preserve the liberty Washington had won for them. "From the cold mansion of death, from the awful bosom of the grave," Washington conveyed a posthumous consciousness of temporal connections; he reminded all that Jefferson, his successor as president, while then "cloathed with immortal honor," would like himself pass from the scene before long. And then who would be left to exhibit "public virtue," who to safeguard against the rise of ambitious men, who to promote rational liberty "before the eyes of the world?"[23]

In the nineteenth century, eulogists continued to project altruism as the primary message meant to be conveyed through the synopsized lives of great Americans. It was supposed that the dominant figures of the founding generation had lived for purposes larger than their personal fame or partisan platforms. While no one again achieved the ethereal dimension of Washington until the martyrdom of Abraham Lincoln, providential purposes were sensationally avowed after the perfectly timed, mathematically implausible departures of John Adams and Thomas Jefferson, who both died on the jubilee of American independence, July 4, 1826.

Elizabeth Gamble Wirt, wife of then U.S. attorney general William Wirt, wrote her husband from Richmond before Adams's death was known in the South: "What a well-timed exit he [Jefferson] made! On the 4th of July and at the *very hour* in which the declaration of independence was first read. There is something very touching in this universal lament for one of our Fathers." She went on to write that the tolling of a funereal bell, once each minute throughout the day, "sounds like choking suppressed *sobbing* breaking forth." Newspapers around the country fixated on the timing of events associated with the coincidental deaths: "It cannot be all chance," more than one pronounced. Adams's reputed last words, "Jefferson survives," were said to have been spoken at the approximate hour when the Virginian expired. "The sound of the Trumpet of Jubilee is reverberated in strange and mysterious echoes," wailed William Halsey, the eulogist in Newark, New Jersey.[24]

There is something extraordinary in the American celebration of a mystifying coincidence and the recourse to providential "last words." Romantic truth could supplant actual fact without any public questioning. Immortalizing Adams's "Jefferson survives" did much to immortalize the founders themselves; an entire generation of ingenious minds profited by the ironic yet revelatory (in a larger sense) "Jefferson survives." Though Adams's last words were "indistinctly uttered," by the admission of John Quincy Adams (in his diary) and by the one witness identified as having been present at the patriarch's deathbed, any uncertainty was left out of eulogies given by Congressman Edward Everett and Salem, Massachusetts, postmaster Joseph Sprague, as well as biographical treatments beginning with Judge William Cranch's 1827 *Memoir of the Life, Character, and Writings of John Adams.* In a republic built on virtuous laws and virtuous speech, the immortality of words exceeded the devotional value of marble and granite statues, as early Americans themselves said conventionally and repeatedly.[25]

Of the many joint eulogies of Adams and Jefferson that were delivered, however, none ascribe godly traits to the deceased patriots. Keenly aware of the pronounced bitterness that the two ex-presidents had shown each other during many of their years on the national stage, William Alexander Duer, in Albany, New York, recommended that his listeners "draw a veil over the frailties of the dead, and cherish the remembrance of their virtues." John A. Shaw, in Bridgewater, Massachusetts, cautioned citizen-mourners, "It is not necessary to exhibit them as faultless: for they were subject to like passions with ourselves." Henry Potter, in Fayetteville, North Carolina, was even more forthright in denying the pair saintliness: "That these great men were fallible, is a truth which none will controvert. To find a being faultless you must rise above this world. Let us bury the faults of our fathers with them."[26]

Instead, the passing of Adams and Jefferson called up nostalgic feeling for the disappearance of a particular age. Affection for the abstract nation, an embrace of civic duty—practical lessons applicable to behavior in a republic—now took precedence over adoration for the dead. "Conscience is absolutely free in the broadest and most unqualified sense," said John Sergeant of Philadelphia, in praise of the nation Adams and Jefferson had fashioned. Epitomizing the nonreligious sense of awe that the coincidental deaths evoked, then secretary of state Henry Clay wrote to the sitting president, John Quincy Adams: "Without indulging in a spirit of superstition, it is impossible to contemplate the dissolution of your father and Mr. Jefferson without believing that it has been so ordered to produce a great moral effect upon the American people, their liberty, and their institutions."[27]

While it is true that the coincidence of the two patriarchs' passing on the fiftieth Fourth of July raised hopeful questions of continued providential intervention in American lives, God's blessing was no longer contingent on beatifying the dead leaders. The lamented pair were humanly esteemed as high-minded sages, "intellectual luminaries"; their advanced age signified that they had been able to "outlive the ordinary measure of humanity." Similarly, a eulogist queried, "Is there not rather cause of devout exultation, that two distinguished survivors of the revolutionary struggle have been spared so long." Adams and Jefferson were, alas, the same as other men, but for the quality of their minds and the extraordinary times into which they were born. Their names may have become "talismanic," as another eulogist put it, but that implied good luck and did not imbue them with divinely wrought power. Immortality was associated not with them, but with their cause—freedom.[28]

The earlier patriarchal nomenclature remained. Adams and Jefferson, as much as Franklin and Washington, were "the Fathers of their country, and benefactors of mankind." As benefactors, they performed civil, not religious, services for the national community. They inspired "gratitude." "We have cause of joy for this abundant cause of gratitude towards our fathers," assured U.S. Senator Felix Grundy in Nashville. Associate Justice William Johnson offered the conventional, fanciful image of Adams and Jefferson looking down upon a duty-bound successor generation, whispering, "Well done, our faithful children." All of these eulogies expressed mystification and commanded a dramatic pause for mourners to study the intended message; but in doing so, they did not rank the dead fathers in a spiritual sense above any other ancestor.[29]

What Providence offered was, instead, a reminder that the Revolution had been a "holy cause," as future president John Tyler pronounced. Felix Grundy delighted that the "principles laid down in the Declaration of Independence have been tested by half a century." With America's "salvation" assured, "What day so fit for them to die!" Massachusetts attorney and author Samuel L. Knapp offered funeral honors to the pair for having "assisted in giving us freedom and fame." It was the national *us* that he celebrated first; Adams and Jefferson were applauded for contributions, not divine inspiration. It was only the "superstitious," he said, who saw the felicitous coincidence as "miraculous." Heaven's hand was present, but it was "judicious" rather than miraculous.[30]

Daniel Webster's three-hour eulogy became the best known. He hoped that the "spontaneous impulse" to mark these two deaths added up to the prospect "that the republic itself may be immortal." The solemnity of the day, to Webster, was occasioned by the wide recognition that a duty had fallen to the generation that was given life, literally and politically, by the founders:

This lovely land, this glorious liberty, these benign institutions, the dear purchase of our fathers, are ours; ours to enjoy, ours to preserve, ours to transmit. Generations past, and generations to come, hold us responsible for this sacred trust. Our fathers, from behind, admonish us, with their anxious paternal voices, posterity calls out to us, from the bosom of the future, the world turns hither its solicitous eyes.

Sacralization of liberty was, again, the paramount devotion. Rather than dwell, as a preacher might, on the certainty of mortality, Webster stressed the duties of citizens. Honoring the dead, as he put it, was evidence that "we do not forget the living."[31]

As profound and commanding as Webster was, there was one less renowned eulogy of Adams and Jefferson, however, which captured in more tremulous tones the romantic transformation that was underway in nineteenth-century America. Peleg Sprague, Harvard-educated congressman from Maine, delivered an exceptionally rich and resilient oration. Images of the universality of death opened it: "They, whose names are associated with all that belongs to us—are intertwined with whatever is dear in the recollections of youth . . . have passed away—the shroud, the coffin, and the hearse have received them." In recalling the meaning of the Revolution, Sprague again evoked images of death by underscoring the bloody destruction perpetrated by the British around the world: Ireland's green fields "scorched by oppression," forcing "emaciated sons" to "crawl" home to share a "communion of wretchedness" with their families; India, too, suffered from British rapacity, "where Ambition has reddened his hands in the blood of millions; and Rapine has rioted on their spoils." These were the rewards of colonized status from which Adams and Jefferson had struggled to redeem America.[32]

These two honored fathers deserved glory for having transcended the passion that had once made them mortal competitors: "In the awful silence of the tomb," Sprague intoned, "passion is hushed, and its fires burn not amid the damp of death." The reconciliation of their late lives marked—and this is especially noteworthy—a "strong sympathy, which death itself was not to sunder, but in which they were to pass together to another world." For this eulogist, as Adams and Jefferson "commingled in peace," their surviving countrymen could also move ahead, "without any thing of the bitterness of despair, and with little even of the poignancy of grief, but with a soothing sadness and a melancholy pleasure."[33]

There was no need to mourn, except as one might mourn the romantic passing of the seasons, "when nature herself is falling to decay, and seems to be putting on the shroud of death." All could feel comforted that an overarching quality of sympathy prevailed as a guiding principle in human hearts as it did in nature—this would succor the nation. The land contained the original patriots' spirits: "Their memorials are everywhere! Their *statues* are man; living, feeling, intelligent, adoring man; bearing the image of his maker; having the impress of divinity. These shall endure. . . . Their *monuments* are the everlasting hills." Like the other Adams-Jefferson eulogists, Sprague celebrated liberty. For him, though, it was both an innate desire and the literal expansion across space. Expansive minds like Adams and Jefferson ultimately taught their posterity by example: "If we inhale the moral atmosphere in which they moved, we must feel its purifying and invigorating influence." The future beckoned.[34]

The sentiments of Daniel Webster and Peleg Sprague conveyed the distinction between private thoughts of eternity and public exhortation on the value of pursuing an active life. For accomplished men of action such as Webster and Sprague, the human mind could perceive the sublime effects of nature but not divine causes. Modest in approaching eternal questions, the eulogists shrank from speculation about the unknown. They served a national audience by celebrating what nature made affectingly real. So while it was mathematically near impossible, the double apotheosis of 1826 did not lead only to explanations involving divine signs. Humans acted in a physical world; the founders' lesson connected native talents to actual deeds.

To jump ahead two decades to the nationally mourned death of Andrew Jackson in 1845, it appears that a further change took place: the intimate life, private character, and unselfish impulses—humanization—enlarged in importance in eulogistic tribute.[35] Jackson was "wholly forgetful of himself and his perils." His passionate attachment to his late wife Rachel, whose portrait cheered him in his own dying moments, symbolized the kind of individual he was to be understood as: "his last breath wafted to heaven a prayer that he might join her! He was truly a good man." His transcendence lay in private devotion, and an imagined humility could be conjured so as to complete the picture: "He declined the honour of an imperial sarcophagus, and only sought a tomb by her side." Just as pictorial representations of Washington's deathbed once sanctified a shared moment of sympathy, the seventy-eight-year-old Jackson's final release from suffering softened and humanized him for a surviving citizenry, who needed the assurance that such transitions proved continuity in republican life. There was at least this comfort in grief.[36]

A fellow Tennessean characterized Jackson's homeliness: "He had lived as a kind neighbour, a true friend, an honest man." The nation-builder had become simply a good man, and words of remembrance constituted true immortality. To Virginian Hugh Garland, Jackson's "manly form" (nothing of a divine quality) was sufficient to awe his countrymen. His greatest accomplishment was "the impress of his character" on the age in which he lived. John A. Bowles, in Lowell, Massachusetts, proclaimed that the name Jackson "awakens echoes and arouses recollections, and kindles emotions, how warmly, how eloquently, in our hearts!" People celebrated an extraordinary ordinary man, eulogized as a beloved national friend. A eulogist in Indianapolis began his address by reporting that Jackson had "expired in the full possession of his senses, surrounded by his friends, expressing the highest confidence in a happy immortality." Gratification for a life well lived insured eternal peace.[37]

Jackson's idealized human qualities were next identified as America's national characteristics. His "firmness" was what made America strong. His "most striking feature" was "an irresistible energy." He possessed an "innate, intuitive faith in human freedom, and in the institutions of freedom." To George Bancroft, the identification of the man with the country was such that "no public man of this century ever returned to private life with such an abiding mastery over the affections of the people." Jackson's was "the last great name, which gathers round itself all the associations that form the glory of America"[38] (Figure 5.2).

Bancroft, along with others, rapturously described a storybook life. Jackson's coming of age mirrored America's, "like the blaze of the sun in the fierceness of its noonday glory," while his mortal departure was "lovely as the mildest sunset of a summer's evening." In a deathbed engraving, he is bathed in a soothing light, his earthly burden removed. Natural metaphors in this case did not suggest transcendence or divinity. Rather, the warrior had finally retreated in peace—his humanity remained behind to exert influence. Jackson's close friend and cabinet appointee, Levi Woodbury of New Hampshire, delivered the common refrain: while "the cold clay sleeps as insensible to our praise and grief as the veteran's sword in its scabbard . . . yet such a life is still powerful; it continues to speak to the world." Like Franklin and Washington, he spoke from the grave. His "bright example" endured, his life story exemplifying "usefulness in true glory, from the dawn of life to its close!"[39]

As was evident in Adams's and Jefferson's reconciliation, the combative Jackson, in death, reputedly lost his partisan character. In Woodbury's words, "how admirably does the grave, thus closed, bury in its bosom most of the enmities and jealousies of a turbid life, and tend to harmonize his countrymen in paying just tributes to his memory." Virginia politician Andrew Stevenson noted that, as with Adams and Jefferson, Jackson's death announced that "America has lost its greatest benefactor and friend." If the collected images amounted to a pacifying bedtime story, Woodbury gave the story its ending:

Figure 5.2. *Grand Funeral Procession in Memory of Gen. Jackson* (1845). Courtesy Tennessee Historical Society Collections, Tennessee State Library and Archives. Though Andrew Jackson died and was buried at his home outside Nashville, so-called mock funerals were held in other parts of the country, such as this public ceremony in New York.

And while a nation bedews with tears the green turf where he sleeps, it is not sorrow without hope; for who can doubt that the same guardian power which has shielded us heretofore through the Washingtons and Jacksons, the Jeffersons and Franklins, that crowd the bright galaxy of our history, will raise up other worthies, and train them suitably to meet every peril which may menace us?[40]

From Franklin's public usefulness and public benevolence, to Washington's superintending grace and confidence, to Adams's and Jefferson's gift of genius, to Jackson's elevated simplicity, eulogists self-consciously produced a catalogue of "American" traits. Doing so, they enshrined select models of private and public virtue to stand as barometers for measuring future moral progress. Death was the moment when an effort was made to soothe, to replace partisan memory with harmonizing images, and to synthesize a grand national purpose.

In life, General Jackson was often associated with General Washington by admirers and campaign strategists, and he was eulogized in such a way as to suggest that in the War of 1812 he had finished the first father's job of ridding the continent of the British, and freeing America to be itself. As the two childless fathers among the nation's chief benefactors, each could be said to have made all citizens his children.[41] Jackson would be "second only to Washington in the hearts of his countrymen," predicted Hugh Garland. "An admiring posterity," said J. G. Harris of Charlotte, Tennessee, "shall make pilgrimages to Mount Vernon in the East, and the Hermitage [Jackson's estate] in the West, to linger around the mounds which contain the illustrious dead, to commune with the spirits of the immortal WASHINGTON and JACKSON." There was a comforting symmetry in such representations.[42]

Everyone who read a newspaper knew that none of this was true. To be simply "firm" and "pure" disguised Jackson's real impulses. He alienated many of those closest to him: among his principal protégés, Secretary of War John Henry Eaton, Senator Hugh Lawson White, and General Richard Keith Call defected to the opposition Whig Party. In Andrew Jackson was contained an extraordinary rage and a taste for personal and political revenge. As a major general, he had ordered disobedient soldiers executed. When the warrior-president needed to see his will fulfilled, he attacked those he construed as enemies; Eaton, White, and Call were all "apostates."[43]

He believed in total solutions, and power unmediated by law. Congressman John Davis of Massachusetts wrote to a colleague expressing equal frustration with Jackson's arbitrary style and with the submissive men, like New Hampshire Senator Isaac Hill, whom the President required around him: "Hill advances him before [i.e., ahead of] the combined character of Washington & Jefferson and I dare say if he would utter all he wishes he would place him over the great ruler of the universe. As the progress of tyranny advances[,] their courage seems to increase & their hopes to brighten. In truth it seems to me they shout with joy at the prospect of conquering the constitution." This was typical of the censure Jackson received. It appeared to some caricaturists that he considered himself a royal personage; it seemed to others that he considered himself God.[44]

There could be only one Washington in the quasi-religious rites of adoration performed by post-Revolutionary Americans. "The finger of an over-ruling Providence, pointing at Washington, was neither mistaken or unobserved," Henry Lee asserted in 1800. Heaven, he amplified, "infused into his mind such an uncommon share of its ethereal spirit" that Washington watched over America with "an equal and comprehensive eye," like the eye of Providence itself. For David Ramsay, Washington was "the chosen instrument of Heaven," to guide his nation, in the biblical manner, "through the storms of war, to the haven of peace and safety."[45]

There was, indeed, only one Washington—one supreme patriarch—in the greater cosmology that the eulogists of the founders had constructed. He received a singular kind of adoration, for he had singularly bequeathed a future to his nation in his farewell address, yielding up power and preparing his own way to heaven. Franklin, though the first patriarch to die, was more readily perceived, over the longer term, as the disembodied "spirit" or native "genius" of America. Jefferson and Adams gave America its voice: they projected the power of Scripture; they provided the transcendent word; their definition of liberty was the catechism of the national creed, meant to resonate in the classrooms of all future generations of citizens. Jackson, chronologically the last of the immortalized founders (technically not a founder), was designated the first apostle of those who preceded him, especially Washington; but here the cosmology crumbled. As a prophet of national harmony Jackson failed because, unlike Adams and Jefferson, his partisan identity could never be shed. His patriotism was consumed by other, less ethereal attributes in the historic memory. He was too bloodthirsty to be remembered as his eulogists wished, and in 1845, when he died, his political successor, James K. Polk, was embarking upon the most expansionist administration in U.S. history, teaching Americans to become accustomed to war. Mid-nineteenth-century America did not comport easily with the mythic harmony of the past.

The cosmology of America's founding luminaries shifted as it evolved. Just as heaven, in our culture, is metaphorically located in the sky without being contradicted by the work of astrophysicists, the legendary identity of a Franklin or Washington could be described as both "sun" and "spirit," without causing confusion among patriot-believers. In this vein, the American "civil religion" that grew from a scholarly discourse in the 1960s, tells an incomplete story; it misses the importance of a spiritual harmony that is other than theological, that connects with the founders' symbolic omniscience.[46]

Then what did the political eulogy achieve? Above all, eulogies of dead leaders helped citizens, at vulnerable moments, come to terms with uncertainties they perceived in their world. As Barry Schwartz has written in his study of the paramount father, "The cult devoted to the adoration of Washington contributed heavily to America's becoming and remaining conscious of itself as a nation." Because Washington had been turned into a sacred object, emotions were manipulated to forge greater unity: "the nation's solidarity presupposed his central, unifying role." The religious historian Gary Laderman adds that Washington's death "regenerated and rejuvenated the body politic." Mourning Washington mixed Christian symbols of resurrection and redemption with Greek and Roman funerary urns—the iconography of the cult of heroes. Americans needed such symbolism to defeat their fears regarding the ultimate instability of the republic, as it headed toward further political division and civil war. As it turns out, the pursuit of millennial happiness, America's ultimate conceit, has also been its most persistent measure of anxiety and bewilderment.[47]

While memory is delusive, it is at the same time emotionally rewarding. In eulogies, words of common lament led to hope of common improvement. The immortal Washington's symbolic children were supposed to be a race of apostles who were wedded to the cause of liberty. Their "liberty" was understood as a set of public manners corresponding to the moderation of power. Their civil religion, then, was really a civil *sensibility*, using symbols of mourning to instill a sense of national belonging.[48]

Chapter 6

The Politics of Tears:
Death in the Early American Novel

Julia Stern

> *Too many tears for lovers have been shed,*
> *Too many sighs give we to them in fee,*
> *Too much of pity after they are dead,*
> *Too many doleful stories do we see*
>
> —*John Keats,* Isabella *(1820)*

Benjamin Franklin is most often identified as a model of success, whose life was a life well lived. Yet in his *Autobiography* there is a death to be considered as well:

In 1736 I lost one of my Sons, a fine Boy of 4 Years old, by the Small Pox taken in the common way. I long regretted bitterly and still regret that I had not given it to him by Inoculation; This I mention for the Sake of Parents, who omit that Operation on the Supposition that they should never forgive themselves if a Child died under it; my Example showing that the Regret may be the same either way, and that therefore the safer should be chosen.[1]

This rather laconic passage is an interstice between two long paragraphs in the second section of the *Autobiography*. The first details the happy resolution of a momentary strife with his brother James, the printer; the second exuberantly testifies to the expansion of his "improvement" club, the Junto, and describes an event that in different literary hands might constitute the central episode around which an entire plot would unfold. By denying the reader the sort of affective detail that was later to be demanded by a reading public intent on dramatically introspective personal memoirs, Franklin delivers an emotionally withholding narrative. What these four brief sentences and the larger surrounding narrative inoculate themselves against is *feeling*. And yet, literary critics consider this scene to be the emotional high-water mark of the entire autobiography.

Given the suffusion of emotion in the early American novel, it is striking that the second installment of the *Autobiography* begun at Passy, France, in 1784, predates William Hill Brown's *Power of Sympathy*—the so-called first American novel—by only five years. But to measure by emotional impact alone the generic distance spanned by Benjamin Franklin and novelists William Hill Brown, Susanna Rowson, and Hannah Foster is to isolate a paradigm shift of amazing proportions. Franklin's is a tale of politically "enlightened" self-interest that fails to grope with the cultural meanings contained in an emerging genre, highlighting what I call the "politics of tears."

Nearly every scholar of American literature writing between 1900 and 1970 ignored the distinctly political character of the fiction of the 1790s. Yet these works certainly were not mindless melodrama meant to opiate an undiscerning reading public desperate for distraction amid the pessimistic projections that punctuated debates over ratification of the Constitution. Popular novels such as *The Power of Sympathy* (1789), *Charlotte Temple* (1791/1794), and *The Coquette* (1797) dealt equally with politics and death, yet were unacknowledged on both accounts by the literary establishment. These novels of threatened virtue and the human will went virtually unread until their rediscovery by feminist critics in the 1980s.

Uniquely hybrid works, novels of the early national period pursued a variety of cultural aims. They were concocted of one part Johann Wolfgang von Goethe—featuring suicidal romantic male protagonists with pistols and copies of *Werther* in hand; one part Samuel Richardson—starring American Clarissas neither drugged nor raped nor wasting over five hundred pages, but conscious, consenting, and undone in the space of three-page chapters; one part English feminist Mary Wollstonecraft in their subversive briefs for female education; and one part continental melodrama of seduction and abandonment.

Readers, it would appear, lusted after death. Conjuring the young and the restless only to dispatch them at their own hands or by childbed fever and, for good measure, blighting their illegitimate offspring in two of every three cases, this literature put morbidity and mortality at the top of its concerns. Between 1789, with the publication of *The Power of Sympathy*, and 1800, when, ending a bulimic burst of literary production, the so-called "father of American fiction," Charles Brockden Brown, completed his fourth Godwinian gothic, the national novel was steeped in sentimentalization.[2] For eleven years, then, dying, death, tombstone inscriptions, mortuary practices, graveyard pilgrimages, and the fetishization of dead heroines constituted the most memorable tableaux within this narrative tradition.

Far from exclusively being thanatological, however, these novels' obsession with death was joined at the hip, as it were, with tabooed sex, particularly the transgression of the most profoundly drawn social boundaries in republican America.[3] We must read politically all representations of dying, death, and funereal practices in the fiction of the 1790s, and in parallel fashion, we also must decode the cultural significance of reprobated erotic conjunctions in these texts. As illicit sexual association between near equals, sibling incest emphasizes horizontal and leveling social relations; the physical union of fathers and daughters, on the other hand, unfolds vertically, on an axis where authority and age surmount powerlessness and youth.

The longings of brothers and sisters for each other remain both unconsummated and punishable by death in the fiction of the two (unrelated) Browns whose work inaugurates and terminates the decade with which we are concerned. William Hill Brown, in *The Power of Sympathy*, and Charles Brockden Brown, in *Wieland* (1798) and *Ormond* (1799), set the margins of any discussion. The incest motif can be seen as a departure from Revolutionary exogamy (sex and marriage between unrelated persons). The Revolution, after all, had celebrated the powerful political trope of colonial separation. Incest, of course, expresses a radically different view. It projects uncertainty about the constitution of the social body in a new republic teeming with potentially mobile immigrants, aliens, and slaves, all of whom theoretically could intermingle and reproduce with members of the founding families.[4] Endogamy, or sex among near equals, represents a dangerously reactionary proposition, in which a culture prevents its own diversification and risks becoming ossified.

Before turning to specific readings of "the politics of tears" in five novels of the early national period, I want to make a bold suggestion: what we might think of as a relatively recent and depraved penchant for vicarious readerly or viewerly rubbernecking over the dead bodies of celebrity heroines actually originates in the fiction of the 1790s. There exists a collective cultural fascination for what I term the "community fetish": the female body drained of all negative associations through the magical hygiene of death. My term pertains not only to Susanna Rowson's fictive Charlotte Temple, an invented figure whose imagined grave at Wall Street and Broadway was routinely visited by actual readers mourning her death; or to Harriet Beecher Stowe's Little Eva, an imaginary character in *Uncle Tom's Cabin* whose messiah-like death was so charged with symbolic power as to have generated an entire critical industry—and, in the words of President Lincoln, ignited the Civil War. There is, as well, the story of two-year-old Jessica McClure, who momentarily appeared as good as dead in 1987 until she was extracted from the well that opened up in her own Texas backyard; Princess Diana, who, several years post-mortem, still commands tabloid covers; and Jonbenet Ramsey, murdered at the age of six on Christmas day 1996 (itself a detail that thickens the mythic, even sacrificial, aura surrounding her killing). The child's hauntingly glamorous image was one that magazine editors would not allow to "go gentle into that good night" of nonpublicity. They are the Charlottes and Evas of the television-tabloid age.[5]

Stolen innocence, an intensely familiar American cultural phenomenon, can trace its emotional origins to fears circulating at the founding moment. The difference between the late eighteenth century and our own time involves the way in which the public expresses its sense of outrage, and how individuals exercise control over how far they will go to empathize. It is a fact that while hundreds of children have been abused and killed in the years since Jessica McClure's well-documented resurrection from the Texas well, most child victims remain unrecognizable,[6] reverting into numbing statistics for the newspaper, disposable faces on milk cartons, or transmographying into the stuff of moving television plots, like the long-running hospital drama *E.R.* Far from serving as community fetishes, these largely nameless children, increasingly ambiguous in the public mind, are the objects of what I call "dynamic woe." The fetish continues to compel collective attention because it substitutes an amplified idealization for an ugly totality.[7] As historical reality, however, dynamic woe meets an averted public gaze. It is this tension—between the obsessive mourning for perfect victims and the refusal to extend that compassion to the mundane deaths of the faceless masses—that has its roots in the eighteenth-century Anglo-American sentimental novel.

In the affective environment of the 1790s, American sentimental fiction begins by paying a peculiar lip-service to the significance of fellow feeling in *The Power of Sympathy*, in which emotion is ironically articulated in an anaesthetized narrative devoid of either warmth or heat. The Anglo-American novel of sentiment reaches its maudlin height not long after in the pathetic tale of betrayal, *Charlotte Temple*. By century's end, this tradition has swerved precipitously into a grimmer mode with Hannah Foster's *Coquette*; while commonly read as a sentimental novel, the book takes on its most powerful significance when understood as gothic fiction. With Charles Brockden Brown's novel of stolen selfhood, *Wieland*, published the next year, the novel is fully absorbed in emotional as well as physical darkness: faulty lanterns, flashes of lightening, and spontaneous combustion afford its only illumination. In this universe, bona fide sympathy is nearly impossible to find.

A recurring motif in this tradition involves representation or narration of the funeral rites held for the doomed protagonist. In each tale, a victim of—almost always—"too much feeling" succumbs. Other dooming conditions include too little food, hypothermia, consumption, and childbed fever. In an affective world, we are led to understand, there is no sustenance for those who live for sympathetic communion.

Like Tolstoy's adage concerning "all unhappy families," no two funerals in the early American novel are alike. Indeed, one could go so far as to claim that the post-partum morbidity exemplified in *The Power of Sympathy, Charlotte Temple,* and *The Coquette* manifests itself in diverse ways. We begin with William Hill Brown's 1789 epistolary work, *The Power of Sympathy,* a novel dappled with the deaths of young and promising figures, who in four digressive tales that form a syncopated plot largely appear as maniacs, suicides, and victims of puerperal fever.

Consider the fate of Ophelia, who, upon being seduced, impregnated, and abandoned by her own brother-in-law, Martin, gives birth to a son. She is abused physically by her tyrannical male parent, Shepard, while receiving "punishment from the hand of a vindictive father [other] than bare recrimination."[8] She finally drinks hemlock and expires in the arms of the very relations who have demanded a confrontation with her "seducer." If in her rebellion Ophelia serves as a figure for unrighteous revolution (having allowed herself to be swept away by a lawless masculine influence), any agency she may have possessed was always, already, circumscribed. Ophelia is caught in a landscape of nonchoice, torn between two unjust authorities: an autocratic, violent father bent on assigning blame and a tyrannical, self-absorbed lover refusing to take responsibility for his actions.

The story of Ophelia, Martin, and Shepard constitutes one of the novel's interpolated *romans à clef,* based on a real-life seduction and suicide scandal that rocked Boston and involved the Harvard-educated lawyer Perez Morton in the role of the villain. Exonerated in the death of Fanny Althorp Morton, he later became Speaker of the Massachusetts House of Representatives and Massachusetts attorney general. That the characters figured are based on members of William Hill Brown's own community makes the political thrust of his tale, its parable of the fatal consequences suffered by those who fail to throw off the yoke of unrighteous power, all the more incisive.[9]

If the subplots of *The Power of Sympathy* afford coded political warnings to readers, the dominant narrative of Brown's novel screams its message in veritable headlines. In a turn of ill fate, the well-born hero Harrington falls hopelessly in love with Harriot, an orphan of unknown origins. In the denouement of the drama, she is revealed to be Harrington's illegitimate half sister, product of an illicit alliance between his libertine father and a lower-class woman. Harrington's passion for the unlikely Harriot swiftly converts the aristocratic youth away from class prejudice, so that he adopts egalitarian views. It is a transformation that requires only twenty pages to effect. Declaring his initial contempt for democracy in an early letter, Harrington writes:

I suppose you will be ready to ask, why, if I love Harriot, I do not marry her. Your monitorial correspondence has so accustomed me to reproof that I easily anticipate this piece of impertinence. But *whom* shall I marry? That is the question. Harriot has no father—no mother—neither is there aunt, cousin, or kindred of any degree who claim any kind of relationship to her. She is companion to Mrs. Francis and, as I understand, totally dependent on that lady. Now Mr. Worthy, I must take the liberty to acquaint you that I am not so much of a republican as formally to wed any person of this class. How laughable would my conduct appear were I to trace over the same ground marked out by the immaculate footsteps, to be heard openly acknowledging for my bosom companion any daughter of the democratic empire of virtue.[10]

Hard on the heels of this expostulation, Harrington has a world-changing experience:

Unhappily at this juncture a lady and gentleman were engaged in a conversation concerning Miss P—— and one of them repeated the words, "a mechanic's daughter." It is supposed the word "mechanic" was repeated scornfully. She [Harriot] heard it—thought herself insulted—and indignantly retired. . . .

I wish people . . . would not dispute for any precedence or superiority but cultivate good nature and sociability. "A mechanic"—and pray whence this distinction!

Inequality among mankind is a foe to our happiness; it even affects our little parties of pleasure. Such is the fate of the human race: one order of men lords it over another. Upon what grounds its right is founded I could never yet be satisfied.

For this reason, I like a democratic government better than any other kind of government; and, were I Lycurgus, no distinction of rank should be found in my commonwealth.[11]

How does Harrington comprehend his political conversion experience? What is it in Harriot that has melted his heretofore hardened, elitist heart? Nothing less than "the power of sympathy," that mystic chord of fellow feeling linking Werther to Grechen in Goethe's *Sorrows of Young Werther* (1774), Heathcliff to Cathy in Emily Jane Brontë's *Wuthering Heights* (1848), and Jane to Rochester in sister Charlotte Brontë's *Jane Eyre* (1847), the seeming stuff of romantic love incarnate.

In William Hill Brown's novel, however, such elective affinities appear to have only biological roots. Thus we learn that what binds Harrington to Harriot is far more than feeling and nothing less than shared paternity. In the overheated emotional climate of the novel, Harriot sickens and dies upon learning the "truth"; and Harrington, bereft in the absence of his sister-lover, takes his own life. His body is found flanked by a copy of *Werther*. In the absence of the dead lovers, the affective atmosphere of the novel takes a decidedly tepid turn, as the final pages of the novel detail the hero's funeral.

Narrated by the impassive Mr. Worthy, tedious sidekick of the excessively romantic Harrington, the concluding epistle is a wonder of suppressed emotion. More a personification of the rational enlightenment than flesh and blood character, Worthy is incapable of providing a visceral reaction to the rites for his friend, for he has neither viscera nor bodily reactions of which to speak. Instead, his response, like many of the putative emotions circulating in the novel, is disavowed and projected onto the bodies of other characters, who are either racially marked or economically disabled.

In place of personal commentary, Worthy offers his perception of the lower classes gathered in grief to express their respect, admiration, and sorrow over the suicide of a privileged young man. One such "rude mechanical" notes that the tragic lover "wast possessed of a too nice sensibility, and a dread of shame. It is only such an one who would take the trouble to kill himself!"[12] The artisan goes on to rue the passing of Harrington, whom he terms a "noble youth," yet one cannot but help sense the resentment that suffuses his lamentation. Equally striking is the utter tone-deafness to class unrest that Worthy reveals in relating this anecdote without commentary.

One finishes *The Power of Sympathy* with unanswered questions, in particular bewilderment over the author's political sensibility. Is the book a brief for "revolution" based on the principle of sympathy, urging new Americans to deconstruct class boundaries through romantic desire? Surely, had the elder Harrington legitimized his transgressive alliance with Harriot's mother, he would have obviated not only the incestuous fate of his children, but he also might have eliminated the very existence of the younger Harrington himself. But might one conclude that Brown's tacit message is conservative to the point of being reactionary? That straying across class lines is what produces the central conflict of the novel in the first place? The deferential graveyard rites marking the close of *The Power of Sympathy* seem to suggest that the classes in the new republic remain relatively impermeable. It is with the collective sorrow represented in *Charlotte Temple* that mourning comes to be imagined as a democratizing experience.

In contrast to *The Power of Sympathy*, *Charlotte Temple* closes with a funeral so full of emotion—and so directly embodied—that the reader feels as if she might be brushing damp grave dirt off the page. In many ways, *Charlotte Temple* offers the purest case of melodrama in the early American fictive tradition. At the urging of her libertine French teacher, Madamoiselle La Rue, a once seduced and abandoned woman who is herself eloping with a soldier, fifteen-year-old English schoolgirl Charlotte Temple is swept away by Montraville. He has been posted to America, where he is to fight in the Revolution. Charlotte literally loses her virtue midvoyage, thereby embodying the seductive dangers of emigration and expatriation as a distinctly Anglo-American cultural problem. Pregnant when she lands in New York, Charlotte briefly lives in the country with Montraville until he falls in love with well-born American Julia Franklin, and abandons his mistress for marriage and martial duty.

Impoverished, starving, and on the verge of delivery, Charlotte walks barefoot to New York City, where she attempts to elicit the sympathy of Mlle. La Rue (who bears greater culpability in Charlotte's seduction than the man who technically deflowers her). Now the respectable Mrs. Crayton by way of a mercenary marriage, she is utterly unmoved, and when the supplicating heroine collapses at her former teacher's feet, the stone-hearted woman turns her away. Horrified by such callousness, the servants of this monstrous mistress carry Charlotte to their meager quarters. There, she gives birth to a baby girl, undergoes post-partum psychosis and childbed fever, and dies calling out her mother's name in a final plea for absolution. Just seconds too late, her forgiving father arrives at the door of this hovel, but his daughter is already a corpse, and he is left to see that she has a proper burial, and her baby a proper home.

In one of those instances of timing so unlikely that it constitutes a hall-mark of melodrama, Montraville, just back from maneuvers, hears

from a neighboring steeple a solemn toll that seemed to say that some poor mortal was going to their last mansion: the sound struck the heart of Montraville, and he involuntarily stopped, when, from one of the houses, he saw the appearance of a funeral. Almost unknowning what he did, he followed at a small distance; and as they let the coffin into the grave, he enquired of a soldier who stood by, and had just brushed off a tear that did honour to his heart, who it was that was just buried. "An pleasure your honour," said the man, " 'tis a poor girl that was brought from her friends by a cruel man, who left her when she was big with child, and married another." Montraville stood motionless, and the man proceeded—"I met her myself not a fortnight since one night all wet and cold in the streets. She went to Madam Crayton's, but she would not take her in, and so the poor thing went raving mad." Montraville could bear no more; he stuck his hands against his forehead with violence; and exclaiming "poor, murdered Charlotte!" Ran with precipitation towards the place where they were heaping earth on her remains. "Hold, hold, one moment," said he. "Close not the grave of the injured Charlotte Temple till I have taken vengeance on her murderer."[13]

What could be more compelling than Susanna Rowson's final image: the repentant seducer, Montraville, kneeling in the cemetery, prostrate before Charlotte's open grave? Rowson makes clear that the spectacle of Charlotte being lowered into the ground forever mars Montraville's prospect of an American future; though united with the sympathetic heiress Julia Franklin (who never knew her mother), he will remain plagued by an incurable melancholy set into motion by his complicity in the ruin of Charlotte Temple.

In a twist of poetic justice, Montraville comes to incarnate as well as to foreshadow the affective response experienced by the audience of the novel. Closing her tale with the figure of Montraville nearly maddened by unremitting grief, Rowson gave fictive birth to real-life readers who so believed in the efficacy of collective mourning for "Charlotte Temple" that they paid for and dedicated a gravestone in New York's Trinity Church. Lovers of the novel (the best-selling American work of fiction until the publication Uncle Tom's Cabin in 1852) traveled to the cemetery throughout the nineteenth century, leaving flowers and notes at Charlotte's "grave."[14] Enacting a fascinating case of life's imitation of art, these pilgrims took literal heed of the pleas of the narrator, who constantly interrupts her story to implore her audience to sympathize, sympathize, sympathize with the wayward Charlotte. By so doing, her readers came to constitute, historically and materially, the narrator's imagined community of bereavement. In their coming together to grieve for the seduced and abandoned heroine, Rowson created a democratic body of mourners, all bound by "fellow feeling."

Charlotte Temple closes with an egalitarian fantasy of sympathy so powerful that it might bind together an imagined audience of Americans of disparate backgrounds. *The Coquette,* published only three years after *Charlotte Temple* and issued by an American press, conceives of republican sympathy in different terms. Written by the wife of a Congregationalist minister in Federalist New England, *The Coquette* offers its readers another tale of seduction and abandonment, based on the real-life case of Elizabeth Whitman, a middle-aged Connecticut poetess and flirt who, deferring marriage until age thirty-seven, ultimately was "ruined" by a local libertine. Ministers throughout New England gave sermons thundering against Whitman's depraved behavior, and she came to serve as an emblem of the dangers of excessive liberty. In the hands of Hannah Webster Foster, however, the historical narrative is complicated considerably: the novel proves far more sympathetic to Whitman's travail than did the sermons emanating against her from the pulpit.

The "virtual" funeral narrative punctuating the final page of *The Coquette* is a textual facsimile of Eliza Wharton's tombstone. After delivering her stillborn illegitimate child in a Danvers tavern in 1788, Whitman died alone, and ignominiously. In Foster's redemptive retelling of Whitman's "fall," the heroine's reputation is resurrected through the public sphere of print, and ultimately through the novelized depiction of the tombstone which details her final penitence.

THIS HUMBLE STONE,
IN MEMORY OF ELIZA WHARTON
IS INSCRIBED BY HER WEEPING FRIENDS,
TO WHOM SHE ENDEARED HERSELF BY UNCOMMON
TENDERNESS AND AFFECTION.
ENDOWED WITH SUPERIOR ACQUIREMENTS,
SHE WAS STILL MORE DISTINGUISHED BY
HUMILITY AND BENEVOLENCE.
LET CANDOR THROW A VEIL ON HER FRAILTIES,
FOR GREAT WAS HER CHARITY TO OTHERS.
SHE SUSTAINED THE LAST
PAINFUL SCENE, FAR FROM EVERY FRIEND;
AND EXHIBITED AN EXAMPLE
OF CALM RESIGNATION
HER DEPARTURE WAS ON THE 25TH DAY OF
JULY, A.D. —
IN THE 37TH YEAR OF HER AGE,
AND THE TEARS OF STRANGERS WATERED HER
GRAVE.[15]

Foster's Eliza Wharton is a belle renowned for her lively wit, poetic gifts, and social charm, who has deferred offers of marriage, claiming that the wedded estate is the "tomb of friendship."[16] As the novel opens, she is negotiating the attentions of two suitors: the minister Boyer, a modest clergyman of Eliza's social class whose censorious attitude toward her economic ambitions and purported "coquetry" mark him as an unlikely match; and Major Peter Sanford, a dashing libertine already reputed to have ruined innocent women. This rake's thrilling company—and depleted bank account—render him an equally problematic future partner. Sanford and Eliza are, in fact, virtually twin characters, sharing not only similar positions in the early national social structure but even the same linguistic patterns, particularly a loathing of "confinement" and a resistance to the "shackles" of matrimony. They exhibit identical yearnings for social elevation and parallel financial proclivities—overspending and lack of income.

After vacillating between the two men, Eliza is caught by Boyer in what he misreads as a compromising position with Sanford. The minister repudiates Eliza, while Sanford marries an heiress to avoid bankruptcy, leaving the heroine in a state of despair. Already suffering from a fatal depression, Eliza ultimately takes up with the married Sanford, "seduced," as it were, by her own failed ambition and thus self-condemned to shame and an anonymous death. She dies far from her erstwhile female friends, whose failure of sympathy had driven her out of the Federalist social fold and into the arms of a man she does not love.

To deliver her baby in secret, Eliza flees her mother's home, succumbing to childbirth fever. She suffers, repents, dies, and is buried offstage by strangers. Her funeral thus offers prosthetic tears: the ending of the book is a sanitary marvel. Deathbed support and burial arrangements are taken up by those anonymous good Samaritans who care for the unwed mother in extremis. The chorus, made up by those fair-weather friends who had previously condemned her insufficiently solemn life, recognizes Eliza's humanity only insofar as it can be incorporated into its own chaste ideology. They value the now-dead Eliza for the public function she performs as a symbol of penitent virtue.

In looking at fictive funeral rituals as indices of feeling in the imagined world of Charles Brockden Brown, we are left with neither anesthesia, nor emotional excess, nor stolen nor misappropriated emotion. Instead, Brown's work is dominated by paranoia—what we might call the rerouting of expressive feeling into self-devouring masochism.[17] Brown's oeuvre is riddled with scenes of death caused by suicide, murder, or plague. But none of these fictive losses is marked by representations of the burial processions, tolling bells, exchanging of gloves, rings, and gifts, or the smoking of tobacco and drinking of rum, which actual funeral ritual in pre-Revolutionary British America entailed.[18]

In Brown's first novel, *Wieland: Or, the Transformation, An American Tale* (1798), Wieland the elder, a religious fanatic devoted to his own heretical Protestant sect, has failed in his seven-year attempt to convert a tribe of Native Americans living in western Pennsylvania. Returning to the rural outskirts of Philadelphia, he builds a great estate using slave labor. Brown mentions this detail only once, in passing. That such a tiny fact of plot should arise in a novel written by a Quaker with abolitionist impulses cannot be an accident, however, and I suggest that it goes far in explaining the political significance of the tragic destruction of the elder Wieland and subsequent members of his family.[19]

Years later, Wieland hears a mysterious command from "his" God, which he ignores. Hours following his act of self-styled "disobedience," which scholars read as a form of Revolutionary defiance, the man spontaneously combusts, dying of mysterious wounds sustained while his body is burning. The reasons for this strange fatality remain unexplained. Nor is any mention made of the elder Wieland's funeral. It is as if Brown depicts the aftermath of Wieland's disaster by striking it out entirely, an event so traumatic to characters and author alike that it cannot be brought into representation.[20]

In fact, Charles Brockden Brown offers readers only two—ever so marginally "proper"—burials, in *Arthur Mervyn: Or, Memoirs of the Year 1793* (1799/1800), and in *Ormond: Or, the Secret Witness* (1799). Both novels take as their subject Philadelphia's yellow fever epidemic of 1793. While both novels detail home burials, we shall focus simply on the "nonritual" that unfolds in *Ormond*. In the back garden of their rented home, during the epidemic, cross-dressing Revolutionary Martinette de Beauvais furtively inters her surrogate father. This act is marked by the fact that Martinette is a woman warrior who has seen service in both the American and French Revolutions. The absolute antithesis of a sentimental heroine, she is a lady who "sheds no tears." And true to form, Martinette buries her "father" with an utter lack of ceremony. Not only is there no funeral procession and no memorializing bells; there are no other mourners to bear witness to Roselli's passing. Martinette must proceed without a casket, and she herself is clothed only in a nightdress, working in the dark. At stake in this funeral service-*manqué* is the fate of sympathy itself: the voyeuristic neighbor, Baxter, who spies on Martinette's actions by peering over the back fence, is undone by what he sees and soon after dies of yellow fever, as if punished for his unrighteous gazing.[21]

What do we conclude from this tiny but supercharged sample of novelistic sentiment? The public exploitation of surrogate emotion in *The Power of Sympathy* and *The Coquette*, the overflow of feeling that threatens to drag the reader into the grave of Charlotte Temple, and the evacuation of feeling in *Ormond*, suggest a cultural shift from an ethos of republican publicity to one of liberal privacy.[22] At the same time, these textual moments reveal the reprobation of certain forms of emotion and the manipulation of collective affect that could be—and was—exploited for political purposes by both major factions in the 1790s, Federalists and Republicans. In much broader terms, as Julie Ellison notes in *Cato's Tears*, it is in the reality of "liberal guilt" and through the enduring power of "vicarious emotion" that the sentiment made famous in the eighteenth century has evolved into that obvious excess of feeling which threatens to overwhelm our contemporary public culture.[23] The spectacles pursued and exploited by an increasingly unfulfilled, intensive, and ubiquitous media will appear no less bizarre to future observers than the novels of the 1790s appear to us. All reflect the persistent centrality of the sentimental in American life.

Part III
Physical Remains

Chapter 7
Major André's Exhumation

Michael Meranze

> *In the centre of the road stood an enormous tulip tree*
> *which towered like a giant above all the other trees*
> *in the neighbourhood, and formed a kind of land mark. Its*
> *limbs were gnarled, and fantastic, large enough to form trunks*
> *for ordinary trees, twisting down almost to the earth,*
> *and rising again into the air. It was connected with*
> *the tragical story of the unfortunate André, who*
> *had been taken prisoner hard by; and was universally known*
> *by the name of Major André's tree. The common people*
> *regarded it with a mixture of respect and superstition,*
> *partly out of sympathy for the fate of its ill starred namesake,*
> *and partly from the tales of strange sights,*
> *and doleful lamentations, told concerning it.*
>
> —Washington Irving, "The Legend of Sleepy Hollow" (1819)

In *Common Sense* (1776), Thomas Paine boldly declared, "We have it in our power to begin the world over again." Independence from Britain, he insisted, would mark new beginnings and create the possibility of retracing the steps of humanity and avoiding prior errors: "A situation, similar to the present, hath not appeared since the days of Noah until now. The birthday of a new world is at hand."[1]

Corpses, however, haunted Paine's new world. Voice of Reason though he was, Paine found the imaginary call of the cadaver palpable and powerful. Reconciliation was impossible, he pronounced, in part because "the blood of the slain, the weeping voice of nature cries, 'TIS TIME TO PART'."[2] On the subject of monuments, he ironically pondered the honors due the disgraced British general William Howe. "The usual honours of the dead," Paine insisted, "are not sufficiently sublime to escort a character like you to the republic of dust and ashes; for however men may differ in their ideas of grandeur and government here, the grave is nevertheless a perfect republic. Death is not the monarch of the dead, but of the dying."[3] In Paine's rhetoric, the dead and violent death shadowed not only the New World but also the very shape of a republic.

Yet, corpses and violence were more than a rhetorical matter. The American republic, after all, was founded amid war and bloodshed. From the remarkable brutality of the fighting between Whigs and Tories in the Southern backcountry, through the intensified struggles on slave plantations, to the unburied bones of rebels who died in Britain's infamous prison ships, the military struggle against British authority left deep scars of death and desolation on the American landscape and in the American imagination. Debates over monuments and memories were deeply charged political issues.[4]

No corpse haunted the early republic more than John André's. On October 2, 1780, the American army executed André, adjutant general of the British army, at their camp at Tappan, New York. His execution marked one of the most traumatic moments of the American Revolution. The autumn of 1780 saw the nadir of the American war effort. André had spent months in secret negotiation with Benedict Arnold, leading to a plan to seize the American garrison at West Point. Dispatched for confidential face-to-face discussions with Arnold, he had been unable to return to British lines and was captured by a group of irregular soldiers. Taken to the American army, André was tried by a board of general officers who sentenced him to be executed as a spy. Despite British efforts to obtain his release, and André's own pleas to be shot as a gentleman rather than hanged as a common criminal, André met his fate at the gibbet. Coming on the heels of the British occupation of Charleston, the news of Arnold's altered allegiance stunned the American Revolutionaries. Simultaneously, André's capture threw the British high command into despair. During André's captivity, Americans struggled to understand Arnold's actions amid widespread fears of further treason. The British, frantically seeking to save their officer, issued threats and offered entreaties, while the Americans purportedly sought to exchange André for Arnold. In the midst of this vortex of politics and emotion, André died a dramatically stoic death at the gallows, a death admired and remembered by many.[5]

Signifying both the necessity of independence and the loss that independence entailed, André's hanged body materialized the collective fate of eighteenth-century Anglo-American empire and the violence that surrounded the founding of the United States. His death triggered an ongoing transatlantic debate. In history, literature, memoir, political argument, and public festival, Americans and Britons aimed to determine the meaning of André's end. Ultimately, however, this debate established nothing so much as the ineradicable conflicts that divided both the new United States and the Atlantic world more generally.

When André ascended the gallows, he enacted a series of roles—as ancient stoic and modern man of feeling, as military hero and bourgeois gentleman, as loyal subject and enduring martyr. Through his very multi-plicity, André became a frame through which Americans and Britons argued the meaning of the American Revolution and the British Empire, the rise of democracy and the perpetuation of aristocracy, the claims of the heart and the rigors of the law, the codes of gentility and the violence of the Revolutionary world. André's execution was a crucial moment in the emergence of the United States. Its afterlife became an enduring symptom of the contested authority of the culture of sensibility in the Atlantic world during the period from the Revolution to the Civil War.

From the moment of his death in October 1780, indeed, even before his death, André's execution figured prominently in contemporary efforts to determine the meaning of the American Revolution. These efforts revolved around the justice of André's fate. Had the Americans been just in their insistence on executing André as a spy? Was Washington just when he insisted on hanging André? The details of these debates are extremely involved. But the general issues can be explained. The British insisted that André, who had crossed behind enemy lines under passports from Arnold, should not be considered a spy (even though he was caught in civilian clothes while carrying vital military information). The Americans, of course, viewed things differently—hence the execution itself. But there was a second recurrent issue. André sought, as a gentleman, to be shot rather than hanged. By this request, he aimed to escape being turned into a spectacle of bodily suffering and dishonor. Washington refused. In this regard, he not only opposed the wishes of the British but of some of his own officers as well—most famously the young Alexander Hamilton. Enamored of André's charm and gentility, they hoped to spare him the ignominious fate of a common criminal—being displayed before thousands in the death throes of the hanged. Hamilton especially viewed Washington's decision with bitterness.

Because of the controversy over André's fate, and because that controversy was fueled in large part by his gentlemanly stoicism, André's execution fused the issues of civility, violence, and revolution in the early republic. Washington's rigor stood at the center of the dispute. Because Washington himself was so committed to the practices of gentility, André's fate was inextricably tied to Washington's reputation. Washington stood as a figure for the new American nation in many contemporary images. Thus, André's execution remained a source of contention between the British and the Americans well into the nineteenth century. The question of violence and the treatment of a corpse was bound to strike deep chords in the political and literary cultures of the early American republic. A new world might have been emerging, but it could not cut its ties to the memory of an archaic ritual or that ritual's material remnant. The dead past could not be so easily put aside.

These issues were literally and figuratively unearthed in 1821. In that year, the British consul in New York decided to exhume André's body and return it to England for reburial at Westminster Abbey. In that same year, a New Yorker by the name of James Fenimore Cooper published his first successful novel—*The Spy*—set in the New York of the Revolutionary War and framed by André's execution. Both André's exhumation and Cooper's novel fueled the ongoing controversy about André's fate. But they did so in a way that focused the controversy on the meaning of violence in a democracy in its relationship to civility and class. In so doing, they revealed anew the persistent and troubled relations between the old and the new, Europe and America, the genteel and the plebeian, violence and the modern political imagination, and the living and the dead.

On the evening of August 11, 1821, James Buchanan, the British consul, made his way from New York City to the small town of Tappan, New York. Buchanan hoped that the cover of night would enable him and one companion to slip quietly into the village, remove the sarcophagus holding André's remains, and return unobserved to New York Harbor. This was Buchanan's second visit to Tappan in the same number of days. The day before he had disinterred André's corpse from its grave of forty years and examined his remains before a wide gathering of townsmen and townswomen. Buchanan had originally intended to return on the following Tuesday and publicly carry André's remains to New York. But having been warned by "a citizen of the first respectability" in the city that "some hot spirits . . . were determined to meet the procession [bearing André's remains] on the way and throw the sarcophagus into the Hudson," Buchanan had determined to return early to Tappan and secretly carry out his task.[6]

Stopping at a tavern near Tappan village for refreshments, Buchanan found—to his dismay—that "some who had witnessed the exhumation the day before" were present, and fearing discovery "took every precaution to avoid coming in contact with the persons at the tavern." One person, however, came up to him and "without any prefatory observation, by way of introduction, asked me, was I not the British consul, as he thought he had seen me the day before at Tappan." Buchanan continued his narrative as follows:

I had no way of retreat; so I told him I was often taken for the consul, and that at times it was very inconvenient to have so close a resemblance to that person. He then began to inform me of the exhumation of Major André, the magnificence of the sarcophagus, and that the whole country would be there on Tuesday to join in the procession. I need not say that I got away from this kind and inquisitive person as quickly as possible, as others were approaching, who, had they been at Tappan the day before, I know not how I should have got clear of these men, more than the lamented André did from those men who met him when he was taken.[7]

Buchanan's words say a great deal and include a remarkable transposition. For what Buchanan and all of his readers knew was that when André failed to escape his captors, the result was his execution as a spy. Imagining himself as André, Buchanan depicted his situation as one fraught with personal danger; he equated his discovery by the townspeople of Tappan with André's capture in the midst of Revolutionary violence. Buchanan thereby implied that the threat posed by discovery was a fatal one.

This was certainly hyperbole. But it was historically significant hyperbole. Linking himself to André and linking the crowd at the tavern to André's captors, Buchanan crucially opposed civility to violence and democracy. Transforming himself into André and the townspeople into his captors, Buchanan, in the narrative, implies that for the civil, confrontation with democracy is filled with danger. And in the process, that danger became a figure for democracy itself.

The danger democracy posed to the bodies of the genteel was an overriding concern to the British consul. Haunting Buchanan's account was the threat of grave robbing. This threat took two forms. First, rumors abounded that the "body had been secretly carried to England." And when the diggers did not find the coffin quickly, Buchanan tells us, "surmises about the body having been removed were revived, and it would be difficult to imagine any event which could convey a degree of more intense excitement." But finding the body removed only one of the fears, he felt. Buchanan next descended to the coffin itself:

. . . which was not more than three feet below the surface, and with my own hands raked the dust together, to ascertain whether he had been buried in his regimentals or not, as it was rumoured among the assemblage that he had been stripped; for, if buried in his regimentals, I expected to find the buttons of his clothes, which would have disproved the rumour; but I did not find a single button, nor any article, save a string of leather that had tied his hair, in perfect preservation, coiled and tied as it had been on his hair at the time. This string I forwarded to his sister in England. I examined the dust of the coffin so minutely (as the quantity would not fill a quart) that no mistake could have arisen in the examination.[8]

André's clothing, in this case, had replaced his remains as the object of anxiety.

Instead of removal, the threat was now exposure. Just as Buchanan feared being revealed in Tappan, so did he fear that André's body had been shorn of its clothing, that his corpse had been left uncovered in death—with the exception of the single string of leather that remained intact. Like André, who worried about the disgrace of the common hanging, Buchanan worried about the disgrace of a common grave.

Buchanan's narrative implied that the Continental army had stripped André of his clothes, denying him in death the dignity that Washington had denied him in dying. Interestingly, Buchanan denies any "unworthy motive" in recording his experience. He was, he insisted, simply ascertaining and propagating the truth as "it may reasonably be inferred, that if stripped, those who permitted this outrage, or who knew of it, had no idea that the unfeeling act they then performed would be blazoned to the world near half a century after the event; or that the future historian should hold up such procedure to the reproval of all honourable men."[9] When Buchanan published his memoir in 1833, his charge stung, and it did not go unanswered. The following year, American James Thacher felt compelled to respond, to try to prove that André's regimentals were not in his grave because they had been returned to his servant in 1780.[10] Thacher, like many others among his countrymen, insisted that André had been treated with exquisite courtesy and granted all due respect.

Buchanan's implicit condemnation of the American army was linked to an explicit condemnation of those plebeian elements who, in the name of American democracy, opposed his efforts. When he had first arrived in Tappan, Buchanan discovered to his dismay that "though I was not expected until the following Tuesday . . . a number of persons soon assembled, some of whom betrayed symptoms of displeasure at the proceeding, arising from the observations of some of the public journals, which asserted 'that any honour paid Major André's remains was casting an imputation on General Washington, and the officers who tried him.'" Buchanan insisted that "these characters were of the lowest case, and their observations were condemned by every respectable person in the village." Still, he "deemed it prudent" to "resort to a mode of argument, the only one I had time or inclination to bestow upon them." He told the "noisy patriots" that he "wished to follow a custom not unfrequent in Ireland, from whence I came, namely, of taking some spirits before proceeding to a grave." The landlord, Buchanan continued, "approved the Irish practice, and accordingly supplied abundance of liquor." The result, Buchanan maintained, was that "in a short time, General Washington, Major André, and the object of my visit were forgotten by them, and I was left at perfect liberty, with the respectable inhabitants of the place, to proceed to the exhumation."[11]

André's remains had mobilized a complex social geography. On the one hand, Buchanan is at pains to separate the protestors from the "respectable." Continuing his story, he reported that "quite an unexpected crowd assembled at the grave . . . a number of ladies, and many aged matrons who witnessed [André's] fall,—who had seen his person,—who mingled tears with his sufferings,—attended, and were loud in their praises of the Prince, for thus honouring one who still lived in their recollection with unsubdued sympathy." Once the coffin was opened, Buchanan allowed "all the people to pass round in regular order and view the remains as they lay, which very many did with unfeigned tears, and lamentation."[12] In this telling, opposition to honoring André marks the absence of sentiment itself. The women of Tappan, like a chorus in a Greek tragedy, speak the voice of the community and represent the natural "unfeigned" emotion of reconciliation.

But as both the term "unfeigned" and the "praises for the Prince" make clear, there is a larger politics at work here. Buchanan places a politics of sentimental memory in opposition to the politics of democracy. For the women of Tappan are only one link in a longer sentimental chain that stretches through New York City across the ocean to England and back again. Buchanan tells us that upon his return to the city with André's remains, "Ladies sent me flowers; others, various emblematic devices, garlands, etc. to decorate the remains of the 'lamented and beloved André'." He sent one "beautiful and ornamented myrtle" to London, where it was deposited near the monument which had been erected to André's memory in Westminster Abbey. The duke of York, in turn, acknowledged the efforts of Reverend Demarat, the owner of the land in which André had lain for so many years. "I recommended," Buchanan says, "that his Royal Highness should convey to him a snuff-box, made out of one of his trees which grew at the grave, which I sent home. But my suggestion was far outdone by the princely munificence of his Royal Highness, who ordered a box to be made out of the tree, and lined with gold."[13] Here André's remains function as the material base for a chain of sympathy that Buchanan suggests knows no national bounds nor class distinctions. André, who died for his king, seems able even in death to recreate the bonds of sympathy that monarchical theory presumed links the sovereign to a subject.

Of course, neither the "matrons" of Tappan nor the "ladies" of New York were royal subjects. And therein lay the other side of Buchanan's rhetorical politics—his attack on the practice of American politics. Buchanan cautioned his readers lest they believe that the people of the United States had acted outrageously, by doing something like hurling André's sarcophagus into the Hudson River. Rather, he insisted that these "hot spirits" were indifferent to André. Writing for a British audience, Buchanan insisted that "it is difficult to explain to those not long acquainted with the United States the motives which govern the action of a democracy, and I am supported in the opinion of some whose judgment I deem sound." Criticizing the newspapers of New York and Philadelphia, he noted that "party feeling in political matters generally runs so high, that the favour of one party is sure to subject its object to the opposition of the other."[14] Between the "noisy patriots" and the political press, the unthinking politics of a democracy had stood in the way of the "unfeigned" sympathies that the "respectable" had shown to André's memory. For Buchanan, democracy is all but unnatural, full of feigned and duplicitous behavior. It is a politics that is insensible to the sentiment of reconciliation.

This critique becomes even clearer when the exhumation is seen in its fullest context. Buchanan was "annoyed" that the state of New York had treated the remains of General Richard Montgomery so differently from those of André. Montgomery, an English-born soldier who came to America during the late colonial period, sided with the rebels and fell in Quebec in 1775, when Americans were trying to conquer Canada. In 1818, New York had arranged, in an act that Edward Livingston referred to as a "great act of national piety," to have Montgomery returned to American soil. Recovering Montgomery's body in Quebec, New Yorkers carried it through their state amid great ceremony, accompanied on their march by military, political, and cultural figures. Following one last great procession through the streets of New York City, the remains were finally deposited at St. Paul's Cathedral.[15]

Buchanan's effort to exhume André had been "inspired," in part, by these events. Buchanan reported that he was "hourly annoyed by contrasts drawn from the conduct of the state of New York as to the remains of General Montgomery—while those of the British soldier, who was sacrificed in the service of his country, in the flower of his youth, *(by a doom, which, in the judgment of many, might have been commuted,)* were abandoned and neglected."[16] Buchanan had hoped for far greater ceremony for André than he in fact received.[17]

For Buchanan, and for Livingston, the remains of André and Montgomery were national relics. The exchange of two military martyrs was a sign not only of national feeling but also, potentially, of international reconciliation. The treatment of the dead became the material of the sympathy of the living. Buchanan imagines a cosmopolitan sympathy that passes beyond national boundaries through the shared sentiments of the genteel and civil. In this resurrection of ties shattered amid the Revolution, the messiness of democratic politics, with its "noisy patriots," was meant to be put aside.

Buchanan's larger narrative replicated an ongoing debate over the meaning of André's execution and, more particularly, the honors owed to André's memory. It did so, however, in a way that diminished the social and political stakes involved in remembering and honoring André. As Robert Cray has demonstrated, the debate over André's exhumation reflected deep social divisions within the early republic, divisions that structured competing memories of the American Revolution.[18] When Buchanan sees "noisy patriots" motivated by liquor and limited by their prejudice, he avoids the political context of André's exhumation—a continuing controversy over the heroism of ordinary individuals in the Revolution.

It was Congressman Benjamin Tallmadge of New York who had triggered this debate on the floor of the House when he attacked the character and motivations of André's plebeian captors. The captors, Tallmadge insisted, were common criminals who would have released André had they been assured of receiving a ransom. The captors' defenders, on the other hand, depicted heroic commoners whose patriotism ran deeper than that of many of the higher-born.[19] In this context, the genteel believed that respect for André's corpse signaled respect for the civility that they believed marked their own class. (Note the genteel New Yorkers' concern for the "lamented and beloved André.") For the plebeian, on the other hand, respect for André's corpse signified an elitist dismissal of the sufferings of the common soldier during the Revolution. André's body, thereby, materialized the political, gender, and class differences of the early republic. And it did so by materializing the connection with the past—a past that remained alive through the memory and the physical remains of the dead.

It is perhaps not surprising that a British official, writing for a British audience in the British *United Service Journal and Naval and Military Magazine*, would link violence and democratic politics in opposition to sentiment and civility. But as Buchanan's mobilization of his genteel New York informants suggests, there were Americans who made a similar equation. One who did—albeit in a remarkably complex way—was James Fenimore Cooper, himself connected through marriage to a prominent loyalist family. In his novel *The Spy*, he engaged in the political debate that Benjamin Tallmadge had stimulated.[20]

Cooper set *The Spy* in the autumn of 1780, after André's execution. The execution is on the minds of all of his characters. The story itself is centered around the Wharton family, which contains a secretly loyalist father, an openly loyalist daughter, a daughter openly on the side of the rebels, and a son, Henry Wharton, serving in the British army. The plot, then, turns largely on the threat of execution and violence. Beyond the actual warfare taking place in New York, three threats take center stage. The first is the danger posed to the Wharton family by corrupt plebeian elements acting under the mantle of patriotism. The second threat is the danger posed to Henry Wharton, who, having come to visit his family, is captured in civilian clothes (as André had been), and therefore condemned as a spy by the Americans. Finally, and perhaps most significantly, a danger is posed to Harvey Birch, a local trader suspected by most Americans of being a British agent (and, therefore, in constant danger of hanging), who is in fact the trusted eyes of Washington and the spy of the novel's title.

These intersecting tales of danger allow Cooper to disassemble and reassemble the André story. Henry Wharton, like André legally a spy because he traveled disguised as a civilian behind enemy lines, is, unlike André, innocent of the charge. George Washington, who officially condemns Wharton (as he had condemned André), actually secretly enables Birch to save Wharton not once but several times; Washington does this because he had been a guest of the Whartons (while himself traveling in an assumed character) and thereby knew Wharton to be innocent. And Harvey Birch, superficially a man who knew no loyalty except to money (thus an apparent confirmation of Tallmadge's critique of André's captors), turns out to be motivated by the highest principle of patriotism. He refuses to accept from Washington any monetary reward for his services.

It is only at the end of the novel that we discover Birch's true nature as well as the fact that Washington, like André, Birch, and Wharton, had assumed a feigned identity in the novel. Here, for perhaps the only time in *The Spy*, revelation is linked with possibility and opportunity and not simply with danger. The scene deserves to be quoted:

"It is now my duty to pay you for these services; hitherto you have postponed receiving your reward, and the debt has become a heavy one—I wish not to undervalue your dangers; here are a hundred doubloons; you will remember the poverty of our country, and attribute to it the smallness of your pay."

The pedler raised his eyes to the countenance of the speaker; but, as the other held forth the money, he moved back, as if refusing the bag.

"It is not much for your services and risks, I acknowledge," continued the general, "but it is all that I have to offer; at the end of the campaign, it may be in my power to increase it."

"Does your excellency think that I have exposed my life, and blasted my character, for money?"

"If not for money, what then?"

"What has brought your excellency into the field? For what do you daily and hourly expose your precious life to battle and the halter? What is there about me to mourn, when men such as you risk their all for our country? No—no—no—not a dollar of your gold will I touch; poor America has need of it all!"

The bag dropped from the hand of the officer, and fell at the feet of the pedler, where it lay neglected during the remainder of the interview. The officer looked steadily in the face of his companion, and continued—

"There are many motives which might govern me, that to you are unknown. Our situations are different; I am known as the leader of armies—but you must descend into the grave with the reputation of a foe to your native land. Remember that the veil which conceals your true character cannot be raised in years—perhaps never."[21]

In having Birch refuse Washington's offer of gold, Cooper validates the reputations of André's captors and by extension plebeian patriotism. Indeed, Birch's questioning of Washington seemingly asserts a moral (if not a social) equivalence between the poor peddler and the wealthy general. Washington's allusions to his search for glory could, from one angle, raise Birch's character even higher than his own.

But Cooper's defense of popular patriotism and democratic insurgency is not as unequivocal as it might seem. Troubling Cooper's depiction of popular patriotism—troubling, too, the historical reality that Cooper fictionalizes— was the presence of those men known as "Cow-Boys" and "Skinners." Cowboys and skinners were irregular groups of men who claimed loyalty to one side or the other (skinners to the rebels, cow-boys to the British) but who, as often as not, used the war as an excuse to plunder. In the novel, a group of "skinners," for example, destroy the homes of both Birch and the Whartons, and they constantly menace Birch's life.

Of course, it is easy to separate corrupt from honest plebeians in the story, and Cooper does so. But while claiming Birch as a figure for American honesty and patriotism, the author throws in one discordant note, a note that returns us to corpses and the ambiguous relationship between the early American republic and violence. Late in the novel, after Birch (at Washington's secret bidding) has escorted Henry Wharton to safety, he finds himself in the company of a skinner. Soon both men are intercepted by a group of cow-boys. At first, the skinner, having proclaimed his intention to turn-coat (another recurrent theme of both the André situation and Cooper's novel), seems more welcome than Birch, who is suspected by all sides. But having recognized the skinner from previous encounters, the captain of the cow-boys decides to hang him in a makeshift gallows in a barn. Here is what ensues after Birch is warned not to aid the skinner:

Birch went no farther than a bush that opportunely offered itself as a screen to his person, while he yielded to an unconquerable desire to witness the termination of this extraordinary scene.

Left alone, the Skinner began to throw fearful glances around, to espy the hiding-places of his tormentors [since he still thought his hanging was simply a trick to extort information]. For the first time the horrid idea seemed to shoot through his brain that something was seriously intended by the Cow-boy. He called entreatingly to be released, and made rapid and incoherent promises of important information, mingled with affected pleasantry at their conceit, dreadful as it seemed. But as he heard the tread of the horses moving on their course, and in vain looked around for human aid, violent trembling seized his limbs, and his eyes began to start from his head with terror. He made a desperate effort to reach the beam; but, too much exhausted with his previous exertions, he caught the rope in his teeth, in a vain effort to sever the cord, and fell to the whole length of his arms. Here his cries were turned into shrieks—

"Help! cut the rope! Captain!—Birch! good pedler! Down with the Congress!—Sergeant!—for God's sake, help! Hurrah for the king!—Oh, God! oh God!—mercy—mercy—mercy!"

As his voice became suppressed, one of his hands endeavoured to make its way between the rope and his neck, and partially succeeded; but the other fell quivering by his side. A convulsive shuddering passed over his whole frame, and he hung a hideous corpse.

Birch continued gazing on this scene with a kind of infatuation. At its close he placed his hand to his ears, and rushed towards the highway. Still the cries for mercy rang through his brain, and it was many weeks before his memory ceased to dwell on the horrid event. The Cow-boys rode steadily on their route, as if nothing had occurred; and the body was left swinging in the wind, until chance directed the footsteps of some straggler to the place."[22]

Cooper forces his reader to confront that which had hung over the entire story—the threat of what Birch, speaking to Washington, called the "halter." Here were the death throes of the condemned, a fate shared not only by the fictional skinner but also by numerous real people during the war—including John André. André, of course, died neither alone nor beseeching mercy. But if Birch served as a double for André's captors, he also served as a more noble double of André himself, who, in a parallel to the self-presentation of Washington, had engaged in espionage in part for glory. Cooper sets out a series of complex, self-reflective identifications. For if Birch is witnessing what would be done to him if captured by the Americans, the fact that the hanging is being done by loyalists also points to a fact shared by Birch and Washington—their mutual fate at the "halter" if the Revolution should fail. To be sure, given the rules that distinguished gentlemen from commoners, that danger was greater for Birch than for Washington; but it does recall Franklin's famous aphorism that "we shall all hang together or hang separately." The violence of the Revolutionary world could not be avoided, nor could the violence of the counter-Revolutionary world.

But then there is Birch's gaze. The issue is not that Birch did not aid the skinner; the presence of the cow-boys made that possibility moot. But why the description of the hanging, and why was Birch unable to leave? Cooper, of course, would make a long and lucrative career out of scenes of violence. But here, he anticipates critics of American culture, from D. H. Lawrence to Richard Slotkin, in linking American democracy to a fascination with violence.[23] If Birch stands in for popular patriotism, does his inability to leave the fatal scene—and from his perspective it was literally a scene—suggest democracy's enthrallment with the violence of its birth? Is Cooper, would-be literary aristocrat, joining here with Buchanan in making violence a figure for democracy itself? Is this the secret revelation of how civil society viewed America's impending course? Does the absorption in the execution and exhumation of André bespeak a repetitive return to the moment of violent birth of the American Republic—a moment inextricably linked to a fascinated gaze on the lost and the dead?

These are, admittedly, questions without any certain or verifiable answer. It is not my intention to endorse the linkage made by Buchanan and Cooper between democracy and violence. Nor do I intend to endorse their opposition between civility and democracy. Instead, I want to suggest that we guard against the presumption repeated by contemporary scholars in assuming these linkages and oppositions. For the increasingly romanticized historical and literary recreations of eighteenth- and nineteenth-century gentility bespeak a flattening of the complexities of the birth of the modern world in the Age of Revolution.[24]

In the eighteenth-century British world, a fundamental genteel conceit had it that when civility began violence ended. This claim, invoked hundreds of years ago and repeated in much scholarly literature today as part of the history of manners and sociability, took shape in numerous discursive and social contexts: from the tradition of belle lettres to the convivial clubs of the metropolis; from the "pleasures of the imagination" to the exploration of the South Pacific; from provincial poetry to *Poor Richard's Almanack*.[25] This cultural claim was, to be sure, always riddled with contradictions—most notably the violence done to self in the name of civility; the violence done to others in the pursuit of civility; and the violence that always, to borrow a phrase, already defined civility itself.

But in the context of Revolutionary upheaval, these contradictions took sharper political and economic form. It was one thing to speak in the name of civility, as the third earl of Shaftesbury or Joseph Addison did, within the context of a post-Revolutionary regime that sought to erase the Revolutionary struggles that preceded it. But it was another in a world so shaped by Revolutionary violence itself. And again, it was one thing to speak in the name of society within a world with a limited political nation, and another when confronted with the existence of a culturally and politically emergent democracy. For the genteel, the repetition of violence and the resurgence of democracy in the context of rippling waves of Revolution recast the meaning and security of civility. And for the genteel, that new situation was riddled less with possibility than with danger.

This was certainly not the way Paine saw it, either in *Common Sense* or in the wartime *American Crisis*. For if corpses haunted his account, they did so in the service of the new, not in nostalgia for the old. And if eighteenth-century civility and democracy seemed in tension, it was not because of the violence of the latter, but because the former, as Paine suggested in his satire of General Howe, seemed ready for "embalming."[26] For Paine, the claims of gentility did not stand in simple opposition to violence; instead gentility itself helped to create forms of counter-revolutionary violence, while lending a blind eye to the violence done in its name.

Ironically, Paine's own fate made his point. Two years before André's exhumation, the controversial political writer William Cobbett had disinterred Paine. Cobbett believed that Americans had shown insufficient respect for Paine's remains, and he sought to have them returned to England for proper burial. Instead, Cobbett became the subject of abuse, from Parliament to the mainstream press, and Paine's bones became the source of ridicule. André ultimately came to rest in Westminster Abbey, the honored servant of imperial power; the Revolutionary Paine's bones sat in a trunk in Cobbett's house till they passed out of history.[27]

André's and Paine's strangely linked and inverted afterlives suggest the disparate violence done in the name of gentility. Our conservative moment makes it hard to remember that. It is a forgetfulness that, while not unprecedented, we would do well to avoid.

Chapter 8

Patriotic Remains: Bones of Contention in the Early Republic

Matthew Dennis

> *Thou, stranger, that shalt come this way,*
> *No fraud upon the dead commit—*
> *Observe the swelling turf, and say*
> *They do not lie, but here they sit.*
>
> —*Philip Freneau, "The Indian Burying Ground" (1787)*

Philip Freneau originally titled his popular 1787 poem "Lines occasioned by a visit to an old Indian burying ground." But its serious subject did not preclude a sly play on words. As the poet observed in a footnote, "the North American Indians bury their dead in a sitting posture." Newcomers— "strangers"—to the new American land, particularly its vast interior, took note of the "swelling turf" of Indian burial mounds, pushed up slightly to accommodate the flexed bodies of single corpses.

Freneau's caution, "No fraud upon the dead commit," addressed those who were fashioning American memory, urging them to be truthful. But what truth might observers of Indian graves tell, and how might that truth help compose a larger narrative of America's rising glory? "They do not lie," Freneau wrote of the literal position of interred Native dead, yet presumably he wished, too, that his readers recognize a responsibility to the truth, that required respect for the silence of the dead—for, as the saying goes, "dead men tell no tales."

Imagining his vanishing Indians as mere "shades," ghosts destined for the Indian netherworld, the "land of shades," he understood what fraud was possible—not simply scholastic deception, but real property swindles as well. The United States could not expand except through the dispossession of Native people. Wishful thinking and official policy already combined to assign living Indians to the past, if not to actual graves; learned memorialists required a retrospective mode in order to prescribe the glorious American future. And, strangely, as they buried Indians metaphorically, they found their mortal remains useful, sometimes as relics, sometimes as artifacts. The Indians' day was done as white Americans claimed their birthright as a chosen people, inheriting the continent that Indians had once (and inconveniently still) occupied. They felt this in their bones.[1]

This chapter examines the political and cultural use of human remains in the construction and practice of nationalism in the United States. It begins with the eighteenth-century attempt among white Americans to account for American Indian remains—both bones and ceremonial mounds—and to appropriate them for their own purposes, challenging or neutralizing claims by Indians to the American landscape. Though American Protestantism might have been expected to perpetuate Puritan aversion to the collection, circulation, and veneration of relics (a practice associated with medieval Catholicism), in fact, new forms of such adoration emerged during the first decades of the republic.

A telling event symbolizes what was happening. In 1808, the New York Tammany Society—a patriotic political association in the days before it became an electioneering machine—staged a grand procession and re-internment ceremony to honor the men whose lives were lost aboard British prison ships moored in New York Harbor during the American Revolution. More than eleven thousand corpses had been unceremoniously dumped nearby at Brooklyn's Wallabout Bay. These remains became holy objects, which served to promote patriotic memory and national feeling. That is, nationalism was in the process of democratizing through the reverential treatment of the thousands of undistinguished bones representing ordinary American patriot-martyrs. In various ways, the remains of common soldiers and sailors—both identified and unidentifiable—would continue to cultivate memory, nationalism, patriotism, and the particular political agendas of memorializers, even though such bones received fewer "rites" than those of elite soldiers and statesmen.

In a contrary way, ancient Indian mounds and Indians' bones were repossessed by white Americans, who found a way to claim them as "ancestors" and to steal their legacy—stealing the continent itself—from living Indian people. The skeletal remains of contemporary Indians and their grandparents were plundered, collected as curiosities, ignored, or plowed over by white settlers. By the end of the nineteenth century, Indian bones became objects of ethnological interest, catalogued by new corps of American scientists attempting to compile a natural history of man. This collection of remains (along with ethnological information and other material objects) represented an assertion of scholarly authority—a sort of intellectual and cultural dispossession that cut Native people "to the bone." It also contributed to the emergence of a racist theory of hierarchy among the peoples of the world, which served both U.S. nationalism and new imperialist agendas.

Though dismissed today by reputable historians and anthropologists, scientific racism has not disappeared completely. It lingers in the efforts of some physical anthropologists to assert their control over Native remains recently discovered or housed (by the thousands) in a wide variety of museums. Such assertions of authority over the natural and human history of North America ignore the terms of the Native American Graves Protection and Repatriation Act of 1990. The controversy over the disposition of "Kennewick Man"—the nine-thousand-year-old skeleton discovered in 1996 along the Columbia River in Washington state—is the clearest case in point.[2]

Peculiar bones figured in the American Genesis story from the early eighteenth century. Skeletal remains of an *incognitum*—later determined to be a mammoth—were unearthed in 1705 along the Hudson River at Claverack (below Albany) and were attributed to a biblical antediluvian giant by authorities who included the Puritan scientist and divine Cotton Mather. According to historian Paul Semonin, such phenomena offered early settlers an opportunity "to incorporate the natural wonders of the New World into their visions of the promised land, to blend the antiquity of their classical learning and millenarian biblical prophecies with the authority of Newtonian science." Fossil remains became "a sign of God's blessing on the New Israel in America."[3]

Like the sacred relics of medieval Christendom that Mather would have abhorred, these bones sanctified the place where they lay. Unlike conventional relics, however, they were not understood to be "alive," or the source of personal power, nor could they effect cures or offer protection. But for Mather and others, the discovered bones identified North America as sacred space. In a sense, this New World Christian geography recapitulated a similar process of incorporation that occurred in northern and western Europe in the early Middle Ages, when those regions were converted and amalgamated into Latin Christendom.[4]

The bones of the American *incognitum* strengthened an emerging American identity as yet enveloped in a larger sense of British and Christian subjectivity. The Claverack relics (and others soon discovered in the Ohio Valley) like those of northern European Christianity, provided a means to circumvent, neutralize, or even expropriate pagan sacred sites and objects. Since proximate Indian inhabitants failed to discern the true meaning of natural remains, they might be seen to have forfeited their claims to them and to the surrounding sacred geography; Christian Americans could repudiate the Indians as unworthy savage interlopers and declare themselves the chosen legatees of North America. The ancient beast's monumental bones thus came to symbolize the new nation's antiquity, distinguishing it from Europe, yet possessing a classical past equivalent to that of Greece and Rome.

Meanwhile, Americans had begun to grapple with another mystery of the continental past. Throughout the southern and middle western Mississippi River watershed, great earthworks and the ruins of ancient plazas and temples punctuated the landscape, as did smaller tumuli. Westering Americans encountered these sites after the American Revolution, as they pushed across the Appalachian ridge and into the valleys of the Ohio River and its tributaries. The mounds fascinated settlers and scholars, both in the U.S. and Europe, provoking the question, "Who were the mound builders?"[5]

Among the first to take up the problem, and to conduct an excavation, was Thomas Jefferson, who went to great lengths to dissociate the ancient earthworks from living Native people. "I know of no such thing existing as an *Indian* monument," he wrote in his *Notes on the State of Virginia*. "Of labour on the large scale, I think there is no remain as respectable as would be a common ditch for the draining of lands." For Jefferson, the burial mounds were unimpressive. "That they were repositories of the dead, has been obvious to all: but on what particular occasion constructed, was matter of doubt," he wrote. To get to the bottom of it, Jefferson had excavated a mound near Virginia's Rivanna River in 1782, some forty feet in diameter at the base, and measuring twelve feet high, "though now reduced by the plough to seven and a half, having been under cultivation about a dozen years." In the end, Jefferson concluded that the barrow was little more than a common ossuary, though he estimated it contained a thousand skeletons and that its stature had derived simply from the repeated heaping of layers of bones, stones, and earth. It was hardly a great engineering or architectural achievement, its contents artifacts of scientific interest, but certainly not relics.[6]

Of the great, moldering structures in the heart of the continent, the grandeur of the ruins invited considerable speculation, though most commentators agreed that they were *not* the work of Indians. Indians, these writers argued, were neither numerous enough, nor had the requisite social and political sophistication, or even the ambition, to build such earthworks and temples. Jeremy Belknap, in an address that inaugurated the Massachusetts Historical Society in 1792, argued, "The form and materials of these works seem to indicate the existence of a race of men in a stage of improvement superior to those natives of whom we or our fathers have had any knowledge." A generation of scholars speculated that the continent had once been the domain of immigrant Egyptians, Hebrews, Tartars, Phoenicians, Hindus, or some other alien race. Certainly it had been the realm of a numerous people who practiced large-scale agriculture, who had developed iron (and possibly steel), and who had mastered advanced building techniques (including the use of bricks), and were accomplished in the art of fortification and defense.[7]

Responding to a neoclassical fantasy current in Europe, Americans could fancifully remake ruins of ancient mounds into grand mementos mori and indulge thoughts about the fall of civilizations. Such speculation served to inoculate themselves against self-doubt regarding their new nation as they confidently contemplated their rise as a glorious new empire. Some of the Ohio mounds became minor pilgrimage sites. With the Indian provenance of American tumuli generally rejected and the sophistication of the mound builders established, American Indians were regarded as invading barbarian hordes. Writing in the *American Museum* in 1790, Noah Webster identified them as "Siberian Tartars": "they were the Goths and Vandals of North America, and drove the more ancient settlers from their territory."[8]

Summarizing American learned and popular opinion alike, William Cullen Bryant celebrated American exceptionalism and the grandeur of its landscape in his 1832 poem "The Prairies." He endorsed American expansionism, as he demoted American Indians from resident heirs to interlopers. Dismissing the real Indians around him on his imaginary gallop across the undulating plains, Bryant asked, "Are they here— / The dead of other days?—and did the dust / Of these fair solitudes once stir with life[?]"

. . . Let the mighty mounds
That overlook the rivers, or that rise
In the dim forest crowded with oaks,
Answer. A race, that long has passed away,
Built them;—a disciplined and populous race
Heaped, with long toil, the earth, while yet the Greek
Was hewing the Pentelicus to forms
Of symmetry, and rearing on its rock
The glittering Parthenon.

Into this idyllic, antique world, "The red man came— / The roaming hunter tribes, warlike and fierce, / And the mound-builders vanished from the earth."

. . . All is gone;
All—save the piles of earth that hold their bones,
The platforms where they worshipped unknown gods,
The barriers which they builded from the soil
To keep the foe at bay—till o'er the walls
The wild beleaguered broke, and, one by one,
The strongholds of the plain were forced, and heaped
With corpses. . . .

Having "Butchered, amid their shrieks" an entire "race," the culpable Indian, in Bryant's words, "Has left the blooming wilds he ranged so long" for "wilder hunting-grounds," pushed there by the advancing foot of white civilization. But the Indians' savage usurpation justified such a crusade. Here was the definitive answer to Philip Freneau, who fifty years earlier had equated the Indians with "the ancients of these lands."[9]

If the romantic ruins of a pre-Columbian civilization could be revered and naturalized, and if mortal remains could become relics suitable for inclusion in cabinets of curiosity, then the bleaching bones of disinherited American Indians could equally be mere trash, at best fertilizer in the cultivation of an empire of liberty in the new West. It had been possible for Jefferson to excavate the Rivanna tumulus without giving a second thought to his disturbance of the Indian dead. Similarly, without remorse, others reduced the mounds, and plowed on, erasing the past and reinforcing the idea that the Indians were a vanishing race.

As in the case with other issues of social and political import, Jefferson's language continues to speak to our concerns. He reported his archaeological exercise in his *Notes on the State of Virginia* with disturbing detachment: "I first dug superficially in several parts of it, and came to collections of human bones, at different depths, from six inches to three feet below the surface. These were lying in the utmost confusion." He recorded with precision that his digging yielded "a scull, which, on a slight view, appeared to be that of an infant, but it fell to pieces on being taken out, so as to prevent satisfactory examination." Methodically, he "proceeded then to make a perpendicular cut through the body of the barrow, that I might examine its internal structure." Though he acknowledged that the sepulcher was well known among the Indians, who would detour a dozen miles to observe it, "with expressions which were construed to be those of sorrow," Jefferson paid such sensibilities little mind. He opened other barrows, too, and found that they contained human bones. If not through excavation, he observed, then through cultivation, burial mounds, "much reduced in their height, and spread in width, by the plough . . . will probably disappear in time."[10]

He was right, of course. Even the great mounds of Ohio, though objects of tourists' fascination, were ultimately destroyed by the new, non-Indian residents. Ironically, as their association with mysterious lost civilizations declined and their connection with Indians became clearer, the earthworks decreased in perceived value—increasingly white Americans literally made molehills out of mounds. Many became mere memories, and the contents of burial mounds, if preserved at all, became simply artifacts serving a new scientific (and imperialistic) knowledge.

Each day, at least six carcases we bore
And scratch'd them graves along the sandy shore.
By feeble hands the shallow graves were made,
No stone, memorial, o'er the corpses laid;
In barren sands, and far from home, they lie,
No friend to shed a tear, when passing by;
O'er the mean tombs the insulting Britons tread,
Spurn at the sand, and curse the rebel dead.[11]

So wrote Philip Freneau, in another of his poems, *The British Prison-Ship* (1781). The *Jersey* and several other inoperative hulks sat out the

Revolutionary War in Brooklyn's Wallabout Bay and proved deadly for many of the American prisoners confined within them. Those who died were unceremoniously buried in the nearest available place—on Brooklyn's shores. With the war's formal end in 1783, the surviving prisoners were released and the *Jersey* was left to rot and sink. Bones were dislodged by wind, surf, and the erosion of the tides and washed ashore.

If Freneau felt a certain romantic regret when pioneers trod over forgotten Indian burying grounds, he was outraged by the boots of "insulting Britons" that waded through the sandy graves of America's Revolutionaries, who were expiring on hellish prison ships in Wallabout Bay. The poet himself had been a captive in one of these floating dungeons; he wrote, then, as a survivor, even before the full spectacle of the tide-swept bones became apparent. At Wallabout, he said, the "mean tombs" had "no stone [or] memorial." And so, Freneau called Americans upon citizens "to rites sepulchral just," that is, to erect respectable tombs and "Place the green turf, and plant the myrtle round." Dead patriots required an honorable place of rest.[12]

Connecticut Congressman Joseph P. Cook, living near Wallabout while attending sessions in New York City, reported in 1785 seeing these abandoned remains shamefully exposed. Congress next took responsibility for burying them, but to no avail. "Walking along the same place, not many days ago," Cook wrote, "we saw a number more which were washed out; and attempting to bury them ourselves, we found the bank full of them." In the early 1790s, as falling embankments continued to strew bones along the shore, Brooklynites resolved to collect the remains and to reinter them in the graveyard of a nearby Reformed Dutch church, below a suitable monument. The plan failed, however.[13]

As the century drew to a close, Americans focused their attention on other mortal remains. On December 14, 1799, the nation lost its greatest hero in George Washington. Through a national rite of mourning, observed throughout the country in mock funerals and elegies, Americans poured out their grief. Congress quickly called for the transfer of Washington's remains to a public tomb in the new Capitol. But some congressmen—particularly Democratic-Republicans—complained that such ostentation was poorly suited to a republic. Congress could not agree, so Washington remained interred on the grounds of his home at Mount Vernon. As it turned out, Americans would debate the merits of their heroes again and again, arguing among themselves about who most deserved memorials. Though they would erect numerous monuments to Washington, they were reluctant to authorize public funds for shrines that might be construed to elevate some citizens above others. Memorials and memorializing continued to play a part in struggles between Federalists and Republicans, and more broadly between republicanism and democracy.[14]

While debating the disposition of Washington's tomb and prospective memorials to his memory, certain New Yorkers continued to worry about the bones at Wallabout Bay. A letter to the *American Citizen* on January 8, 1803, acknowledged, "It is always with rapture I hear the name of Washington spoken of by my countrymen." but "what do we want of inanimate monuments erected to his memory; it seems as if without a pile of stone we should forget him[?]" The eponymous national capital, the writer argued, was monument enough. As to a Washington monument in New York, he was adamant that something else be accomplished first: "let us bury the relicks of our brethren, who gloriously fell in arms in defence of their country, lying within our view above ground, a reproach to humanity, to say nothing of patriotism." At Wallabout, "the remains of the patriot . . . [are] exposed to every indignity, for the want of a common grave." Democratizing public memory, he urged that the bones be gathered up "with that respect due to sacred worth." Of the prison-ship dead, he added, finally: "Let them not be forgotten in death—they are all worthy and deserving,—in so doing you will act consistent and worthy of yourselves. To erect a monument to their chief [Washington], before they have a common grave, you would deservedly draw on yourselves, a reproach never to be wiped away."[15]

A week later, "Humanitus" wrote in the same newspaper, "The circumstances of the human bones scattered in the sand, and bleeching on the shore of Long-island, in the neighbourhood of the Wall-about-bay, is a sight that still shocks every stranger that visits this part of the island." Citing a proverb, "What is the duty of everyone to do, is generally left undone," the pseudonymous contributor beseeched his fellow citizens to take action, lest their own shame match that of the British: "does not twenty years neglect of the bones of the victims . . . proclaim our own disregard of what is decent and humane?" Appropriate reburial and commemoration of these ordinary sailors and soldiers was a public obligation: "While we immortalize the conqueror [that is, Washington] with a statue, let us not refuse the unfortunate soldier a grave!"[16]

Certainly these sentiments were politically motivated. They implicitly challenged the Washington cult, which Federalists sought to monopolize to their advantage. The New Yorkers sought instead to elevate common men as worthy, republican heroes. The sanctification of Washington seemed contrary to American republicanism. Among those criticizing the Washington cult (not without personal motives) was his former vice president and successor, John Adams. On February 25, 1808, Adams wrote to Benjamin Rush, parodying the adoration of the Divus Washington, "When my parson says, 'Let us sing to the praise and glory of G. W.,' your church will adopt a new collect in its liturgy and say 'Sancte Washington, ora pro nobis' [Saint Washington, pray for us]." Adams added that if the Washington mausoleum proposal had been passed by Congress during his presidency, he would have been "obliged to do the most unpopular act of my whole unpopular life by sending it back with a negative and reasons."[17]

During Jefferson's presidency, tension mounted in American cities following the *Chesapeake* incident of 1807, when the British, in search of Royal Navy deserters, attacked an American frigate near Norfolk Harbor. Republicans anticipated renewed war with England and found reason to remind the public of Britain's perfidy and insensitivity. Recalling the Wallabout prison ships excited New Yorkers once more. Meanwhile Federalists and those who opposed Jefferson's trade embargo sought not to aggravate feelings toward Great Britain; these groups suspected Republicans—most notably the New York Tammany Society—of a dangerous partisanship. (Of course, both sides acted in passionate partisan political fashion while claiming only pure and upright motives.)

What is most important for our purposes is the activity of the Tammany Society in this regard, as it transformed the prison ship remains into political relics—"the relicks of our brethren." Their public veneration, like that of holy relics of yore, offered legitimacy and power to those who controlled them. If repossessed Indian mounds and artifacts helped white Americans lay claim to a continent, then the sacred remains of Revolutionary prisoners aided plebian Americans' quest for political authority within their new nation.[18]

It was in 1803 that the Tammany Society first took up the cause of the Wallabout martyrs, sending a memorial to Congress, which was presented by Representative Samuel J. Mitchell. It recalled the prison dead to the nation's memory and requested an appropriation for their interment, in a tomb "neither lofty nor sumptuous, nor magnificent." The memorialists appealed at once to American classical fantasies and to well-established republican values:

If the ancient Grecian Republics—if Athens, the noblest of them all, raised columns, temples and pyramids to commemorate those who fell in the fields of Marathon and Platæa in defence of their country; can America be backward, and yet just, in paying her tribute of respect to the memories of citizens, who, equally patriotic and meritorious, perished less splendidly, in the prisons of unheeded want and cruel pestilence [?].[19]

But Mitchell informed the Tammany Society that, given the competition for monuments—for deceased Generals Wooster, Herkimer, Davidson, Scriven, Mercer, Nash, and De Kalb—"I dare not hold out to you any warm encouragement." The congressman observed that "some are of the opinion that Congress ought not to appropriate public money for such purposes," and that there were others who believed the art of printing "has superceded the use and intention of monuments." If commemoration as a whole was called into question, it seemed that the ordinary heroes of Wallabout were likely to be a low priority for national legislators.[20]

The Tammany Society continued its efforts in earnest in the winter of 1807–8, under the approaching shadow of conflict with Great Britain, and with assurances that it did so only because "others to whom the task with equal if not greater propriety belonged" had failed "to undertake its execution." In its official account, Tammany went to great lengths to sound positively nonpartisan: "They [Tammany] have been anxious to avoid the appearance of an ostentatious display before the public, and would cheerfully have lent their humble aid to any measures which the general or their state government might have adopted on the occasion. Being disappointed in their wishes . . . they have at length resolved to originate measures on this subject."[21]

The Tammany Society and its Wallabout Committee represented the bones as holy relics, deserving of adoration. Their official account employed language that seemed to mirror the terms of worship common to medieval Christianity. It urged the American people—"more enlightened in their views, more exalted in their stations, and more dignified in their native character"—to imitate and improve upon the ways that other nations have celebrated their heroes, "with the zeal of enthusiasm and the fervency of religion, [and to] preserve and perpetuate their memory and embalm their bodies rendered sacred and venerable by the actions performed." To fail to do so would entail a national descent "beneath the darkness and barbarity of ages that are past." By this strange twist, republicanism was "modernized" through the "enlightened" veneration of relics.[22]

The Tammany Society dispatched a circular, inviting other "patriotic Societies and public bodies . . . together with the citizens at large" to join in their initiative. In an effort to gather more information, the committee asked for the names, places of birth, age, rank, and family lineages of the prison ship dead, "together with such circumstances respecting each as may be interesting." "This information is indispensably necessary," the circular explained, if the indistinguishable bones of common patriots were to be transformed into something more noble.[23]

Support and financial contribution poured in. Only Federalist organizations held back any testimonials. First- and second-hand accounts of former war prisoners turned up, such as that sent by Alexander Coffin, Jr., who was incarcerated on the *Jersey* and other prison ships in Wallabout Bay. Coffin's short memoir was reprinted by the Tammany Society and became a print memorial if not one carved in stone.[24]

Funds materialized more quickly than anticipated, enabling the Wallabout Committee to lay the cornerstone of a new vault for the remains on April 13, 1808. The festive event began at Brooklyn ferry with a procession of United States Marines, followed by a body of citizens, a committee representing various societies, the Tammany Society's Grand Sachem, the orator of the day, the Wallabout Committee, and a detachment of artillery. Fixing the site in patriotic time, the engraving read, "This is the corner stone of the vault erected by the Tammany Society or Columbian Order . . . Year of the discovery the 315th, of the institution the 19th, and of American

Independence the 32nd." Music, gun salutes, and a stirring oration—"a speech highly animated and appropriate"—marked the occasion.[25]

Finally, with the vault completed, another extraordinary procession took place six weeks later, moving through lower Manhattan, across the East River into Brooklyn, and back again. The day began with the blast of cannon. Flags hung at half-mast, thirteen minute guns fired, the city's bells "pealed a solemn funeral toll," streets swarmed with people, and military and public bodies began their assembly as spectators "crowded the windows of those houses by which the procession was to pass." A broadside had announced the events as a "GRAND & SOLEMN FUNERAL PROCESSION." And it was indeed led by a trumpeter mounted on a black horse. He wore a helmet ornamented with flowing black and red feathers; he held the trumpet, with a black flag attached, in his right hand. The flag bore the motto in gold letters: "Mortals Avaunt! 11,500 Spirits of the Martyred Brave, Approach the Tomb of Honour, or Glory, or Virtuous Patriotism!" He was followed by the chief herald, on a white horse, aided by a "Citizen" and a naval character, each carrying his own silk flags "of the American stripes, with crape, & c." Next marched other escorts, military detachments, bands of music, drums and fifes, and citizen soldiers marching with "reversed arms, being the custom on all funeral occasions." The Republican Greens performed the *Grand Wallabout Dead March*, composed by Captain James Hewitt. Then appeared the grand marshall, the clergy (poorly represented), the Wallabout Committee, the Tammany Society itself, and the "Thirteen Coffins, filled with the Bones of immolated American Patriots." Some 104 "Revolutionary Characters," eight per coffin, assisted as pallbearers.[26]

In a place of honor following the sacred coffins was "The Grand National Pedestal"—a large float, drawn by four horses, carrying messages on each of four panels and supporting a colossal flag with a massive globe on its staff, itself surmounted by an American eagle in a cloud of black crepe. Some said that even the eagle "seemed to morn!" The parade continued with some three hundred of "Neptune's hardy Sons—the American Tars." In an extraordinary tribute to men classified as the "lower sorts," the official account reported, "These brave Republicans of the ocean, to the contemplative mind, was a most affecting sight—it was truly interesting indeed—that sight alone drew the sympathizing tear from every eye:— These worthy, these patriotic tars, were inspired with one soul! they were steady and true, as the needle to the pole; the most exact order, and the greatest harmony were observed in their ranks." The mayor, governor, and other political figures, including diplomats followed. Significantly, "The Citizens, of all classes, here in deep and solemn silence walk'd, four abreast . . . each wearing crape on the arm, and carrying a cypress branch in the hand." The report thus continued to emphasize the procession's democratic character: "In this assemblage, composed of the inhabitants of a large, opulent and enlightened city, all distinctions of politics, of religion, of wealth, or family, were buried in the general sentiment of sympathizing sorrow."[27]

When the procession reached the sacred site at Wallabout, there stood a stage draped with black crepe. The thirteen coffins were placed in front, and the dedication begun by the Reverend Ralph Williston, who echoed the Wallabout Committee's sentiments regarding the prison ship dead as "holy martyrs" and their remains as relics. Dr. Benjamin De Witt delivered the funeral oration. "Too long, alas! have the rites of sepulture been denied to these remnants of the bodies of the valiant, who died in the contest of freedom," he pronounced. "Shall the rich man, who dies in luxury and splendor, amidst the comforts of the world and the friends of his bosom, have his name engraven on a costly tomb? and shall no monumental marble tell the untimely death of the poor patriotic tenants of a prison?" The speaker answered his own question: "Yes, they shall be remembered with affection—their names shall be immortal—the spirit of seventy-six hath reanimated the souls of our revolutionary veterans, and kindled a flame of patriotism in the bosoms of the rising generation."[28]

De Witt's admonition was universalized: "By this awful view of death, ye are admonished that ye also are the subject of mortality." He urged his hearers to "do unto the dead, as ye wish the living to do unto you, when ye pay the last debt to nature." This was a strange inversion of Thomas Jefferson's famous line to James Madison in 1789, " 'that the earth belongs in usufruct to the living;' that the dead have neither power nor rights over it." The prolonged neglect of the Wallabout all too literally bore out Jefferson's point, but the Tammany Society's festive rite in 1808 invoked the power of the dead through their relics, which they hoped might perform a political rather than a religious magic. If Jefferson's notion was utterly democratic—undermining the sanctified status of the founders' original intentions—it also implicitly challenged the sanctity of history and memory. But perhaps Jefferson realized that history and popular memory were plastic, useful to those who sought an enlargement of the political sphere.[29]

In the end, the unprecedented pageantry of May 26, 1808, went nowhere. Fund-raising languished, mourners lost interest, other heroes and causes rose and fell. The Wallabout vault was largely forgotten. By the 1820s, the town of Brooklyn had grown so much that it encroached on the tomb; an alteration of the grading of Jackson Street pressed against the walls of the vault, causing concern among residents that mephitic gases emanating from the sepulcher could cause widespread illness. Benjamin Romaine, former treasurer and Tammany grand sachem, stepped in to buy the site; he refurbished it and added an antechamber and other adornments. Romaine ultimately used the vault as a burial place for himself and his family. After he died in 1844, the tomb again fell on hard times.

Brooklynite Walt Whitman, in his *Leaves of Grass*, commented on the once celebrated bones deposited in the old vault in Brooklyn, "mark'd by no special recognition":

Greater than memory of Achilles or Ulysses,
More, more by far to thee than tomb of Alexander,
Those cart loads of old charnel ashes, scales and splints of mouldy bones,
Once living men—once resolute courage, aspiration, strength,
The stepping stones to thee to-day and here, America.[30]

Eventually in 1908, on the 100th anniversary of the Tammany Wallabout ceremony, a new Martyrs' Monument—a 198-foot column over a crypt— was dedicated in Fort Greene Park by President William Howard Taft, as twenty thousand spectators looked on. After that, the monument and os- suary were forgotten and neglected until 1993 when controversy over a proposal to construct a garbage incinerator nearby awakened the public and inspired new efforts to remember the prison-ship dead.[31]

Ironically, like Indian remains and mounds, these patriotic dead were overrun by the tread of encroaching urban pioneers. The fate of the Wal- labout martyrs today must seem not so far removed from that of the ancient remains of America's Native people. A western poem of 1876, di- rected to the nation's centennial year celebration, says it well:

I hear the tread of pioneers
Of nations yet to be,
The first low wash of waves, where soon
Shall roll a human sea. Behind the scared squaw's birch canoe,
The steamer smokes and raves; And city lots are staked for sale
Above old Indian graves.[32]

Bones and the nation are linked symbolically: graves of ancestors stake claims to the national landscape and its history. They are political relics, deployed (though not always self-consciously) to gain control of the na- tion's collective memory, and in support of particular cultural and political agendas.

Chapter 9

A Peculiar Mark of Infamy: Dismemberment, Burial, and Rebelliousness in Slave Societies

Douglas R. Egerton

Southern trees bear strange fruit,
Blood on the trees and blood at the root,
Black bodies swinging in the southern breeze,
Strange fruit hanging from the poplar trees.

—*Lewis Allen, Billy Holiday, "Strange Fruit" (1939)*

As dawn broke on August 20, 1796, Sheriff John Moseby led William Harris, "a notorious thief" and an African American, from the Richmond city jail. A "great crowd of Spectators," white and black alike, had gathered to witness the macabre spectacle. Moseby set about "blindfolding and tying up the criminal," before bundling him into "the Cart." The sheriff mounted next and accompanied Harris on the short but symbolic parade to the town gallows, near Fifteenth and Broad Streets.[1]

The black man died, an example made of him. But at least he died unbroken and physically intact; as far as the record indicates, he remained so after death. In many parts of the South, however, white judges commonly sentenced rebellious bondmen to be turned over to local surgeons for mutilation following their execution, a practice that had little to do with the training of young doctors. In extreme cases, or in times of servile unrest, white authorities resorted to torture and dismemberment while the accused remained alive. Africans, and many African Americans, believed that an unnatural death, or the failure to observe proper burial rites, doomed the soul to wander forever in the desolate waste of the damned, unable to serve as that protecting ancestor to whom later generations might appeal for assistance. Some discerning magistrates adjudged that a refusal to allow bondwomen to bury their husbands constituted a proper lesson; other slaves, forced to watch public executions, would be thus dissuaded from further resistance. To discourage slaves from committing crimes, purveyors of southern "justice" operated according to a terrifying logic.

In theory, domination over enslaved bodies was the responsibility of individual masters, though their power emanated from colonial or state laws enjoining slave owners to maintain a docile labor force. Eighteenth-century English statutes varied from colony to colony, but all condoned a ghastly variety of tortures. Branding, burning, hamstringing runaways, amputating limbs, castrating accused rapists, and conducting private executions were recognized tools of the American master class. In Middlesex County, Virginia, a minister and two of his flock beat and kicked to death one of the clergyman's bondmen who had attempted to run away. Another master chopped off the toes of a slave for "lying out and doing Severall Misdemeanors." Down the coast, in Charles Town (later shortened to Charleston), South Carolina, urban masters consigned their recalcitrant slaves to the 1768 workhouse, known formally as the House of Correction. Sensitive owners, one resident of the town observed, frequently ordered "refractory slaves" to the workhouse "with a note from the owner directing a specific number of lashes to be given." The "whipping-room" was constructed of double walls filled with sand to muffle inmates' screams. Masters who preferred not to do their own whipping paid a price for their squeamishness: each visit to the workhouse cost a lordly twenty-five cents.[2]

As the most visible sign of patriarchal command in Charleston, the imposing, tax-supported workhouse served to remind the lowcountry's black majority that the line between private and public authority was an exceedingly vague one. The planter-politicians who drafted the colonial statutes that allowed their overseers—or the workhouse warden—to carve off the ears of a belligerent slave were the same men who convened county courts when plantation punishments failed to enforce racial control. Because Southern courts tried slaves as both men *and* property, it followed that their sentences focused more on the body than on the accused as human agents. When a Greene County, North Carolina, court found a slave named Scott guilty of murdering another bondman, it sought not to rehabilitate the man but rather to discipline the body. Scott received the biblical thirty-nine lashes, "severely but not barbarously inflicted," at five different places in the county, before a large M (for murder) was branded on his right cheek.[3]

If North Carolina magistrates employed Scott's battered body as a symbol of the rule of order, he was nonetheless lucky to have preserved his body from mutilation; he had, after all, only murdered another slave. On the other hand, American courts were traditionally ferocious when white lives were threatened. In 1712, a group of enslaved Coromantee torched a building in New York City's east ward and murdered ten men who came to extinguish the fire. Prosecutors moved swiftly to deter other conspirators.

Fourteen slaves marched to the gallows. Two others burned at the stake, and one more roasted for ten hours over hot coals, while another pair of conspirators were broken on the wheel and left to starve in public. The mere hint of a conspiracy was often enough to attract white vengeance. On the eve of the Revolution, Charleston authorities accused Jeremiah, a free black harbor pilot, of urging area slaves to join the British in the event of war. After two months in the workhouse, Jeremiah was bloodied into a confession by the warden. A city court sentenced him to be "hanged and afterwards burned."[4]

The royal governor of South Carolina, Lord William Campbell, doubted that Jeremiah's trial, based as it was on evidence obtained after eight weeks of torture, "deserves the name" of a fair hearing. But colonial magistrates, empowered by the Negro Act of 1740, cared little about what went on behind the thick walls of the workhouse. Their concern was rather with the majesty and ritual of the courtroom itself. The building, an imposing square block with heavy iron bars, was designed to intimidate lowcountry bondmen. When jailers dragged terrified or broken slaves through its dark entrance, a judge was able to play the role of secular deity, as the presumably impartial arbiter of men's fates. Seated severely on their high-backed chairs, magistrates regarded themselves as the final bastion of order and hierarchy when plantation authority broke down.[5]

If Southern magistrates donned robes as ominous and omnipotent justices, the wives and families of accused bondmen were cast in the role of a terrorized audience. To best illustrate their power—and the deadly risk one assumed in challenging it—most slaveholders required that blacks witness the execution of their fellow bondmen. Early American hangings, like their English counterparts, were always public affairs. Hangings were at once a potent symbol of the power of the state over individual black bodies and a bloody lesson of the futility of resistance to white domination. Nothing was more successful in inducing passive behavior than to be forced to watch fathers or husbands or friends dangling from the end of a noose, helplessly kicking. When an Alabama court sentenced a slave named Dabney to swing, area masters herded their slaves toward the execution site. According to diarist John Horrey Dent, more than two thousand people heard an obviously broken Dabney publicly confess "that disobedience had bro[ugh]t him to the gallows, and [he] advised his colored brethren to take warning by his case and be obedient."[6]

When the accused was not merely a homicidal slave who had slipped poison into his owner's soup, but a politicized rebel who enjoyed immense popular support in the slave quarters, there was always danger in bringing together large numbers of grieving bondpeople. On September 12, 1800, when Virginia authorities executed six black revolutionaries, including General Gabriel's brother Solomon, for the crime of "conspiracy and insurrection," mounted militia were obliged to form a circle around the gallows "to keep off the crowd." Flashing sabers had the desired effect, and the rebels, according to one journalist, marched toward "the gibbet amid the singing of hymns, and the wails of their fellow slaves and friends who were allowed to crowd the space outside the line of military."[7]

The need to demonstrate white mastery over black bodies was especially evident in the urban South, where the constant crack of the overseer's whip was everywhere heard and only unseen within the maze of winding streets and back alleys. When Charleston authorities executed black abolitionist Denmark Vesey, together with five of his chief lieutenants, on July 2, 1822, Warden John Gordon staged an elaborate parade up King Street toward the town gallows north of the city boundary. Twelve-year-old John Adger later remembered that "immense crowds of whites and blacks were present at the scene." One genteel lady "greatly feared they would [make] some attempt to excite further rebellion; but they did not attempt it." Mayor James Hamilton hoped that Vesey would demonstrate the sort of penitence that Dabney later expressed in Alabama, but he was a disappointed spectator insofar as the condemned remained defiant. They "met their fate," he sighed, "with the heroic fortitude of Martyrs."[8]

As Vesey's stoic courage in the face of death demonstrated, the mere hanging of black "martyrs" not only failed to deter further resistance to enslavement, such displays actually emboldened some witnesses. As a man who associated with native Africans like Monday Gell, an Ibo, Vesey undoubtedly knew that many West African societies encouraged young men to act out a haughty disdain for physical pain or death. Learning to endure ritual scarification without crying out was an important step in puberty rites meant to direct a boy's social integration. When Coromantees rose up against their Caribbean masters in 1701, terrified planters were astonished at their willingness to assault heavily fortified lines. "Intrepid to the last degree," marveled Christopher Codrington, "not a man of them but will stand to be cut to pieces, without a sigh or groan."[9]

Thirty-five years later, masters on Antigua witnessed a similar expression of fearlessness when Hercules, an enslaved carpenter, was found guilty of conspiracy. Authorities employed every gruesome method imaginable to break his spirit, but by "living up to his name," as Hercules' master put it, the execution—like Denmark Vesey's in the next century—served only to impress his fellows with his heroism. "In above four hours upon the Rack," wrote his master, "not a groan or Sigh came from him," and he stared at the iron bar "which broke and mangled his Limbs as if he rather enjoyed than feared it." Dismayed planters feared that the tale of Hercules' quiet dignity would live on in the plantation quarters in later years. "He died the bravest of all," complained another planter, "for he never winced, all the while his Bones were breaking."[10]

Hercules' stunned master undoubtedly thought his slave most unusual, but the stories related by discouraged whites across the Americas indicate that he was not. When Carolina magistrates informed Rolla Bennett, the domestic servant of Governor Thomas Bennett, that he was to swing with Vesey, he "exhibited no fear." When the same court asked fellow conspirator Peter Poyas if he truly "wish[ed] to see his master and family murdered," Poyas "only replied to the question by a smile." On the day of his execution, he "even laughed when first brought out of the Jail & preserved this State of mind to the last." Fourteen days later, the condemned rebel Bacchus marched toward the gallows, "laughing and bidding his acquaintances in the streets 'good bye.' "[11]

As they observed such displays of bravado, many among the American master class came to understand that hangings often failed to satisfactorily control their enslaved labor force. Some form of retribution *beyond death* was deemed necessary. Although few Euro-Americans developed what might now be regarded as a sophisticated (anthropological) cognizance of West African culture, numerous whites, and especially those involved in the trading of black bodies, displayed considerable knowledge of African religiosity. According to William Bosman, a Dutch trader based in Elmina, Africans from the Gold Coast region "take it for granted that the deceased are immediately conveyed to a famous river," somewhere in "the inland country," where "their god inquires what sort of life they have lived." If their answers proved acceptable, the deceased were "gently wafted over the river, to a land abounding in all kinds of happiness." Similarly, the Kongo also regarded death as a journey from the physical to the spiritual realm. For Kongo peoples, departed ancestors, or *bakulu*, resided in an underworld found beneath wide riverbeds or lake bottoms; this notion allowed Christianized African Americans to regard the River Jordan as the boundary between the world of the living and that of the dead.[12]

Africans who died unnaturally, or who were dismembered upon death and so failed to receive the proper burial rites, were in danger of having to wander forever in the desolate waste of the undead. European veterans of the African trade learned early on that mutilation of rebel bodies was a far more effective deterrent than the cat-o'-nine-tails. As one ship's master put it, African mutineers "believe that if they are killed and not dismembered, they shall return again to their own country"—a belief that might encourage captives either to rise up against white crews or dive overboard in an act of suicide. West Africans did not regard suicide as an unholy act that placed the soul in jeopardy; among the Yoruba, suicide bestowed "great credit and honor" to those who found the courage to end a burdensome existence. But the public mutilation of corpses, as captains soon discovered, pacified those below decks rather quickly.[13]

Both English common law and West African rulers relied upon dismemberment as an extreme form of punishment. British culture shared a consensus attaching a deep importance to the post-mortem care and integrity of the corpse at burial. Traitors were subject to quartering and beheading. A 1752 act of Parliament gave judges the discretion to order a murderer's body to be dissected. English monarchs displayed the heads and disinterred bodies of their enemies: the corpse of regicide Oliver Cromwell was hung from the gallows three years after his death, and the head of seventeenth-century Native American rebel Metacom, in Massachusetts, was displayed on a pole. African rulers attached a significant political and religious meaning to the act of beheading; an Asante king decorated his throne with a solid gold head, representing an enemy killed in battle. This was meant to remind his subjects that decapitation would deprive them of the opportunity to pass whole into the spirit world of the African heartland.[14]

There is suggestive evidence that white masters learned the important connection between dismemberment and the afterlife. Whereas English magistrates meted out sentences of dismemberment to the white working class, American courts of the late eighteenth century reserved posthumous torment for black bodies. In at least twenty-six cases, Virginia courts ordered sheriffs to display executed slaves' heads on poles in public places. Of course, Virginia county courts sentenced numerous whites to the gallows in colonial Virginia, but no evidence exists of white corpses either being decapitated or drawn and quartered.[15]

White authorities who put down an 1811 slave revolt in Louisiana resorted to the wholesale mutilation of black corpses in the explicit hope of preventing further rebelliousness. Already-executed bondmen were decapitated, and their heads, spiked onto stakes, lined the banks of the Mississippi River. Enslaved Africans often returned the favor. In September 1739, Kongolese rebels in South Carolina broke into Hutchinson's store near the Stono River bridge in search of muskets and powder. Next, the rebels marched south toward Spanish Florida, but not before killing the two storekeepers, Robert Bathurst and a Mr. Gibbs, and depositing their heads on the front steps.[16]

The practice of decapitating black corpses was hardly unique to the North American mainland. In Jamaica, during what came to be known as Tacky's Revolt of 1760, the rebel leader was shot while trying to rejoin his soldiers. Triumphant authorities marched with his severed head to Spanish Town, where they displayed the trophy atop a tall pole beside the main highway. Significantly, several of Tacky's "countrymen" risked their own lives by stealing into town and removing the head, as they were "unwilling to let it remain exposed in so ignominious a manner." Sixty-three years later, planters in Demerara brought two captured rebels to the gallows at Cumingsbergh to the tune of a "dead march." After swinging from the gibbet, the bondmen, Natty and Louis, were decapitated for public display.[17]

Random exhibits of African heads no doubt frightened less assertive bondpeople into submission, but the strategy succeeded only so long.

Some courts tried to formalize mutilation by resorting to England's Murder Act of 1752. This law allowed judges to release corpses to surgeons for dissection, in an attempt to deter premeditated murder. Although young doctors ordinarily found it difficult to learn about the inner workings of the human body, the preamble to the act made it clear that its most troublesome provision had little to do with the training of surgeons. Rather, Parliament found it "necessary that some further Terror and peculiar Mark of Infamy be added to [capital] Punishment." For the English and Anglo-American ruling class, no better metaphor existed to justify their mastery. The more "this plague of crime" grows, observed William Forster, "the more resolutely will the good magistrate . . . administer the roughest correctives."[18]

The use of American surgeons in this manner was most effective when undertaken against Africans who had but casual contact with Christian theology. Such was notably the case in July 1822, when South Carolina magistrates delivered the corpses of many of Denmark Vesey's adherents "to the surgeons, for dissection." Charleston editor Isaac Harby prayed for the practice to be continued long after 1822: "Let the body be always at the disposal of the Court," he wrote, "separate from the advantages of medical science which may be derived from the delivery of the body to the surgeons." Well aware that even Vesey's most hardened followers dreaded the prospect of mutilation, Harby added that "capital executions would be regarded with much more terror than they now are: and consequently be much more effectual to the prevention of crimes."[19]

Harby was probably right. Chief among Vesey's lieutenants was Jack Pritchard, a woodworker and, according to trader Zephaniah Kingsley, who purchased Jack in 1805 in Zinguebar, a "Conjurer [and] a priest in his own country [of] M'Choolay Morcema." When the magistrates sentenced Pritchard to hang before being turned over to the surgeons, the African apparently lost all courage. He begged for his sentence to be stayed for "a fortnight longer," and when he was denied, he pleaded again, this time for one week. The doomed man "continued earnestly to solicit until he was taken from the Court Room to his cell." His body, like that of most of his fellows, was dumped into a shallow grave along Line Street. The dismembered remains soon attracted vermin, leading white residents to complain to the city council about "the offensive manner in which many of the culprits have been interred."[20]

If genteel Charlestonians were offended by the smell of rotting corpses, Jack Pritchard's widow was far more offended by the desecration of her husband's body. The slave community reasoned that respect for the deceased connoted respect for the living. The surgical dismemberment and careless internment of the African priest who had acquired the name Pritchard in America was not merely a form of terror; it was a calculated expression of contempt toward black Carolinians. When Charles Manigault discovered that one of his slaves had drowned himself to avoid a beating, he refused to allow others to pull the bloated corpse from the water. A ghastly buoy, it remained afloat until the tide finally carried it off, the drifting reminder of Manigault's disdain for his human property.[21]

Unlike their owners, the enslaved appreciated their responsibility to the deceased. While African beliefs about the afterlife varied, most accepted the unnerving truth that not everybody would reside with the spirits in the afterlife. Dismemberment at the hands of one's enemies was, however, only one way in which the dead might be kept from crossing the great river. Any unnatural death ruled out passing into the next world: infants, who had yet to demonstrate their conformity to the rules of society, might be ineligible. Thus, long and complex funeral ceremonies took on special significance in African life, and failure to adhere to death rituals could hinder entry into the world of one's ancestors. A proper burial insured both the serenity of the soul in the spirit world, and the ability of the living to summon ancestral power for the good of the surviving family. Without a fitting funeral, men like Jack Pritchard or Manigault's drowned slave threatened to become wandering spirits—*zumbi,* in Kikongo—doomed to haunt the living, and perhaps even to do harm or to kill.[22]

By tradition, women played an important role in this process. Some plantations retained the African custom of delegating the responsibility of preparing the corpse to a single woman, and in some cases it was regarded as taboo for any other person to touch an unprepared corpse. As most funeral rites required not merely the cleaning of the body but also the preparation of special ritual foods, it commonly fell to groups of older women to control the memorial process and preserve ancient cultural institutions.[23]

Death in the Old South predated embalming. Enslaved women, according to Cordelia Thomas of Georgia, washed the corpse "with hot water and home-made soap" before "wrapp[ing] 'em in windin' sheets." Black carpenters "measured de corpse and made de coffin." Caskets were simple, crude boxes, Julia Larken remembered, "made out of plain pine wood, lined wid black calico" and sometimes painted "black on de outside." As the carpenters worked, women laid out the corpse on a cooling board, "a long straight plank raised a little at de head, and had legs fixed to make it set straight."[24]

Burials were held at night. Here, curiously, the interests of masters and slaves coincided. Few planters cared to give their workers time off to attend day funerals, owing both to their concerns about productivity and their desire not to demonstrate a greater respect for the slave dead than masters actually felt. But abundant evidence indicates that African Americans, too, as black Carolinian Caleb Craig recalled, preferred that interments be held at night. Evening services allowed bondpeople from neighboring plantations to attend funerals. In the early eighteenth century, a time when

Africans had as yet little familiarity with Christianity, funerals were held after dark, an indication that the origin of this practice probably lay in West Africa. Night funerals lasted well into the twentieth century.[25]

In the half-century after the American Revolution, enslaved black Christians routinely insisted that graves be dug on an east-west axis, so that the deceased would not be buried "crossways ov de world." As late as 1936, Emmaline Heard of Georgia remarked that "folks are always buried so that the head faces the east." That way, Heard explained, "when the Judgement Day come and Gabriel blow that trumpet everybody will rise up facing the east." During the Civil War, white abolitionist turned Union officer Thomas Wentworth Higginson helped to arrange a mass funeral for several black soldiers. As the coffins were being lowered into the large hole, an aged slave leaned over to whisper that he "must have their positions altered—the heads must be toward the west." Once again, funerary customs apparently reflected an earlier practice, wherein captured Africans wished their bodies to face east, toward the spirit world of their ancestors.[26]

The Christianization of the slave community did not, of course, erase an earlier spirituality. Rather, it fused Euro-American faiths with African religiosity. Just as the Mandingoes followed a solemn, graveside service with singing and dancing to appease the soul of the departed ancestor, Old South funerals turned quickly from sadness to festivity. Mourners often poured a bottle of spirits over the headboard so that the deceased might absorb the liquor. Along the Georgia and Carolina coasts, where the number and density of Africans allowed for the greatest retention of African culture, a ceremonial drum often broke the somber mood after a funeral. Its rhythm lightened the sorrow of the community and encouraged the congregants "tuh dance aw sing." According to one Mississippi slave, within moments of the funeral the mourners "would be jumpin' high as a cow or mule."[27]

When the sun rose, slaves left the graveyard to return to the fields, but not before carefully decorating the mound with bits of broken crockery, shells, bottles of liquor or medicines, and even tools which a deceased craftsman might require in the next life. For a people who were allowed to acquire little in the way of property, tools were coveted items; in Zinguebar, Jack Pritchard had boarded the slave ship clutching his carpentry tools as tightly as he did his amulet pouch. Placement of treasured possessions on the grave completed the funeral ceremony and placated the departing spirit. "I don't guess you be bother[ed] much by the spirits if you give 'em a good funeral," advised Sarah Washington, "and put the things whut belongs to 'em on top of the grave."[28]

More than any other practice, the decoration of graves revealed the power of collective memory. Africans on both sides of the Atlantic painstakingly mounded and smoothed the graves, before embellishing each in a unique fashion. In many parts of Africa, survivors buried meaningful belongings with the dead, such as weapons necessary for defense along the path to the spirit world, or food to eat on the way. Ornamental items, like beads, were placed atop the grave. E. J. Glave, who traveled throughout Zaire in 1884, observed mourners ornamenting graves "with crockery, empty bottles, [and] old cooking pots." Twenty years later, a missionary in Gabon described a graveyard that could well have been found in South Carolina: "over or near the graves of the rich are built little huts, where are laid the common articles used by them in their life—pieces of crockery."[29]

Southern whites, including DuBose Heyward (normally an astute observer of lowcountry folkways), regarded funerary adornments as nothing more than "a strange litter" of "futile weapons that had failed in the final engagement with the last dark enemy." However, black Southerners understood the "strange assortment of crockery and glass" to be sanctified messages left by the living to pacify departed spirits. Long after Euro-Americans abandoned the idea, Africans and their descendants believed that the dead could, for better or for worse, continue to affect the lives of their families.[30]

As considerable numbers of former slaves later observed in interviews conducted under government auspices, failure to observe proper funerary customs could have dire consequences. "Dem t[h]ing tha' people call ghostes, dey is evil walks," worried Washington Dozier of South Carolina. "I know dis much, de sperit uv de body travels on [and] dat de truth." Like the Fanti peoples of the Gold Coast, who dressed the deceased in burial garments appropriate to their rank in life, Dozier understood the need to assure the dead a proper reception in the next world. George Vanderhorst, another lowcountry slave, understood that danger all too well when he decided to save his neck by testifying against Jack Pritchard in 1822. Perhaps fearing that Gullah Jack's powers as a "conjurer" would only be infuriated by the surgeon's knife, he begged the magistrates to send him "far away from this place."[31]

Even the smallest failure to appease the dead might doom the spirit to wander. As infants were far too young to undergo either African rites of passage (or later, in the American South, to become active congregants in a Christian church), the death of a child required special attention to custom. Following the death of her baby, Emmaline Heard continued to hear it cry at night. Her neighbors suggested that the coffin had been incorrectly interred. When it was unearthed and opened, Emmaline "found the baby had been buried wrong; the head was facing west instead of east." Once "the box" was turned around and reburied, the distraught mother "never heard it cry no more."[32]

Tales of angry spirits were not restricted to Africa. In the late seventeenth century, many Protestants in the west country of England stubbornly refused to believe that the duke of Monmouth (Charles II's illegitimate Protestant son) had been executed after his capture in 1685. Belief in his survival lasted until the reign of George III, by which time Monmouth would have been more than one hundred years old. Across the Atlantic, in colonial New Jersey, whites condemned an unnamed slave to be burned at the stake for decapitating his master with an ax. As evidence, white authorities pointed to the unassailable fact that when the slave was forced to touch his master's head, blood flowed from the ears and nose of the corpse; the master's angry, enraged soul, they believed, was testifying from the next world.[33]

If New Jersey farmers regarded a surge of blood as lawful evidence, it remains that the Protestant Reformation was slowly eradicating a belief in ghosts over much of the North Atlantic world. By denying the existence of a purgatory through which troubled souls might wander, English theologians argued that at the moment of death, all beings rose to heaven directly or else descended to hell, never to return to the world. Popular sentiment in Britain expressed concern that the soul might sleep in the grave until Judgment Day, when body and soul rose together—thus explaining much of working class animosity toward dismemberment. But if many common folk continued to fear apparitions, educated skeptics like Thomas Hobbes dismissed the possibility of spirits as rank superstition. It thus appears likely that the persistence among Southern whites (especially upper-class Anglo-Americans) of a belief in spirits, was due to their extended contact with African Americans. In South Carolina, where whites were not only a minority population but were raised by slave mammies, educated planters often took it as gospel that angry spirits stalked the living. When Florida planter William J. Keitt was murdered by his slaves, several of the suspects escaped hanging because Keitt's brother "believed them honest & guiltless." Diarist Mary Chesnut was told that Keitt's ghost materialized long enough to castigate his brother for releasing "the two rascals who cut his throat," and her only response was to record what she heard as a "*true* story."[34]

Despite the obvious differences of power and authority between black and white, American slave societies became, as numerous scholars have noted, a world forged by master and bondman together. Both races came to fear the wrath of the wandering dead, even as this fear provided white magistrates and white surgeons with a special form of terror that reached beyond the gallows. For all of her lack of Mary Chesnut's education, former slave Minerva Edwards echoed the white diarist's sentiments when she explained why she and her husband had fled their Texas farm during Reconstruction. The former owner, a white planter, "was real mean," she recalled, and had "choked his wife to death." Minerva and her husband Anderson attested that they often "heered peculiar noises by night," and on one occasion they "seed the woman whut died come all 'round with a light in [her] hand." The Edwardses abandoned the estate without even bothering "to gather that crop." Shortly thereafter, their friend Charlie

Williams "git drunk" and fell asleep in the abandoned house. "That woman come in and nigh choked him to death," Minerva added. "Ain't nobody ever live in that house since we is there."[35]

Yet, even the dread that Minerva Edwards felt decades after seeing an embittered ghost failed to deter the most resolute slave rebels. In 1831 the notorious Nat Turner was so determined to attain liberty during his life, and so disdainful of the prospect of wandering for eternity in the land of the undead that, according to oral tradition, he sold his body to Southampton, Virginia surgeons and used the money to buy ginger cakes as a last meal. According to William Sidney Drewry, who interviewed aged residents of the county in the late nineteenth century, "many citizens [were] still living who ha[d] seen Nat's skull." In the end, despite the best attempts of the master race to employ dismemberment and posthumous mutilation as forms of class control, it was Mary Chesnut who experienced nightmares, and Nat Turner who marched bravely to the hanging tree.[36]

Part IV
After Life

Chapter 10

Immortal Messengers: Angels, Gender, and Power in Early America

Elizabeth Reis

> *There are* Thousands of Thousands, *yea* Myriads of Myriads *of them. This we are sure of.*
>
> —*Increase Mather, Coelestinus.* A Conversation in Heaven *(1713)*

Angels adorn headstones in cemeteries across America. Their association with death and heaven is conventional. In early American religious history, however, the notion that such supernatural beings could appear on earth was complicated by questions of gender and claims of authenticity. Belief in angels took various forms, reflecting the shifting power of individuals and groups in American life. Though various religious traditions confirm angels in their theology, Americans have gradually incorporated personal angel encounters into their popular beliefs and practices. This chapter explores the phenomenon of angel belief with particular attention to early Americans' changing ideas about death and personal salvation.

The revolutionary Swiss cleric John Calvin emphasized the centrality of God in heaven and contested the power and significance attributed to angels in the medieval world. In Calvinist New England, not surprisingly, angels appeared rarely in the lives or writings of either ministers or lay people. Certainly angels were part of the biblical panoply, and Puritans hardly ignored the supernatural; Satan and devils regularly intruded into their spiritual lives. Puritans worried about the fate of their souls after death and searched constantly for providential signs that would reveal God's final decree, but this searching did not invite benevolent angel appearances that might have foretold their future. In fact, ministers and laity alike were much more apt to interpret providential signs as evidence of God's displeasure. The rare angel appearance was regarded with skepticism, especially if it was received by a woman. For New England ministers, women's encounters with angels in the seventeenth century were invariably suspect, likely delusions conjured by the evil angel Satan rather than visitations authorized by God. Just as women's bodies were weaker than men's, so, too, were their souls considered more fragile and vulnerable to satanic attack.[1]

By the time of the Great Awakening, when popular revivals spread across the American colonies in the 1730s and 1740s, angel sightings had become a more common feature in believers' writings. Angels appeared to encourage people with regard to their prospects after death. Now carrying happy news of assurance, angels were no longer seen negatively. As Christians became more comfortable in their hope of heaven, angels increasingly (even up to the present) confirmed ordinary people's intimate and favorable relationship with the divine, while making salvation more tangible.

Greater optimism about salvation at once empowered and constrained female believers. What better way for women to prove their spiritual legitimacy, to make their voices heard, than by the intercession of an angel—an event formerly associated with biblical miracles? But in the eighteenth century, a woman's ephemeral spiritual authority was rarely translated into worldly power because a sighting was too often a deathbed vision that was followed by death. An angel sighting might confer power, but it offered no long-term institutional gain in legitimacy if the empowered female host was to be physically diminished or shortly dead.

By the early nineteenth century, as attitudes toward death, dying, and the afterlife shifted and heaven seemed to become more accessible, believers continued to use angel visitations to relieve anxiety about the hereafter. At the same time, these visitations became a way to distinguish beliefs and practices, or to advance religious objectives. Shakers, Spiritualists, Catholics, and Native Americans all wrote about angelic intercessions that often contradicted traditional Protestant teachings but which, nonetheless, comforted those who were facing loss or confronting their own mortality. Such encounters provided a greater measure of legitimacy and power to the viewer than was the case earlier. At their séances, for example, Shakers invoked angels who revealed the nature of heaven to participants. But only those who conformed to the Shaker program of celibacy were told they could experience that heavenly bliss which angels announced.

Increasingly in the nineteenth century, angel visitations were disassociated with proximate death. Not only did sightings become more common, one could converse with these heavenly beings and live to tell the tale. Representative of this change was the radical proposition of Emanuel Swedenborg (1688–1772)—as voiced by his nineteenth-century interpreters—that death could wait, that one could see angels in this world. Moreover, comporting with a growing sentimentalization of religious culture, departed loved ones could stay near or could return as angels. This transformation of deceased family members into angels allowed believers to reconstruct families beyond the grave.

Angel sightings posed a dilemma for mainstream ministers. While the presence of angels in the Bible made it increasingly difficult to denounce their existence, clergy feared the potential chaos that an increase in angel sightings would bring. And, so, they delivered sermons and wrote treatises attempting to control the impact of the fantastic accounts available in the popular press. Yet some religious leaders vocally promoted angel appearances. Unlike the common people, who were most interested in salvation, religious elites tended to fear angels as a means by which their authority, and the new faiths they founded, might be undermined. But belief in angels, even if tempered by the advice of ministers, was only to increase its hold on the popular imagination.

To understand trends in angel belief in America, we must begin with the Puritans. No serious student of the seventeenth century would deny that New Englanders lived in a "world of wonders." We no longer picture Puritans as stodgy churchgoers, wedded mechanically to theological beliefs and practices, with little sense of the supernatural.[2] Rather, Puritans attuned themselves to the implications of their natural surroundings which they endowed with supernatural power. Wonders and providences were God's messages; that is, Puritans explained and ordered their lives by observing and attending an array of communications thought to convey God's designs. Visual occurrences—earthquakes, droughts, floods, thunderstorms, and comets—were all credited to a mysterious, manipulative God. Likewise, maleficia—iniquitous acts magically perpetrated implicitly or explicitly with Satan's aid—marked extraordinary distortions of the natural world by the devil.

But not all wonders were considered equal. Indeed, seventeenth-century Protestants believed that the age of miracles had ceased in the biblical period. For revelation, the Puritans relied instead on the centrality of the scriptures.[3] They looked to God's providences for knowledge and guidance, but they distinguished between those wonders emanating directly from God, and miracles, as in Roman Catholic tradition, which they interpreted as human or diabolical manipulations.[4] Even elite forays into what we might call "magic" for healing purposes were suspect, and they were only justified when carefully handled by skilled practitioners who were presumed to be revealing God's wishes. People sought knowledge of divine designs, but this certainty was impossible; asserting such knowledge or attempting artificially to alter heavenly arrangements was a damnable offense.[5]

Around 1685, when the leading Puritan divine, Cotton Mather, saw an angel, he recorded his surprise:

A strange and memorable thing. After outpourings of prayer, with the utmost fervor and fasting, there appeared an Angel, whose face shone like the noonday sun.

His features were those of a man, and beardless; his head encircled by a splendid tiara; on his shoulders were wings; his garments were white and shining; his robe reached to his ankles; and about his loins was a belt not unlike the girdles of the peoples of the East.

Mather's vision of a winged, beardless angel sporting a "splendid tiara" is startling, and virtually unprecedented.[6]

Puritan ministers like Mather usually read portents and wonders negatively as signs of God's displeasure. They could accept the devil coming to earth. Direct intercessions by angels or by God were another matter. Cotton Mather's learned father, the Reverend Increase Mather, warned that angels must never be worshipped, and of this much he was sure: "The Angelical Nature is invisible to bodily eyes."[7] Yet despite his father's reservations, Cotton Mather saw an angel in glorious splendor.

Despite their skepticism, Puritan ministers sometimes attributed miraculous healing to divine intervention, tentatively linking curing to angels. Increase Mather noted that biblical characters, such as Daniel, had been healed in this manner, and suggested that ordinary people might also benefit from angels. In *The Angel of Bethesda*, the first complete medical guide in the American colonies, Cotton Mather recounted tales of several people who had received remedies through dreams as they slept. He pointed to men and women so miserably ill that doctors could do nothing to save them, yet who achieved full and dramatic recoveries due to "the Wonderful Work which He had wrought upon" them.[8] Mather cautiously, but unshakably, suggested the direct involvement of angels, though in doing so he feared arousing "Unwarrantable *Superstitions, or Affectations*." And he admitted, "It is possible there may be more of the *Angelical Ministry*, than we are *Ordinarily* aware of." Angels operated covertly, *"Behind the Curtain,"* he suggested, by "Impressions on the Mind" of physicians, providing them with information about cures available only through this kind of "Insensible Manuduction." Indeed, he hinted, his very own book, *The Angel of Bethesda*, might in fact have been a product of the guiding hand of angelic ministry.[9]

Angels' powers were as broad as they were elusive. Increase Mather denied them any independent activity but nonetheless suggested they could be useful to the faithful. "There are *Thousands of Thousands*, yea, *Myriads of Myriads* of them," he contended. "This we are sure of." Angels were "serviceable" to believers, that they might better serve God; thus they wielded extraordinary power, enough "to manage and apply all the *Elements*, to make Thunders and Lightenings, and Earthquakes!"[10] They answered the prayers of believers and provided protection against enemies. They relieved people of "Wants, of Straits, of Difficulties."[11] Like God, angels watched over. Yet at other intervals, they simply watched. Increase Mather warned, "Remember, that the Angels are the Spectators of your Behavior.

Behave your selves, as having the Eyes of the Angels on you. Often think, *Is not an Angel standing by?*"[12]

How could one know if supernatural interference was demonic or angelic? Ministers and laity alike struggled with this question. Increase Mather was particularly concerned with trickery: "How easy then is it for *Daemons*, who have a perfect Understanding in *Opticks*, and in the Power of Nature to deceive the Eyes, and delude the Imaginations of Silly Mortals?"[13] Despite angels' invisibility, he believed that "Good Angels do not hide themselves in the dark under ambiguities, but declare their messages clearly."[14] Yet for Increase and Cotton Mather alike, an angel's credibility seemed to depend on what its message was and to whom it was offered.

Two examples illustrate both Mathers' wariness in instances when angels visibly or audibly declared their messages to ordinary people especially women. In 1694, an unnamed female congregant in Boston's North Church heard a voice, which she initially assumed to be that of an angel. At first suspicious that the woman might be the victim of a "loose Imagination," Cotton Mather came to believe that the "Invisible Whisperer" was indeed angelic when it told the woman secrets that she otherwise could not have known. Later two factors caused Mather to change his mind and ultimately doubt the genuineness of the vision. First, under the alleged angel's guidance, the young woman appeared no longer interested in visiting Mather, believing as he put it, "the Lord had made her *Pastor.*" Second, the spirit spread malicious gossip that Mather deemed inconsistent with the behavior of a benevolent angel. He became convinced that the voices "had no Angelical Aspect," and warned his parishioner to ignore the voice. Heeding his advice, she said to her apparition, "I desire no more to hear from you; Mr. Mather saies you are a Divel, and I am afraid you are. If you are an Angel of the Lord, give mee a Proof of it." The spirit in this case was unable to provide the required evidence and never returned, satisfying Mather that he had successfully aborted "Witchcraft of the most explicit sort."[15]

Another unnamed female North Church parishioner saw an angel while she sat in Cotton Mather's study awaiting his religious counsel. Entering a trance-like state, she revived to describe "a most Glorious Appearance of An Angel in a Shining Apparel." Mather admonished her to be cautious of diabolical appearances, and after she left he shared his apprehensions with his father, who concurred that Satan might be involved. Later, at an all-female prayer meeting, she was visited again, this time by more than one angel, bearing messages for both her and Mather. One of the spirits directly confronted Mather's skepticism: "Our Friend Mather is Apt to doubt we are good Angels, but tell him for to Convince him that we are these things, for he'll be here in half an hour, that he's now Studying Such a Sermon on Such a Text, and that such and such Thoughts have occur'd to him lately, for we are assisting him in his Composure of and lately

Suggested such thoughts to his Mind." The angel's prophecy turned out to be accurate. Upon his arrival, Mather admitted that he had been studying that particular sermon. In the end the angels told the woman that because their appearance troubled Increase Mather, "we will[,] because we loath to grieve him, never visit you anymore."[16]

In both of the above cases, the sighted angels authenticated themselves by knowing things otherwise unknowable to their subjects. But it was precisely such secret knowledge that made angel sightings suspect. Puritans construed any sort of providential experience as a revelation, a dangerous step toward claiming certain intelligence of God's plans for the future. Given their belief in predestination, in which one's spiritual destiny—election or damnation—remained unknown to mortals until Judgment Day, Puritans simultaneously searched for divine determination and shunned alleged demonstrations of spiritual assurance. They wanted to know their futures after death but tried to content themselves with ambiguity, searching instead for signs that might provide hints (but never absolute certainty) of their ultimate fate.[17]

Cotton Mather's personal angel sighting, though dramatic, remained within the bounds of theological plausibility because the spirit did not speculate on Mather's destiny. Instead the shining, winged figure dressed in white foretold Mather's great influence on earth through his writings. "The fate of this youth should be to find full expression for what in him was best," said the angel, and he predicted Mather's authority would spread "not only in America, but in Europe" as well. Mather had no trouble justifying his own angel sighting, even though it contradicted his father's insistence on the invisibility of angels. "I do now beleeve," he wrote, "that some *great Things* are to bee done for mee, by the *Angels* of God."[18] If angels were indeed bound to help him, he vowed in return not to abuse the privilege: he would continue to do God's work by making himself more useful to the sick and poor. Mather was quite conscious of his responsibility to be discreet, confiding in his diary that he would conceal "with all prudent Secrecy, whatever extraordinary Things, I may perceive done for mee by the Angels, who love Secrecy in their Administrations."[19]

As a powerful minister, Cotton Mather had confidence in what he saw and in his right to see it. He had less confidence in the visions of his parishioners, especially if they were women. Precisely because women were considered more likely to succumb to Satan's temptations, they were thought *less* likely to be the direct or particular beneficiaries of angelical apparitions. Increase Mather most doubted those reports in which women alone had seen angelic visitors; in his view, it was more likely that Satan had simply deluded the women. He reasoned, "if those White Angels appear to Females only, who are the weaker Sex, and more easy to be imposed on, that renders the case yet the more suspicious." In "former dark ages," he rationalized, many women achieved fame due to "pretended Angelical Apparitions and Revelations." Like many other Puritans hostile to Catholicism, Mather seemed to be referring to female Catholic mystics, like Teresa of Avila, whom he presumed to have received spurious revelations. He urged his Protestant readers to rest assured: "if ever an Age for Angelical Apparitions shall come, no question but men, and *not women only* will be honoured with their Visage."[20]

The elder Mather thus projected what came to pass in the next century, when an age of angelical apparitions did arise. And, as he anticipated, both men and women claimed to see these divine beings. Eighteenth-century didactic verses and spiritual narratives betray a shift in religious world view: through the miraculous intercession of heavenly messengers, inspired souls searched more actively, and more optimistically, for a guide to the afterlife, confident that they were among the saved.

Stories of angel visitations, told privately in intimate circles when a family member neared death, illustrate ordinary people's use of the supernatural to assuage their fears of the unknown. In February 1712, the Reverend Joseph Standen wrote about his own son's repeated visions during a smallpox epidemic. The boy, only nine years old, was desperately ill. The father described how "his Pain & Torment was so great that his Face seemed convuls'd with the sudden Twitches and Agonies which almost every Moment he suffered . . . he went blind and had purple blotches mixed in with the pox, some as broad as the Nail of one's finger." Throughout his illness, the boy seemed aware that death was imminent and he continually asked to be delivered from his ordeal. The father explained how an angelic vision of the boy's four brothers, one of whom had already died, seemed to calm him and prepare him for death. The father maintained that his son was "certainly awake & this story he always told the same way with many particular circumstances." Convinced of his salvation—and of his father's similar confidence—the child passed away peacefully.[21]

Private angel encounters may have been encouraged by the publication of angel stories, which revealed similar optimism about salvation. *Heavenly Damsel,* published anonymously in the 1750s, portrayed a girl's active search for her ultimate destination, rather than a passive wait for divine grace: "Her Thoughts her Words her Actions were divine/ *How to gain Heaven she spent all her Time.*" And for this she was rewarded. On her way home from school one day, she had stopped to read and contemplate Matthew 27, when a "Person in bright Rayment, whose Hair was as White as Flaxen and whose Face shone like Gold approached her, and spake unto her." The angel said, "Dear Child when thou of Life are dispossest, Thy Soul shall go into eternal Rest, With God and Christ, with Saints and Angels dwell." Surprised by the angel's presence and made ecstatic by his message, the girl related the unusual event to her mother and went to bed. True to the angel's word, she became ill the next day and not long after died, calling for the blessed angels to guide her to the hereafter.[22]

If in the seventeenth century certain knowledge of one's future, however conveyed, signaled damnation, by the Great Awakening in the 1730s, angel sightings and accompanying divine revelations no longer carried negative connotations. Such visitations were still extraordinary, literally a matter of life and death. Nevertheless, people across the colonies were beginning to experience access to the supernatural that was more widely shared.

One cause for this change was the democratization of American religion.[23] Established churches felt the challenges of new denominations such as Baptists and Methodists; ministerial authority eroded, and church membership expanded as the religious world became diverse and inclusive. Frequent angel sightings must be considered part of that popularizing trend. By the mid-eighteenth century, believers *could* see angels, find themselves transported to other worlds, tell others about their journeys, and even preach based on the new authority vested in them by God and his angels. Spiritual travelers defined themselves as a new elect. While most people remained unsure of what would happen to their souls after death, those who were privileged to visit the supernatural world held to the conviction of their certain salvation.

When any person, male or female, claimed to see an angel, a series of events were set into motion. "Seekers" tried to convince others of the reality of their apparitions, of their own sincerity, and of the genuineness of their religious conviction. When successful, even the weakest individual could gain validation by convincing others of an angel's presence. In 1792, Polly Davis, a young woman from New Hampshire, saw an angel. She recorded her experience, confirmed by several witnesses, in a pamphlet entitled *A Faithful Narrative of the Wonderful Dealings of God Toward Polly Davis*. Before her encounter with the angel, Polly had suffered from a terrible sickness and felt apprehensions about God. After the visitation, she miraculously recovered and was so convinced of God's presence in her life that she was moved to tell others about her new-found conviction.

Davis's severe illness and miraculous recovery form the heart of her tale. She had spent days "seized with convulsions which came upon [her] with such violence." When the spell abated, she related visions of a horrible pit and damned spirits: "I have seen hell naked before my eyes, and fully expected to plunge into it. The sight was dismal beyond description. It was a region of most dismal darkness and smoke. . . . I heard the groans of the damned spirits, which indicated that agony and distress which is beyond all utterance or conception." Readers are set up to expect a catastrophe.[24]

Just as she was about to "plunge into the dismal gulf of darkness and misery," Davis's savior took her by the hand and brought her to heaven, where "every object which opened to my view appeared to be clothed with inexpressible beauty." The Lord told her to return to the world and warn others. He promised her recovery, but only after she endured further illness. Davis vacillated for sixteen days when suddenly, "to the surprise of the bystanders, she spake out in plain and audible words and said, *Stand by, and let me get up!* Immediately upon which she sprang from her bed, and walked the room with astonishing nimbleness and alacrity, praising God." Her explanation was simple: she had just seen an angel "standing in white," who foretold her immediate recovery and said that she should go out and carry the Lord's message.[25]

As the religious world expanded, angels became part of the cultural repertoire of all Christian faiths.[26] Indeed, angel encounters were frequently the means by which evangelical Protestants and other Christians separated themselves from older, harsher religious ideologies. Sometimes reacting unequivocally against the "cruel doctrine of Reprobation," members of various sects interpreted an angel's presence as the denial of Calvinist orthodoxy, implying that one could know one's fate, if only one were willing to listen to angels.[27]

New religions on the social margins, such as Shakerism or Spiritualism, used angel sightings to persuade as well as to instruct. Claims of supernatural visions fortified the faith of adherents and helped to convince potential disciples that theirs was the one true path to heaven. Mother Ann Lee, the controversial founder of the Shaker Church and a vigorous proponent of celibacy, used her angel visions as a test of her followers' confidence in her and in her faith. According to one disciple, "At Watervliet, in 1780, Hannah Cogswell and others being present, Mother Ann said, 'I see another angel sounding a trumpet. Hannah, do you believe that I see these things?' Hannah answered 'Yea.' Mother said, 'Blessed are they that have not seen and yet believe.' "[28] Mother Ann Lee's angel sightings need to be understood within the context of her unorthodox interpretation of Christian doctrine: God and the spiritual powers governing the universe were composed of complementary principles, female and male.

Mother Ann Lee used her angel encounters to renounce sinners and their sins, and she promised audiences with angels—female and male—as a spiritual reward. Bent on admonishing those among her flock who still sinned, Mother Ann Lee announced revelations she received with regard to certain members' lack of purity. She tried to convince one family that a woman who lived with them, whom they had assumed to be chaste and honest, actually "lives in whoredom with married men, young men, black men, and boys." The charges against this particular woman proved true, after which, according to her supporters, "faith in Mother was strengthened, beyond a doubt, that Mother had the revelation of God, and was able to see what creatures had in them."[29]

This kind of testimony compounded. One adherent, Lucy Prescott, recounted that "while the Brethren and Sisters were worshipping God in the dance, Mother came into the room and sung awhile. After they stopped dancing, Mother said, 'The room over your heads is full of the angels of God. I see them, and you could see them too, if you was redeemed from the nature of the flesh.' "[30] Another women reported, "The winter after the gospel opened Mary Moseley was at Watervliet in the room with Mother Ann, and Mother said, 'I see the room full of angels, and they are female angels.' Turning to Mary, she said, 'You must leave off sinning, and serve the living and true God.' " The way in which Mother Ann Lee's followers recalled her angelic visitations in 1816, when Shakers collectively published their recollections, suggests the extraordinary kind of control the Shaker leader brought to bear as she established her legitimacy and the authority of the church: "If you were without sin, you would be blessed with angels, as I am," declaring her own divine election and admonishing her followers to heed her example.[31]

The work of angelic apparitions was not limited to personal transformations in the early republic. Angels could carry divine messages of salvation intended for entire groups of people, especially the powerless or the socially and politically afflicted. Handsome Lake, a prophet among the Seneca Indians of western New York, saw three angels who inspired him to create a new religion, after his people had been devastated, economically and militarily, and he himself had sunk into a state of drunkenness and despair. Handsome Lake's apocalyptic visions, beginning in 1799, initiated not only a personal but a tribal metamorphosis, rescuing the Seneca from cultural defeat emanating from their having sided with the British during the Revolutionary War. Angels appeared to him in a fashion hardly different from early nineteenth-century Protestant encounters with angels; in his case, they interceded to aid a weak man near death and a disempowered people on the verge of political and cultural dissolution.[32]

As in all the above accounts, Handsome Lake's testimony was designed to confer upon him credibility and authority, despite how implausible the story might appear. Indeed, one Quaker observer remarked that he saw no reason to question the veracity of Handsome Lake's revelations. Even *white* men were known to have visions, he conceded. The angels who appeared to Handsome Lake were not dressed in white, nor were they female: they arrived in the form that would have been most compelling to a Seneca audience, "three middle-aged men dressed in fine ceremonial clothes, with red paint on their faces and feathers in their bonnets, carrying bows and arrows in one hand and huckleberry bushes in the other."[33]

Handsome Lake was first visited on his supposed deathbed. The angels who came to him explained that they had been sent by the Creator to help him in his despair, owing to his "constant thankfulness." They offered their prescription for a full recovery, and they prophesied that the Indians would enjoy a place in heaven. With the inadvertent encouragement and legitimation of Quaker advisers, the visions of Handsome Lake fundamentally reordered Seneca society.[34]

Otherworldly visions continued to challenge the mainline Protestant clergy, as angel appearances multiplied. No ministers denied their existence, but whether or not angels physically traveled to earth was another matter. Theologians published treatises and delivered sermons that dealt with angels' capabilities in heaven and their relationship to the living. Most emphasized angel invisibility, while at the same time admitting that on rare occasions angels did appear to help sinners. By detailing the form in which angels might materialize, and by arguing what kind of people they might visit, clergymen may have further encouraged angel sightings while hoping to deter them.[35]

Professor of theology A. D. C. Twesten was explicit in this regard: "If an angel is to communicate anything to us," Twesten wrote in 1844, "he must appear in some such way as in the form of a man talking."[36] And that, indeed, is how angels generally appeared to believers—recognizably, as men. Most of the eighteenth- and early nineteenth-century vision stories were told by men and featured male angels.[37] Yet curiously, illustrations that accompanied written texts often presented a female angel, or at least an androgynous one. Theologians preferred to depict male angels, and they countered increasingly popular artistic representations of female angels with long flowing hair by reminding readers of angels' biblical origins. The author of a piece published in 1838 in the Protestant journal *American Biblical Repository* asserted: "The Scripture never makes mention of female angels. . . . In the Scriptures the angels are always males. They were so represented, not to mark a distinction of sex, but because the masculine is the more honorable gender."[38]

No one did more to "normalize" angel sightings, and to depict these apparitions as resembling mortal men and women, than the eighteenth-century thinker Emanuel Swedenborg. His *Treatise Concerning Heaven and Hell* was reprinted seven times between 1837 and 1854. In it, he claimed that he could "converse with angels and spirits in the same manner as I speak with men."[39] Despite countless critics, including those who judged him insane, Swedenborg had many American adherents in Jacksonian times, who responded eagerly to his visions of angels. If mainstream Protestantism equivocated, Swedenborg held nothing back, sensuously describing angels' remarkable sense of touch, sight, and sound.[40]

Among nineteenth-century popular visionists, the Spiritualists followed Swedenborg's lead in offering distinct, gender-balanced descriptions of angels. In their journals and pamphlets, accounts of angels abounded. These angels were generally departed spirits of loved ones, hence some were male, others female. The publishers of spiritualist literature treated their audience as converts and made no strained attempts to prove that angels of all kinds abounded.

In the 1853 *Book for Skeptics*, one publisher noted in his prefatory remarks: "I have conversed with spirits who said they were once residents on this earth, whose physical bodies have long since commingled with the dust, but that now they are angels and in possession of other bodies, and of a continued state of existence, being clothed with immortality." The author of this particular work, J. Everett, took more precautions than his publisher, lest his readership include skeptics. He begged readers to consider the possibility of otherworldly intrusions, assuring that angels communicated with him often, in a voice he could hear, and in his own language. He had even seen their writing. He posed: "Were you to present a blank sheet of writing paper to an invisible being, with the request to write you a communication, and it should be intelligibly written, in your presence, in far less time than you could read it, would you not believe that a spirit was with you on this earth?" According to Everett and his publisher alike, an age of revelation and miracles was about to begin; the world was on the "threshold of the revealments which are yet to be made by angels."[41]

To be sure, Everett could not have imagined the vast changes in the nineteenth-century religious landscape as newcomers, particularly Catholics, arrived in greater numbers. Catholic writers, like Spiritualists, had no difficulty espousing the reality and ubiquity of angels and the comfort they delivered, especially at the time of death. Catholic angels were visible, androgynous spirits. They talked directly to their charges. They explained clearly (especially to children) their purpose on earth.

Catholic children's literature was filled with short stories designed to teach children about the hereafter and their relationship with God. Angels came to dying children, easing their fears about heaven and encouraging them to trust in God, even if he remained imperfectly understood. In one such tale, an angel visited a young girl whose brother was dying. The angel assured the girl that her brother would be happier in heaven: "We see glorious resplendent lights flashing in Him, and breaking in blazes of glory, as if ten thousand suns were rising, and ten thousand suns were setting in Him all at once. We call these the storms of divine light, though they are not confused and violent like what you call storms on earth."[42]

The girl then asked if God ever touches the angels (a question that seemed out of place in an otherwise didactic story about death). The angel replied in sexually suggestive language:

Sometimes we feel God touching us, and I cannot tell you what it is like. The great seas, which we have in us instead of hearts, tingle all through, and the waves cease to beat upon the shore, and the harp sinks down into the deep, and there comes such a calm, such a silver calm, throbbing, throbbing, throbbing in the deeps, that the sea drinks in all our light, and a beautiful night, a beautiful darkness, comes over our spirits; and if you could look into heaven at that moment, you would see the grand power of God all stretched out with great bands round the spirits of the

mightiest Angels to prevent their breaking, and spilling their seas, and dying of unspeakable blessedness, because of this little gentle touch of the dear God.[43]

The angel helped the little girl with her confession, and then the child
wept, thinking about her brother so near death. Her tears were not of sadness, according to this tale, but rather happiness that her brother would
soon be in a holy and happy place. The earthy sensualism and assurance
of heavenly reward in this angel's message is a far cry from the careful
prophesying of Cotton Mather's visitation.

Nonmainstream believers—New Church Swedenborgians, Shakers, Spiritualists, and Catholics—had their own styles of spiritual communication
that ran counter to traditional Protestantism. But gradually, the radical understanding of angels became America's notions of angels. By 1850, representations of angels were appearing on stereograph pictures, on greeting
cards, and in ladies' magazines. Angels had become metaphors for feminine sensibility, and the angels themselves were by now primarily female.
They were of the kind that Mother Lee had seen, with long flowing hair
and white robes, far removed from Mather's masculine, loin-girded angel.
The feminization of angels was a piecemeal process, and by no means completely consistent, though it had developed in unison with a kinder and
gentler religious sensibility: salvation was potentially available to all believers now, and both women and men could justify their optimism about the
future state by claiming an angel all their own.

Chapter 11

"In the Midst of Life we are in Death": Affliction and Religion in Antebellum New York

Nicholas Marshall

> *The sorrow for the dead is the only sorrow from which we refuse to be divorced. Every other wound we seek to heal, every other affliction to forget; but this wound we consider it a duty to keep open; this affliction we cherish and brood over in solitude.*
>
> —*Washington Irving, "Rural Funerals" (1819)*

In February 1830, Amelia Lewis Curtis died at the age of twenty-three in rural Yates County, New York. Amelia's death naturally produced anguish in her father. A teacher in local district schools, John Lewis left a record of the trauma brought on by the loss of his recently married daughter. His diary records that the day following her death was one "of deep mourning, of sorrow, of unutterable grief, to our poor bereaved family." Lewis was left with the hope that the family would be able to "bind up their broken hearts," bend to the will of God, thank Him for the chastisement, and use it for good among the living. For a week after he received the news, however, Lewis could not bring himself to teach his classes. During that time, he professed the further hope that, in time, all the family would "join the dear departed child in realms of endless bliss." When Lewis's eldest son came home a few days later, the appearance of his "dear son" caused "great joy."[1]

Amelia's death impelled Lewis to include a short essay in his diary, attesting to the significance of Christianity. He described his faith as a "religion of sympathy," founded on "the principle of human wretchedness":

It meets man in every species of sorrow and affliction. It takes him by the hand when deserted by human supports. It pierces the clouds which throw a melancholy gloom over the path of life and opens before the "way worn travellor" a "full hope of immortality."

This was a depressing vision of the trials endured in everyday life, but the diarist perceived that there were great benefits to the living as well as the dead contained in the teachings of Christianity:

Let us reflect upon this peculiarity of our holy religion, and consider what an advantage we obtain, by possessing it. All the human race are suffering, in some way, or in another. We cannot enter a family and be permitted to know what is passing within it, without perceiving that there is a worm corroding the root of their comforts—some poisoned arrow penetrating their breasts—some intolerable burden subduing their strength. To such how suitable is the invitation of our compassionate *Saviour.*

Lewis decried the preaching of cold, abstract doctrine. "What a mockery of human misery! what a want of duty! what a loss of time!" he lamented. He preferred that church which took the sufferer by the hand and "conduct[ed] him to the *Saviour!* Let us lead him to the wells of salvation! Let us pour the healing balm into his bleeding heart, and assure him that there is *One* who sympathizes with his sorrows." Given the wretched conditions of everyday life, Lewis believed that Christ's sympathy was the basis for a useful religion.[2]

John Lewis's reaction to Amelia's death exemplifies a significant trend in the social relations and religious practices of the antebellum era. According to Lewis, his society was suffering from constant intrusions of sickness, misfortune, and premature death. Indeed, the private papers of other ordinary Americans living in New York state confirm his impressions.[3] Diaries and correspondence from the antebellum period were saturated with discussions of affliction. Constant illness and frequent death were the most significant elements in the lives of the common people, far outweighing any other concerns, including the problems associated with economic change. Lewis's loving commitment to his family, especially to his wife and children, also documents a more general trend found in personal writings. An increasingly sentimentalized culture had spread, emphasizing the importance of close, deeply affectionate familial relationships.

Overwhelming experiences with affliction were not unusual in the antebellum era because of a debilitating new disease environment. The physical suffering discussed in personal writings coincided with a dramatic decline in the health status of Americans in general. Life expectancy varied greatly in colonial America depending on the region and period, but the years between 1750 and 1790 appear to have witnessed generalized, gradual increases. After 1790, however, life expectancy in America actually began falling, declining from about fifty-six in 1790 to forty-eight in 1860. Simply put, early nineteenth-century Americans experienced earlier deaths and increased physical suffering at the hands of diseases such as typhoid, scarlet fever, and tuberculosis. It was their geographical mobility that led to the increased incidences of these fatal diseases. Americans' height, another important indicator of general health, dropped precipitously after the late 1820s. On average, Americans had shrunk nearly one and a half inches by the time of the Civil War, a statistic most likely reflecting the nutritional effort spent in childhood fighting disease.[4]

The medical profession could do little to help people when they faced ill health. The bleedings and purgings recommended by Dr. Benjamin Rush in the late eighteenth century continued to be the primary methods of treatment—although increasingly, doctors and the public understood the futility of such practices. During a yellow fever epidemic in 1854, for example, one doctor was taunted on the streets: "The wiseacres abused me at the corners for being old fashioned," he complained, "and for killing my patients with Lancet and Calomel." New therapies attempted (without much success) to ameliorate the health crisis. These included hydrotherapy, botanical cures, patent medicines, and diet reform. In 1860, Oliver Wendell Holmes suggested that "if the whole materia medica, *as now used,* could be sunk to the bottom of the sea, it would be all the better for mankind,—and all the worse for the fishes." It would not be until later in the century, when germ theory became known, that real advances in medicine began.[5]

The problem of affliction specific to the antebellum period is vividly revealed in a letter written in 1842 by Emeline Hicks to her cousin Alice Barber, who had just reported the death of a daughter. In response, Emeline attempted to comfort Alice by offering an image of "little Mary" in a better world, adding that such affliction served a purpose, keeping one's eye trained on religious duties. Moreover, in that Alice had noted that her own health was precarious, Emeline stressed that the death of Mary meant that Alice would have her "little rose bud" waiting to greet her when heaven beckoned. As Emeline's mother had recently died, Alice referred to that event in her letter describing Mary's death. Emeline reacted: "You say you are aware that I am not a stranger to grief, but you are not aware of one half," going on to reveal that her son Adelbert had died since her last letter had told of her mother's death.[6]

There was nothing extraordinary in this exchange. The simultaneous occurrence of a serious decline in health and the sentimentalization of loving relationships created enormous pressures within Protestant religion. Americans like John Lewis increasingly viewed Christianity as a support to be relied on during seemingly never-ending cycles of emotional distress. Traditional doctrines of predestination could not be sustained, and so a new, more sympathetic religion was replacing the older one. No longer was God's main purpose to divide humankind into saved and damned (with only a small portion thought to be in the former category). Instead, God chose to suffuse the society with love and care in an effort to save all that could be saved. The ultimate goal for Christians was to find their place in a domesticated heaven. As long as they were prepared—having experienced saving grace—all loved ones would be reunited in a heaven, as so many put it, "where parting is no more." The drone of physical and emotional pain, taking its toll in daily life would finally be overcome in this soothing afterlife.[7]

In the face of sickness, suffering, and death, New Yorkers sought assurance and relief in their religion. Diaries and correspondence offer compelling evidence that such affliction propelled many into serious religion, while creating needs that altered interpretations of the Christian heaven. The increasing perception that human agency could deliver a conversion experience, and thus ensure passage to heaven, created a new dynamic within social groups. In order to secure a reconstituted circle of loved ones in the afterlife, many felt an obligation to convince loved ones that saving grace had to be speedily attained. The pressure of sickness and death added to the tension built into relationships between those who felt the assurance of grace and those perceived to be on a path to perdition.[8]

Because the hand of death could fall without warning, New Yorkers increasingly acknowledged the necessity of spiritual preparation. The seemingly constant memento mori heightened anxiety about the condition of souls and helped launch people into churches for the purpose of finding saving grace. An Otsego County man found signs of his own mortality all around him in the last few months of 1848. The construction of a new home served to remind him that "very soon all the earthly habitation that I should want would be but a few boards nailed together in the form of a small box lined with a few yards of linen all consigned to the clods of the valley." A month later, he heard of the death of an old schoolmate and friend. This news produced a "very peculiar sensation," having seen the deceased in good health just a few weeks previous. "O how uncertain is life," he remarked in his diary that evening, "and yet man live quite as heedless as though their life was guaranteed to them." A week later, the friend who had informed this anonymous diary keeper of the old schoolmate's death, himself died. "This," the puzzled and troubled survivor wrote, "shows the importance of . . . improving every opportunity to inform upon the mind of poor dying mortals the importance of being prepared to die for we know not but those whom we today converse with may tomorrow be in eternity." Every illness and death he learned of compounded his sense of the need for preparation.[9]

Henry Clark Wright's experience as a boy in Otsego County, earlier in the nineteenth century, illustrates new problems associated with separation by death, as well as the transition from a Calvinistic interpretation of death to a softened perception of a loving God who provided for his flock. Wright lost two loved ones by his seventh year: his mother died of "apoplexy" when he was only five—his house had "ceased to be a home when my mother was carried out of it." Only two years later, his older brother died of "brain fever," leaving the survivor with vivid memories of having watched as the silent boy stopped breathing. As an adult, Wright recorded his disapproval of the way death had been treated in those years; he had been told that God had taken his brother away as punishment for sin. This form of theology had "shrouded death in gloom and horror." He eventually came to see his brother's death as "gain to him, and that he was gone to a brighter, more joyous and more active scene of happiness." Wright was becoming reconciled to God, whereas earlier he had felt only distance and anger. "Natural death is not a natural calamity," he claimed, but "the fruit of divine love and goodness." It was merely a "change of mode of existence—an introduction to a higher, more happy, and more beautiful state of being." Recalling his own early struggle, he determined that death "should be presented to children as an angel of love and beauty, and not as an insatiable monster, existing only to devour."[10]

Serious illness and death frequently prompted conversion experiences. When George Kaercher came to the United States in 1828 from France, he worked as a farm laborer and hauler of iron ore. At the age of fifteen, as he remembered, Kaercher did not feel close to God. However, "the sudden death of Mrs. Richard Smith, a few friendly remarks of a Christian friend, a prayer meeting, and the drawing of the Holy Spirit led me to the foot of the cross." Peggy Dow, wife of the famous itinerant Methodist preacher Lorenzo Dow, spent most of her early years in Oneida County, living with a sister following the death of their mother. As a young girl she was "at times very unhappy, for fear I should die, and what would become of my soul!" At the age of fifteen, Dow began a two-year battle with sickness. Fearing that that she "should be called to pass the dark valley," she worked hard to achieve saving grace.[11]

Like Kaercher and Dow, William Pratt turned to religion after a trying period of sickness and death within his circle of loved ones. During the period in which he kept his diary, the twenty-year-old Pratt worked on his family's farm in Steuben County. He had previously attended district school and the local academy. In early 1843, soon after commencing the diary, his uncle Ebenezer became seriously ill. After a visit during which he helped move the "perfectly helpless" older man, William reported that he had never beheld "a more distressing looking person." When Ebenezer died the next day, William noted that, because of his religion, "death had no terrors" for Ebenezer. Two days later, he helped celebrate his sick cousin Ira's twenty-first birthday, a celebration tempered by William's prediction that Ira had "seen his last birthday." After noting two more deaths a few days later, William announced young Ira's demise, induced by "bleeding from the lungs." The "sad and affective" event was "*melancholy, melancholy* indeed," that a young man just about to enter public life had been "thus early called away." William determined then and there a good, if hidden, purpose, had to lie behind the act, though a "dismal cloud" still hung over the family.[12]

It was the death of his cousin Ira that transformed William's religious life. First, he had a long conversation about religion with a friend and attended church in the evening. Ira's funeral the following day prompted more deep questioning. How strange and short life was, William noted in his diary: "Friends are separated. Youthful associations are broken up, and the ties of kindred are sundered. Yet we seem not to feel it as we ought, but rush on in heedless pursuit of this thing or that, forgetting for what we live and almost wholly regardless of the fact that 'in the midst of life we are in death.' "[13]

William attended church services regularly over the next week: "I took the anxious seat deeply impressed with the importance of attending to the subject of religion," he wrote on Sunday evening, "and hope and trust that I have given my heart to God." Soon thereafter, he began to express his feelings publicly, proclaiming to his diary, "I found peace to my soul and enjoy that happiness which I never before experienced and which the world knows nothing of. I humbly hope and trust that I have set out in the service of God and that my sins have been washed by the atoning blood of Christ."[14]

Ira's death proved to be part of a series of events resulting in William's conversion. He marked the second anniversary of his brother Joel's death. A few weeks passed, and the sudden illness and death of a student at the local academy prompted him to write further of "providence." William grimly reflected on the course of his life over the past six years, noting the anniversary of the death of his "only and beloved sister," that was a beginning of sorts—a death from which all subsequent deaths dolefully cascaded. " 'Twas then the cup of affliction, hitherto untasted, was presented to my lips of which I drank and deeply too." How quickly life had changed for him since the time, not long past, when "four youthful cousins lived":

The hopes of all were high. Their prospects fair and bright. Mary, Joel, and Ira, where are they? Yonder church yard tell full well. . . . But let me not indulge in melancholy reflections, but rather let the anniversary of the dying day of each serve to remind me of the shortness and uncertainty of life and of the necessity of working while the day lasts that whence Death shall overtake me I shall be ready and waiting for the coming of the Son of Man.

William Pratt paid heed to his eternal future, viscerally reminded that his worldly existence could end at any moment. He found peace, a respite from the pain of loss, in faith.[15]

Like William Pratt, Susan Fox felt the soothing hand of grace amid loss of family members. Born in 1803, she lived most of her adult life in the vicinity of the village of Weedsport, caring for her ailing parents. She became a member of the Methodist church at the age of fifteen, yet for the next eight years "enjoyed but a small share of the comforts of religion." Then, she later recalled, "in mercy the Lord afflicted me, by taking two of my dear brothers from me at once. This was through grace the means of my seeking the Lord with all my heart until his blood was applied to the washing my soul from all unrighteousness." Susan understood that her religion was best experienced in the presence of deep wounds.[16]

When she was in her mid-thirties, Susan's vision of the bounties of a higher plain of existence worked to inspire a wish to die soon, so that she might leave behind the difficulties of worldly existence. Heaven represented a resting place, where pain ceased to exist, and where death lost its horror and, indeed, became desirable. Soon after her conversion, Susan grew fearful that she might offend God and have her blessing revoked. She therefore prayed for an immediate death: "I had an assurance if I went then," she wrote a few years later, "all would be well." When Susan heard an especially invigorating sermon, she experienced a powerful calm and inspiration that she identified with a heavenly essence. Such "bliss" felt like "weeping" her life away, "the losing sight of earth the forgetting every thing as it were but God." With the sustenance of faith, "I had a view of my better home," she wrote in her diary. "O! when shall I get to possess it." To "leave the busy world" was a "privilege." In times of sickness, she felt even closer to heaven. One sudden attack of fever brought visions of death to her mind, a death "disarmed of its horror." Remarking on the final days of a friend's suffering from consumption, she wrote: "How cheering the thought that the weary pilgrim will soon get a place of rest where the inhabitants shall no more say I am sick."[17]

Death is omnipresent in Susan's diary: "One friend after another is called to their reward"; "one after another is going into eternity"; "death is all around us taking without distinction to grade or condition saint or sinner, youth, or the aged"; "death is taking its victims all around us." The thought of going to a place "where parting is no more" became increasingly appealing. When her friend Jane Griggs died soon after marriage, Susan remarked on the sorrow her death evoked, yet she found comfort in the knowledge that Jane had "believed she would soon meet her friends in heaven, although there in so much health." After another friend died, Susan wrote that the prospect of meeting friends "makes heaven look inviting." In 1842, a beloved brother-in-law was "cut down in prime of manhood when he seemed most needed." If she felt great anguish at the separation, "the thought of a reunion, sweeter the bitter cup of sorrow and adds a stronger tie to hearts." A year later, one of Susan's childhood friends died a "triumphant death." Present at the deathbed, Susan told her friend that she would "be at the gates of the celestial city to welcome the others [her circle of friends] when they arrived." The dying woman clasped her arms together and replied, " 'So I will embrace you when you come.' " Several months after this scene, Susan's mother died. The prospect of their "re-union" "animated" Susan's soul. The beauty of heaven as a gathering place of old friends and family members gave Susan relief and hope.[18]

New Yorkers worked hard to encourage religious commitment in those they loved. The high rates of sickness and death meant that there was real urgency in the project of directing family and friends to their saving grace and conveying the vision of a happy heavenly reunion. Letter writers expended large supplies of ink trying to convince those dear to them of the errors of their ways.

Silas Scott exhorted his brother Warham to seek God's mercy by pointing to the instructive passing of their father. In the letter from home that informed Warham of the death, Silas explained that their father saw a shining vision beyond the grave, and Silas had "a bright evidence of meeting him one day, eternal joy, where parting will be no more." Silas pursued his point by setting "the natural ties" and "sweet meetings" of the mundane world against the greater promise of a heavenly reward:

if our hearts are prepared by grace how much nearer our ties and the prospect of meeting in that eternal world of joy where Jesus our saviour is truly consoling—brother shall I have your company or must we be separated after death—oh brother consider if you never have accepted of offered mercy. May you enlighten your understanding and you accept of offered mercy that you may be happy here and happy in eternity.

Many years later, when Silas himself had just died, his son John wrote a letter to his uncle Warham, who, it appears, had yet to heed the call. John reminded him that no one knew when the moment of death would arrive, and thus there could be no delay in preparation. He acknowledged that Warham was a moral man, but added forcefully, "if you have not had your heart renewed by grace divine you are not ready to go and I wish you would look and see how the case is between you and your god for this is a loud call to you." John was persistent with his uncle: "I hope I shall so live and you too, that we may meet my father in heaven."[19]

The diary of Lucy Stoddard for 1860 is as blunt. On New Year's Day she wrote, "Ah! how many that were happy one year ago; to-day are miserable; many who promised themselves a long and prosperous life then are to-day lying beneath the clods of the valley." At the end of the same year, she noted, "how many times have I dropped the tear of sympathy as friend after friend has been laid in the grave." From January to December, Stoddard encountered nearly two deaths per month, several times using the common phrase "in the midst of life we are in death." Her primary religious goal was the conversion of friends and acquaintances. When one sickened, for example, she groaned, "Oh I can not bear the thought that she should appear before the Judgment Seat unprepared." After attending church one day, she noticed "how many do not see that they will soon be judged." And again, "how I shudder when I think that perhaps *some* of those that we daily associate with, and are bound by the nearest ties may be then parted from us forever." At the close of one week, Stoddard felt "an unusual feeling of sadness on account of the spiritual welfare of [her] friends." She prayed, hoping that each death in the neighborhood would lead to the repentance of others.[20]

The personal papers of New Yorkers demonstrate the significance of high death rates in the urgent enterprise of converting souls. Historians, however, have not recognized this fact. In the main they have interpreted the increasing membership in Protestant churches as a product of some form of social anxiety caused by fading economic prospects in rural areas, class tensions in cities like Rochester, the challenges of a newly mobile and rapidly changing society, and the needs of a liberal, democratized citizenry. Though these arguments are subtly argued, they are not firmly rooted in the recorded experiences of ordinary Americans. The anxiety that diaries and letters reveal is more immediate and relevant: the deaths of loved ones and local acquaintances served as stark reminders of the need for religious preparation.[21]

The common desire for a sympathetic religious experience had a pronounced impact on society within New York state. Affliction seems to have encouraged a general indifference to denominational rivalries. The personal writings of New Yorkers show a startlingly eclectic pattern of church attendance. Churchgoers may have selected a primary congregation, but the diverse range of denominations appearing in the pages of individual diaries strongly suggests that useful preaching was sought and spiritual assurance found. People attended a variety of meetings and became less particular about their denominational affiliations.[22]

Some New Yorkers attended only one Sunday church meeting and limited their participation to two churches. Samuel Mariner, for example, regularly alternated between Presbyterian and Baptist services. Others, however, noted their attendance at three or more churches during short periods of keeping a diary. Over the course of several months in 1843, Cornelia Smith visited Quaker, Baptist, and Methodist churches. Benjamin Gue managed to attend meetings in the late 1840s in five denominations: Methodist, Quaker, Baptist, Congregational, and Universalist. Many New Yorkers, in fact, made a regular practice of attending the meetings of several different denominations on the same day. This practice may have reflected a simple desire to hear more preaching on a given Sabbath than one church provided, yet it also reveals that the religious experience outweighed the fine points of doctrine. On January 4, 1844, John Bower attended the Presbyterian church in the morning, the Episcopal church in the afternoon, and the Methodist church in the evening.[23]

The nonsectarian religious practice of rural New Yorkers indicates that frequent sickness and early death significantly linked daily life and religious concerns. Above all else, these Americans sought saving grace to ensure reunion with loved ones in a place "where parting is no more," and to soothe the pain associated with a lifetime of affliction. Entering into doctrinal debates could only distract one from the primary goal of finding assurance (and promise) in the various houses of God. Those who hungered for a general sense of security found sustenance in a generalized religious practice, taking as much as they could from the many sources that eased their afflictions in a medically primitive environment.

Historians have generally viewed the antebellum fascination with illness and death as a direct outgrowth of a sentimental, if not maudlin, literary culture.[24] A debate centering on Harriet Beecher Stowe's classic *Uncle Tom's Cabin* (1851) consigns many scholars to one of two possible interpretations. The two scholars most responsible for this dichotomy are Ann Douglas and Jane Tompkins. Douglas characterized the rise of sentimental religion and culture as a retreat from the intellectually sophisticated reasoning found in Calvinist preaching. In her view, tears and sympathy washed away the powerful meaning of the Puritan faith, resulting in the "commercialization of inner life." In contrast, Jane Tompkins saw sentimental literature as a legitimate intellectual exercise. She argued that writers like Stowe offered their female readers a compelling "jeremiad" of salvation. Rather than an escape from reality, Stowe's jeremiad expressed the larger cultural myth that the suffering and death of the innocent female empowered women to "work in, and change, the world." But, in fact, this feminization of religion has emphasized a false dichotomy, that religion was either debased by the intellectual simplicity of sentimental preaching, or that the softening of religion was the means by which middle-class women acquired social power.[25]

The death of "little Eva" in Stowe's novel has frequently been used as an example of the sentimental revolution. Yet, for the purpose of this discussion, Eva's actions are less important than those of her bereaved family members in the days following her death. When Stowe describes the responses of Eva's parents, she reveals the two competing interpretations of sentimental culture. Her mother, Marie St. Clare, expresses a mawkish, self-absorbed, and ultimately passive display of grief mainly intended to attract others' concern with her suffering. She "lay on her bed, sobbing and moaning in uncontrollable grief, and calling every moment for the attention of all her servants. . . . she was fully convinced that nobody on earth did, could, or would feel it as she did." Marie portrays the view of the debasement of religious expression, a self-serving faith devoid of real sympathy or larger intellectual and theological concerns. In contrast, Tom, the St. Clare's devoted slave understood that it was Eva's father, Augustine St. Clare, who in his own quiet way endured genuine feelings of loss. Augustine fully appreciated how his daughter's death helped him reevaluate the role of religion in his life, and he worked to change the world through her sacrifice, offering a more optimistic, empowering portrait of death and religious faith.[26]

On October 10, 1851, another little Eva died. This one, however, was not a fictional character. She was Eva Carr, the daughter of an anonymous central New Yorker who kept an account book that has survived. Until that grim October evening, his little book contains only business transactions. Then, ten pages of heartfelt grief suddenly appear: "Great God what an affliction," wrote Eva's father. "How I worshipped my lovely, intelligent child is known only to Him above. . . . Great God can I ever become reconciled to the loss of my dear angel of a child. God what great sin have I committed that I should be visited by so severe an affliction." Affliction threatened to overwhelm Carr, much as it did Augustine St. Clare.[27]

The need for sentiment and sympathy came from the real need to deal with death. A clearer understanding of demographic reality leads us to consider how the combination of religious concerns and a fairly static medical knowledge created a generalized emotional crisis. Mobility meant that rural Americans were not as closed to the outside as they had been in the previous century. If they could not stop the spread of disease among a roving, more commercial population, they could find solace in the only permanence that their society offered, and that was found in local churches where salvation was sought and the possibility of heavenly relief from suffering was easily anticipated. Reading and writing their own personal narratives of loss served a useful purpose in daily life. Narratives of loss found a welcoming audience. The private papers of ordinary Americans plainly demonstrate for us that many sought relief in a more soothing religion that had adapted to meet their emotional needs.

Chapter 12

The Romantic Landscape: Washington Irving, Sleepy Hollow, and the Rural Cemetery Movement

Thomas G. Connors

> *Then look around, and choose thy ground,*
> *And take thy rest.*
>
> —*Lord Byron, at Missolonghi (1824)*

Romantic ideas about death and landscape shaped antebellum America's solution to the practical problem of urban burial. The rural cemetery proved popular with strollers who appreciated the picturesque setting and varied monuments, a tableau designed to appeal to the sensibilities of the age.[1] This important and practical innovation may be traced in the language and experience of Washington Irving (1783–1859), whose romantic tastes informed his responses both to the urbanization which threatened his parents' vault in Manhattan and the question of how to preserve the natural environment of a place he had made famous: Sleepy Hollow.

Irving's beliefs on burial practice emerge in his journals, letters, essays, and fiction. These in turn may be measured against the actions he took to arrange his family's secure entombment. Both his words and deeds embody the romantic notions about death that later made "Victorian" a byword for "morbid" and defined the sentimental expressions of grief that marked the century. His relationship with Tarrytown reflects a similar evolution from imagined to created landscape, where Irving's mind may yet be found in the geography of his home at Sunnyside and the cemetery at Sleepy Hollow.

Irving's opinions on appropriate ways to mourn and bury the dead developed as he reflected on what he observed during long sojourns in Europe. Like many other nineteenth-century travelers, he regarded the tombs of the famous (including St. Paul, Charlemagne, and Ferdinand and Isabella) to be worthy of his attention. In his journals, he described wooden crosses in a Swiss graveyard, copied epitaphs from an English churchyard, and inspected the monuments of Winchester Cathedral with a discerning eye.[2] In Rome he visited the Protestant Cemetery, "a solemn—melancholy place" that deeply moved him as it would later affect the poets John Keats and Percy Bysshe Shelley.[3] He preferred the simplicity of this graveyard to the display of Catholic saints' remains for veneration inside churches. In Syracuse, he anticipated Mark Twain's later comic exasperation with popish relics in *Innocents Abroad* (1869).[4] In the cathedral, Irving saw

a thigh bone of one of the disciples but I forget his name. By the way these disciples must have been an uncommon bony set of fellows. I have seen no less than five thigh bones of St. John the Baptist, three arms of St. Stephen and four jaw bones of St. Peter.

In Catania, Sicily, he ended a lengthy description of the cathedral's treasures—including the heart of St. Agatha—by noting that "in this sanctum santorum I had my pocket picked."[5]

If Irving found little to venerate in displayed fragments of saints, he was no iconoclast either. In Avignon, France, he met with "the severest disappointment" upon discovering that the tomb of Petrarch's *"belle Laura,"* which he anticipated finding "guarded with the utmost veneration, as reflecting celebrity on the place and attracting the particular curiosity of Strangers," had instead been "utterly demolished during the time of the late revolution." This sacrilege was too much: "Never did I curse the revolution, its authors and its consequences, more than at that instant; this is a cruel instance of the indiscriminating fury of the wretched rabble who predominated in that period of devastation, when the arts and sciences . . . were arrested and their . . . choicest specimens defaced & destroyed."[6]

In the letters and journals written during Irving's early travels, and especially in *The Sketch Book* (1819–20), can be found many examples of such ruminations on burial practices and monuments, supporting passionate judgments that would later inform the choices he made for his own family. The sketches on "Westminster Abbey" and "Rural Funerals" supply particular insight. His comments on the former are grounded in a romantic taste for the medieval. Irving entered Westminster through its gloomy and crumbling cloisters, where everything bore "marks of the gradual dilapidations of time, which yet has something touching and pleasing in its very decay." He recommended wandering there by the light of a full moon. Emerging into the abbey's magnificent Gothic interior, he felt "a profound and mysterious awe . . . surrounded by the congregated bones of the great men of past times."[7]

Awe quickly gave way to a moral lesson on the fleeting nature of fame and to an equally critical commentary on monuments and personalities. In contrast to the indignation he felt at Avignon, the petty vandalism he saw at the abbey—graffiti on kings' tombs, a head missing from Henry V's effigy—provided examples of how powerless the mighty are in death. As an American republican, Irving may not have found the desecration of royal tombs altogether displeasing.[8]

Recent attempts at memorial sculpture received Irving's scorn. He preferred medieval effigies:

They have an effect infinitely more impressive on my feelings than the fanciful attitudes, the overwrought conceits, and allegorical groups, which abound on modern monuments. I have been struck, also, with the superiority of many of the old sepulchral inscriptions. There was a noble way, in former times, of saying things simply and yet saying them proudly.[9]

One of the finest pieces of sculpture in Westminster Abbey, Roubillac's mid-eighteenth-century tomb of Lady Elizabeth Nightingale, appeared "horrible rather than sublime" to Irving. From the vault's door, a shrouded skeleton (Death) aims a spear at Lady Nightingale, who sinks into her frantic husband's arms.[10] Irving admired the skill of the sculptor but strongly disapproved of the message. As a restorative, he set forth his sentimental views on mourning and commemoration of the dead:

Why should we thus seek to clothe death with unnecessary terrors, and to spread horrors round the tomb of those we love? The grave should be surrounded by every thing that might inspire tenderness and veneration for the dead; or that might win the living to virtue. It is a place, not of disgust and dismay, but of sorrow and meditation.[11]

For Irving, the conditions for "an honored and peaceful grave" were met in the pastoral setting of a country church, celebrated in *The Sketch Book* in "Rural Funerals." (In another essay, he confessed to be "fond of loitering about country churches.")[12] He found that funeral services in the English countryside elevated the mind through a "purity of sentiment and the unaffected elegance of thought." The "stately and frigid" urban funeral, in contrast, offered only "a gloomy parade [of] mourning coaches, mourning horses, mourning plumes, and hireling mourners, who make a mockery of grief" (as Dickens did in satirizing the same scene almost two decades later in *Oliver Twist*).[13] This seemed to Irving only the hollow appearance of sorrow; it was empty, insincere, and short lived. The pace of life in the city would not stop for death, nor pause to honor memory. After the crepe splendor and purchased tears, the deceased was quickly forgotten.

In the country, as Irving tarries, death rings true. Like the bell that tolls it, death fills the air "with its pervading melancholy over hill and vale, and saddens all the landscape." The author was intrigued by the rural custom of decorating the grave with flowers, turf, and evergreen. Each flower, each color symbolized some precise shade of grief or melancholy. Irving appreciated how carefully the plots were tended, signs, to him, of faithful remembrance. Here, he felt certain, death transformed love into a "truly spiritual affection [that] rises purified from every sensual desire, and returns like a holy flame, to illumine and sanctify the heart of the survivor." The "woes" and "delights" of "the love which survives the tomb" somehow balanced each other. Here, death perfected the deceased, erasing defect and resentment. As "the voice from the tomb" was "sweeter than song," Irving urged his readers to "go to the grave of buried love, and meditate!"[14]

Literary pilgrimages called forth a tone that was even more personal. As Irving had written in "Westminster Abbey," poets evoked a "fonder feeling" than "the great and heroic." He felt a special "companionship between the author and reader" when he visited writers' tombs. Sir Walter Scott's family vault, set amid the ruins of Dryburgh Abbey, had once been a part of the ancestral estate; all except the right of burial had been sold away. Irving visited the site only once, in 1817, and his reaction was naturally muted because he was accompanied by Scott himself, who found the abbey's current owner a bit too enthusiastic in anticipating his eventual interment there. On the grounds of Scott's home at Abbotsford, however, the American writer stopped to observe "a small antique monument" which stood over the grave of one of his host's favorite greyhounds.[15]

At Newstead Abbey, Irving found that Lord Byron had gone further. The poet had buried his favorite dog on the site of the ruin's high altar, and asked that he be interred there as well. When Byron's body arrived back from Missolonghi, Greece, in 1824, his family demurred, preferring that he rest in the family vault in Hucknall Torkard church instead. Irving duly made the pilgrimage and firmly agreed with the executors' "better judgment and feeling in consigning his ashes to the family sepulcher, to mingle with those of his mother and his kindred."[16] This may strike us as strange: surely Byron by rights should rest in some iconoclastic or exotic setting rather than the Whig calm of an English parish church. Yet Irving's response is consistent with his other words and actions in conceiving the ideal of a family plot in a rural churchyard. His comments on visiting Shakespeare's grave are instructive:

He lies buried in the . . . chantry of the church, and never had a poet a more enviable grave. Thus to come back and lay his dust at the place of his nativity—To be treasurd [sic] up in his native town & to be the theme & pride of his townsmen and then such a place of sepulture. The church is one of the most beautiful old country churches in England and its situation is almost unrivaled. It stands on the banks of the Avon. . . . The elms at the bottom of the burying ground droop their branches into the water. . . . The yard is green, the very tomb stones are half covered with moss—small birds were fluttering & chirping about every fissure of the old walls and rooks were sailing and cawing about the spire.[17]

In Irving's opinion, Shakespeare had chosen an ideal grave—with his family in his hometown parish church on the Avon's banks.

In Irving's native New York, no park-like churchyards awaited along quiet riverbanks. The Irving family vault in front of the Brick Church in a deteriorating neighborhood in lower Manhattan held no charm. Thus the returned tourist gave a great deal of thought and energy to insuring that he and his family would rest in rustic tranquility, in a place full of history and legend. But what insurance? Irving provided his own: a celebrated short story, penned only a year after his visit to Scott's Abbotsford.

Washington Irving wrote "The Legend of Sleepy Hollow" far from the Hudson, in England. According to his nephew and biographer, Irving worked out the framework for the tale in a discussion with his brother-in-law, Henry Van Wart, over a year before he sent the completed manuscript to his brother Ebenezer in New York, at the end of 1819.[18] He found his ghost in German legends of the supernatural, but the setting came straight from the pleasant memories of his adolescence. The story imagines the picturesque region to have been rich in folklore, superstition, and quaint custom, the perfect setting for a duel between the sturdy Dutch frontiersman and the smarmy New England schoolteacher.[19] In the Hudson Valley and Catskills, Irving found his literary hinterland, where pockets of oral tradition remained to be mined, away from urban and industrial revolutions. Later he would freely admit that his alter ego "Geoffrey Crayon" had been "beguiled by his predilection for the haunts of his youth, and by the certain taint of romance, whenever any thing connected with the Dutch was to be described."[20]

Irving had first visited this area in 1798, at the age of fourteen, sent north to escape an epidemic in New York.[21] The image of the infected, diseased city left behind contrasted with the pure and lush environment of Tarrytown. Forty years later, he could keenly remember his joy in exploring the forested hollow. The landscape of "The Legend of Sleepy Hollow" would be an example of geography imitating literature, or at least exploiting it. By contrast, the growth and renewal of Manhattan carelessly swept away relics of the past remembered from Irving's childhood and celebrated in his *Knickerbocker's History* (1809). Across the ocean in Britain, he took comfort in believing that the hollow had not changed, and by setting his comic ghost story there, he made it sacred ground and ensured the preservation of its rural atmosphere.

"The Legend of Sleepy Hollow" climaxes at the bridge by the churchyard, where the Headless Horseman hurls his flaming head at Ichabod Crane. According to Irving's yarn, the horseman, said to be a Hessian decapitated in a nearby skirmish, lay buried in the churchyard (and later local tradition identifies the tombstones of the "original" Brom Bones and

Katrina Van Tassel there).[22] Irving mixes actual geography and history with legend and imagination. The whole region is presented as "drowsy, dreamy" and "bewitched," untouched by changes brought about by progress. Irving felt that in "such retired Dutch valleys . . . population, manners, and customs remained fixed," while the "incessant changes in other parts of this restless country, sweeps by them unobserved."[23] As he grew older, Irving begrudged every alteration in the region, bestowing a mythic identity upon the Hudson Valley. His storytelling prompted the romantic reimagining of the region by other artists, most notably Thomas Cole's landscape paintings and Andrew Jackson Downing's pastorally inspired architecture.[24]

In "The Legend," Irving took advantage of the role the area played as a military frontier in the Revolution, drawing on history and inventing legend. At a "haunted" stream along the road from Sleepy Hollow to Tarrytown, Major John André had been captured in 1780, setting in motion the events leading to his execution, across the river at Tappan. André, whose remains were conveyed to Westminster Abbey in 1821, grew into a tragic and romantic figure of the war. Irving drew on the vagueness of oral tradition to invent the story of the horseman, a Hessian mercenary, and the "nameless battle" in which he lost his head. At the Van Tassel ball in "The Legend," old veterans reminisced about their adventures as young soldiers fighting the British. Irving's comment reveals much about his own role as the region's storyteller and popular historian: "Just sufficient time had elapsed to enable each storyteller to dress up his tale with a little becoming fiction . . . in the indistinctness of his recollection."[25]

The landscape of "The Legend" did exist, as did the central feature of the church, churchyard, and bridge. The old Dutch Church, described by Irving in his later essay "Sleepy Hollow," was built in the late seventeenth century by Frederick Phillipse, the Dutch colonist whose estate embraced the region and who rested in a vault under the church (Figure 12.1). In the story, the churchyard's "grass-grown yard, where the sunbeams seem to sleep so quietly" would seem a tranquil place to lie. Irving thought it so, though as a boy he had heedlessly romped there: "I blush to acknowledge the thoughtless frolic with which, in company with other whispers, I have sported within its sacred bounds, during intervals of worship, chasing butterflies, plucking wild flowers, or vying with each other who could leap over the tallest tombstones; until checked by the stern voice of the sexton."[26]

The burial ground of the old Dutch Church had been used since the mid-seventeenth century and, in Irving's day, many of the early inscriptions in Dutch had not yet crumbled into illegibility.[27] At this place, Ichabod Crane made his final dash for the bridge beyond which the ghost could not follow him. Here, religion, death, and nature converged in a landscape seared into readers' imaginations by the fiery light of the horse-

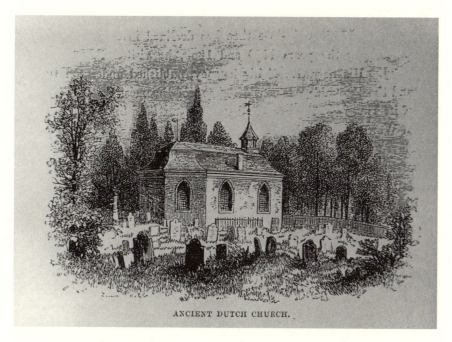

ANCIENT DUTCH CHURCH.

Figure 12.1. "Ancient Dutch Church," from Benson J. Lossing, *The Hudson from the Wilderness to the Sea* (1866).

man's jack-o'-lantern head. In time, the acclaimed author would return to the place where he had set his story and make it his own.

In 1835, when he returned from years abroad followed by a Western adventure, Washington Irving decided to find a home and settle down. He designed his own romantic house, garden, and family tomb, putting into practice what he had written about. Not surprisingly, he took Abbotsford, Walter Scott's estate, as his model. Scott had grown up in Edinburgh, had bought a farmhouse in a hilly region south of the city, and gradually turned that place into a Gothic fantasy of a house, which he renamed after a nearby ford used by medieval monks. Irving's admiration for Scott's home began in 1817 when he visited Abbotsford and spent several days with his host touring nearby ruins and picturesque sites.[28]

The parallels between Abbotsford and Irving's Sunnyside are too many to be dismissed as coincidental. Both writers enjoyed escorting visitors around the grounds to admire the scenery and hear their recounting of local legends. For Irving, this typically culminated in a visit to the old Dutch Church and the scene made famous in "The Legend of Sleepy Hollow." Inside his drawing room, Irving hung a steel engraving of Scott's literary circle, thus linking the two writers' homes as literary shrines. Thrilled by the chance to meet Irving, journalist Theodore Tilton tellingly proclaimed that "a visit to Sunnyside is equal to a pilgrimage to Abbotsford."[29]

The transformation of Irving's estate began in 1835 when the author purchased an eighteenth-century Dutch tenant cottage he first called "Wolfert's Roost" on the Van Tassel estate—the same family described in "The Legend of Sleepy Hollow." Aided by his neighbor, architect George Harvey, Irving gave free rein to his romantic tastes in remodeling it into "Sunnyside" over the next dozen years. He created an eclectic mix of Dutch Colonial gables, Gothic trim, and Tudor chimney stacks, with an annex inspired by a Spanish tower (Figure 12.2).[30]

As to the grounds, Irving's taste ran to the picturesque style of eighteenth-century English gardening, "marked by irregular and seeming naturalism." The lawn beside the house overlooked the Hudson River. He reworked the riverbank, clearing away rocks and trees, while adding steps and benches. Paths wove through wooded areas along a creek and cove. Above the house, a dam held back the waters of a tiny brook to form a pond christened the "Little Mediterranean." The creek then cascaded through an ice pond and miniature gorge on its way to a cove opening into the Hudson, so that the house faced water on two sides. Behind the house, dependent buildings led up to fields used for Irving's small farm, providing pastoral scenery and potential income. Andrew Jackson Downing, the most influential architectural writer of the day, thought Sunnyside "almost the beau ideal of a cottage-*ornée*" (small villa residence), set in a model landscape:

There is also a quiet-keeping in the cottage and the grounds around it, that assists in making up the charm of the whole: the gently swelling slope reaching down to the water's edge, bordered by prettily wooded ravines through which a brook meanders pleasantly; and threaded by foot-paths ingeniously contrived so as sometimes to afford secluded walks, and at others to allow fine vistas of the broad expanse of river scenery.[31]

In a recent study of Sunnyside's landscape, Robert Toole concluded that Irving "manipulated the property's components to create a unified composition that melded a modest farm into a wider setting dominated by nature."[32] Irving took both solace and pride in his own creation: "Here I am, rooted on the banks of the Hudson, in a cottage which I have built, myself, amidst grounds which I have laid out and trees which I have planted, amongst the scenes of my boyhood and about which I have scribbled in later years."[33] He identified himself with the Hudson, rather than his native New York City, emphasizing the river which linked his romanticized childhood to his chosen home and best-known works.

Though he had created his version of Abbotsford, Irving could not duplicate Dryburgh Abbey, the ruined medieval church housing Scott's ances-

Figure 12.2. Washington Irving's Sunnyside. Photograph by Thomas Connors, 2001.

tral tomb. The Irving family vault at the Brick Church in New York had neither the rural scenery nor the security of Dryburgh to commend it. Even before a new rural cemetery was proposed at Sleepy Hollow, Washington Irving had already planned to establish a family plot there. In June 1838, when his brother Peter died, Irving arranged for the body to be taken up river by "Union Steam boat . . . to be deposited in a temporary grave at the Episcopal church" in Dobbs Ferry, "until I can have a family vault erected there."[34] If at this point his intent was to build a vault in Dobbs Ferry, within a few years his mind was set on Sleepy Hollow. Writing his brother Ebenezer from Madrid in 1842, he directed the landscaping of Peter's temporary grave, while imagining a new family burial ground on the hillside next to the old Dutch churchyard:

I mentioned, in a former letter, my wish that you would have an iron railing put around the gravestone of our dear brother Peter, and a gravestone within, with a simple inscription of his name, age, date of his birth, &c. Have honeysuckles and shrubs planted inside of the inclosure, that they may, in time, overrun it. I had intended to have his remains transported to a family vault or burying ground which I contemplated establishing at the old Dutch Sleepy Hollow church. Even now, perhaps, it might be as well to buy of the Widow Beekman a few yards square of the woody height, adjacent to the north end of the burying ground, and have it enclosed with a paling for the family place of sepulture. I think a family burying place, with a gate opening into the main burying ground would be preferable to a vault. . . . Our dear brother's remains might be conveyed to the above-mentioned place. Think of all this, and carry it into effect. It is the thing that lies near my heart. I hope, some day or other, to sleep my last sleep in that favorite resort of my boyhood.[35]

Here he visualizes the family plot he later created—its iron fence and white marble stones, simply inscribed with names and dates, and standing on the hillside a few yards above the northern edge of the old churchyard.

Irving knew all too well the dank family vaults in the churchyards of lower Manhattan. Not only his parents, but the remains of his intended bride, Mathilda Hoffman, who died of consumption in 1809, lay there.[36] New York's insatiable growth threatened his parents' vault, but it was not until 1853 that he took the actions he had vowed a decade earlier. Plans to widen the narrow streets near City Hall condemned the vaults in front of the Brick Church, including the one in which Irving's parents lay. Before the church and vaults were entirely destroyed, Irving had his family's remains safely entombed at Sleepy Hollow.[37]

Quoting lines from Lord Byron, the author wrote his niece: "Then look around / And choose thy ground / And take thy rest." These words had gone through his head, he said, as he was selecting a family plot in the new cemetery, one that should be shaded by a grove of oaks and "just on the edge of the old church yard."[38] On September 29, 1853, Irving personally oversaw his parents' reburial. Popular historian Benson Lossing further romanticized the event: he reported that as the grave of Irving's mother filled with dirt, the son leaned against a tree, covered "his face with his hands and wept as tenderly as a young child." He had been unable to attend her original entombment, thirty-six years earlier, when he was in England. Lossing added another anecdotal gloss to the story, claiming that Irving's Scottish nurse, Lizzie, was interred in his mother's grave. It was his nurse who had boldly stopped George Washington in a New York shop, asking the president to bless his young namesake. Here, history and legend, childlike innocence and the prophesy of his later fame, were symbolically connected in this account of filial and maternal love, even in death.[39]

In Irving's sentimental geography, the plot to the left of his mother was to contain his own grave. On his left, a space remained for his surviving brother Ebenezer. On his mother's right, he buried his father, and then Peter, who had been moved from Dobbs Ferry. This accomplished, Irving told his niece that he could now "look forward with serene satisfaction to being gathered at last to a family gathering place, where . . . my dust may mingle with the dust of those most dear to me." He had reunited most of the household of his youth "in that favorite resort of my boyhood." In death he could return to the warmth of home, surrounded by the "ashes" of those he loved, in a tranquil landscape, in which death itself represented a nostalgic return to his own idealized memories of childhood.[40]

The genealogical geography of the Irving plot mapped out his family tree. His parents lay in the center of the plot, flanked by two bachelor sons, Peter and Washington, who in turn rested beside married brothers, William and Ebenezer, and their wives. While Ebenezer's family occupies the eastern half of the plot, and William's fills much of the western portion, certain relatives were placed in sites that highlighted their unique relationships to family members. William's son, Pierre Munro Irving, who became his uncle's secretary and biographer, is buried at Irving's feet, while his beloved nieces rest above his head. The relationships emphasized in the original allotment of the Irving graves remained the organizing principle for much of the next century.[41]

The development of a separate and far larger garden cemetery north of the historic churchyard had received Irving's fervent public support from the start. What may at first seem strange to us—that Irving would welcome the commercial development of Sleepy Hollow as a place of burial—in fact proves the close link between the rural cemetery and the municipal park. The first American rural cemetery, Mount Auburn (1831), in Cambridge, Massachusetts, continues today to carry on its dual function as an arboretum and cemetery. In Concord, where a well-loved natural beauty spot was dedicated as Sleepy Hollow Cemetery in 1855, Ralph Waldo Emerson warmly extolled the preservation of this environment:

Our use will not displace the old tenants. The well-beloved bird will not sing one song the less, the high-holding woodpecker, the meadow-lark, the oriole, robin, purple finch, bluebird, thrush, and red-eyed warbler, the heron, the bittern will find out the hospitality and protection from the gun of this asylum, and will seek the waters of the meadow; and in the grass, and by the pond, the locust, the cricket, and the hyla, shall shrilly play.

Irving believed that the rural cemetery at his Sleepy Hollow would accomplish the same end.[42]

The catalyst for Sleepy Hollow Cemetery was a gravedigger's spade that turned up old bones in a plot thought to be empty. It became instantly clear that the old Dutch churchyard would soon be full. After much talk, twenty-five of the area's most prominent gentlemen convened in the long room over a Tarrytown store in 1849 and subscribed their names to the roll as charter members of an association to develop a rural cemetery adjacent to the old churchyard. Irving and eight others served as trustees on its board.[43]

It was Irving, of course, who proposed the name, to capitalize on the notoriety of the place. He hoped that the "worthies" organizing the project were "already aware of the blunder they have committed in naming it the

Tarrytown instead of *Sleepy Hollow* Cemetery. The latter name would have been enough by itself to secure the patronage of all desirous of sleeping quietly in their graves." Incredibly, the trustees waited until five years after Irving's death in 1859 to follow his advice. Claiming no "pecuniary" interest in the venture, Irving publicized the project in the *Knickerbocker*, in 1849, wishing it success, "as it will keep that beautiful and umbrageous neighborhood sacred from the anti-poetical and all-levelling axe." Obviously, preservation meant fending off tasteless capitalism from the "sacred" spot.[44]

The *Knickerbocker* quickly complied, praising the cemetery's natural beauty in clichés of the picturesque: "a succession of woody eminences and tranquil dells; a charming spot, breathing the very spirit of seclusion and repose." It was, in short, a scene of variety, pleasing to the nature-loving eye. The ground had already been divided into sections "appropriately and tastefully" renamed to evoke sylvan, park-like images: Woodland Hill, Forest Shade, Shady Dell, Mount Hope. Other sections highlighted the area's heritage: Irving Ridge, Hudson Hill, Battle Hill, Tarry Grove. Of course, the historic setting, "by the quaint old Dutch church, toward the entrance to Sleepy-Hollow," adjoining "the little grave-yard where so many of the fore-fathers of the hamlet sleep," added to its appeal. Beyond its natural and sentimental attractions, Sleepy Hollow offered convenient access from the city by steamship or (shortly) rail.[45]

The new cemetery's design carried all the characteristics of the American rural cemetery of the mid-nineteenth century (Figure 12.3). Its roads wound around hills, through glens, and along the Pocantico River. It was divided into marketable sections, and the topography was labeled to appeal to the era's tastes. Battle Hill, named for the earthen remains of a Revolutionary redoubt, commemorated vague traditions of a local skirmish.[46] The cemetery map remains a testament to the world of nineteenth-century cultural literacy, drawing on biblical, patriotic, and literary geography: Gethsemane, Monticello, Ben Lomond, Gibraltar, Tivoli, Cashmere. The change of name to Sleepy Hollow Cemetery in 1864, of course, did no harm in underscoring its authentic romantic appeal. Nor did the Washington Irving Memorial Chapel, erected in 1922, with stained glass windows depicting the author and the adventures of Ichabod Crane.[47]

Even Washington Irving's Tarrytown could not be spared jarring intrusions of progress, contaminating a once "pure" environment with eyesores and strangers. From time to time after he began to live there, Irving commented on these changes in letters to the *Knickerbocker*, disapprovingly assessing, for example, the new pulpit and Greek revival portico added to the Dutch Church, or the French style of dress worn by the women in the congregation that had replaced "the primitive garbs of homespun manufac-

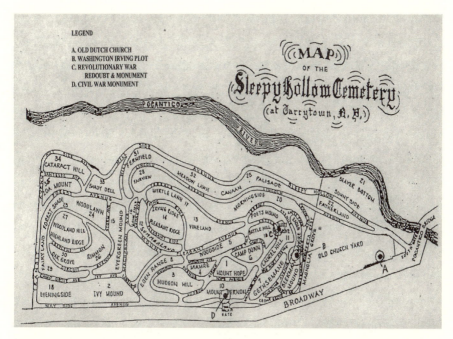

Figure 12.3. Map of the Sleepy Hollow Cemetery. Collections of the Sleepy Hollow Cemetery, Sleepy Hollow, New York. This map is based on a 1960 version, modified here to reflect how the cemetery appeared in 1860.

ture and antique Dutch fashion." The church sexton, a boyhood friend and fellow antiquary, decried "the appalling revolution that was taking place," as steam transportation turned languid Tarrytown into a bustling river town. Irving sadly believed the region's fate had been sealed: "How can I hope even Sleepy Hollow can escape the general inundation? In a little while, I fear the slumber of ages will be at an end . . . and the antiquarian visitor to the Hollow, in the petulance of his disappointment may pronounce all that I have recorded of that once favored region, a fable." A rural cemetery, of course, was Irving's solution to the problem.[48]

More changes were to trouble Irving as observer and creator of a fabled landscape. The deepest blow must have been the railroad which sliced along the Hudson's shore in 1847, separating Sunnyside from the Tappan Zee and turning his cove into a marsh. Though "quite in despair," he kept a low public profile during construction. He complained in one letter, however, that "if the Garden of Eden were now on earth, they would run a railroad through it."[49] Irving commented as well on the new Croton Aqueduct which bridged Sleepy Hollow: "Not far from the old Dutch haunted church, and in the heart of the wood an immense culvert or stone arch is thrown across the wizard stream of the Pocantico." He even attempted a comic reworking of his "Legend," editorially inserting immigrant Irish workers in place of Ichabod Crane. The laborers, called "Paddies" and speaking "an unknown tongue," were cast as stage Irish stereotypes, slow-witted, superstitious, drunken, gullible, and prone to pratfalls. In the tradition of Brom Bones, locals "grieviously harried" the workers as they staggered from the "Whisky-shop in a neighboring village" back to the "Colony of Patlanders" in the hollow, frightened by glimpses of headless fiends who eventually grew bolder, "occasionally tripping up, or knocking down, the unlucky object of their hostility." As a result, the "Paddys" no longer ventured out of their "shantys" after dark. Irving warned that if his crudely caricatured Irish were to grow "tired of being cut off from their whisky," they would then delay construction of the aqueduct. He now seemed to delight that life imitated his art, and that his story still haunted the hollow.[50]

Nevertheless, Irving consistently mourned the loss of the place as he had once known and imagined it. As early as March 1839, he wrote to the *Knickerbocker* as "Geoffrey Crayon," having found that the landscape of his imagination had been illusionary:

It is true, the romance of youth is past, that once spread illusions over every scene. I can no longer picture an Arcadia in every green valley; nor a fairy land among the distant mountains; nor a peerless beauty in every villa glistening among the trees; but though the illusions of youth have faded from the landscape, the recollections of departed years and departed pleasures shed over it the mellow charm of evening sunshine.[51]

Irving's death on November 28, 1859, and his funeral a few days later, received national attention. The events were prominently illustrated in *Harper's* and *Frank Leslie's* magazines (Figure 12.4). Henry Wadsworth Longfellow delivered a warm memorial address in Boston shortly afterwards, and in 1876 was inspired to write "In the Churchyard at Tarrytown," a tribute (which, despite its title, reveals no conclusive evidence of its author having visited Sleepy Hollow). If Longfellow never paid his respects at Irving's tomb, many other pilgrims and admirers did.[52] The earliest illustrations of the gravesite all show floral offerings. Benson Lossing's depiction includes two women in heavy mourning dress and a prose description of "wreaths of withered flowers . . . killed by the frost and buried by drifts of lately departed snow. These will not remain, for all summer long fresh and fragrant ones are laid upon that honored grave by fair hands . . . these sweet tributes of affection" (Figure 12.5).[53] Souvenir hunters less sweetly chipped away at two of Irving's tombstones, before the current one, rounded to deter future blows, was erected around 1900.[54]

The landscapes that Irving fastidiously undertook to realize at Sleepy

BURIAL OF WASHINGTON IRVING IN HIS FAMILY LOT AT THE CEMETERY, NEAR TARRYTOWN—THE LAST MOURNER AT THE GRAVE—FROM A SKETCH BY OUR OWN ARTIST.

Figure 12.4. "Burial of Washington Irving in his family lot at the cemetery, near Tarrytown." Printed in *Frank Leslie's Illustrated Newspaper*, December 17, 1859. This image depicts "the last mourner at the grave."

Hollow and Sunnyside quickly became cultural icons. Currier and Ives printed pastoral scenes of the old Dutch Church, the Sleepy Hollow bridge and mill dam, and four of Sunnyside alone. Andrew Jackson Downing called Irving's cottage and grounds "even more poetical than any chapter of his *Sketch Book*." Oliver Wendell Holmes described Sunnyside, "next to Mt. Vernon, the best known and most cherished of all the dwellings in our land." Visiting in 1905, Henry James still "seemed to hear in the summer sounds . . . the last faint echo of a felicity forever gone."[55]

The property passed through the descendents of Ebenezer Irving until 1945, when it was acquired by John D. Rockefeller, Jr., who opened Sunnyside as a museum two years later. Restoration has removed a later wing and rebuilt some outbuildings, and the grounds maintain the feel of Irving's original landscape.[56] Meanwhile, Washington Irving's youthful illusions of Sleepy Hollow survive in the national consciousness as a haunted landscape instantly called to mind as the setting for the climax of Ichabod Crane's terrifying chase. Indeed, Sleepy Hollow is so vividly imagined that many would guess it to be a fictional place.

There is truth in such confusion, as Henry James knew: "The place is inevitably, today, but a qualified Sleepy Hollow," he wrote. "The Sleepy

IRVING'S GRAVE.

Figure 12.5. "Irving's Grave," from Benson J. Lossing, *The Hudson from the Wilderness to the Sea* (1866).

Hollow of the author's imagination was, as I take it, off somewhere in the hills, or in some dreamland of old autumns, happily unprofanable now."[57] Modernity has expropriated Irving, whether in the stone monument showing Ichabod's pursuit, erected near the bridge, or in the naming of the local high school team as the "Horsemen." In 1996, the city of North Tarrytown, even slower than the cemetery's trustees had been, changed its name to Sleepy Hollow. Even so, Washington Irving's vision exists. The ancient churchyard, the rural cemetery, and the natural beauty of Rockefeller State Park in the hollow, all remain within reach of the picturesque garden of Sunnyside. In these places, we can yet know what the mid-nineteenth-century historian Benson Lossing felt as he passed the late author's home on his journey up the Hudson: "Around that cottage, and the adjacent lands and waters, Irving's genius has cast an atmosphere of romance."[58] By force of imagination and pen, he had permanently altered the landscape.

Notes

Introduction

1. Among recent treatments of death that take in a variety of perspectives, see Sheila M. Rothman, *Living in the Shadow in Death: Tuberculosis and the Social Experience of Illness in American History* (Baltimore, 1995); Robert V. Wells, *Facing the "King of Terrors": Death and Society in an American Community, 1750–1990* (Cambridge, 2000); Christine Quigley, *Modern Mummies: The Preservation of the Human Body in the Twentieth Century* (Jefferson, N.C., 1998); Stephen Prothero, *Purified by Fire: A History of Cremation in America* (Stanford, Calif., 2001); Jay Ruby, *Secure in the Shadow: Death and Photography in America* (Cambridge, Mass., 1995); Deborah Smith, " 'The Visage Once So Dear': Interpreting Memorial Photographs," *Dublin Seminar for New England Folklife, Annual Proceedings* 19 (1994): 255–68; Karl S. Guthke, "Talking Stones: Anthologies of Epitaphs from Humanism to Popular Culture," *Harvard Library Bulletin* 10 (Winter 1999): 19–69; Richard E. Meyer, ed., *Ethnicity and the American Cemetery* (Bowling Green, Ohio, 1993); Lynn Rainville, "Hanover Deathscapes: Mortuary Variability in New Hampshire, 1770–1920," *Ethnohistory* 46 (1999): 541–97; Kirk Savage, *Standing Soldiers, Kneeling Slaves: Race, War, and Monument in Nineteenth-Century America* (Princeton, N.J., 1997); Gail Holst-Warhaft, *The Cure for Passion: Grief and Its Political Uses* (Cambridge, Mass., 2000); Deborah A. Lee and Warren R. Hofstra, "Race, Memory, and the Death of Robert Berkeley: 'A Murder . . . of . . . Horrible and Savage Barbarity,' " *Journal of Southern History* 65 (1999): 41–76; Gary Alan Fine, "John Brown's Body: Elites, Heroic Embodiment, and the Legitimation of Political Violence," *Social Problems* 46 (1999): 225–49; Christine Daniels and Michael Kennedy, eds., *Over the Threshold: Intimate Violence in Early America* (New York, 1999); David T. Courtwright, *Violent Land: Single Men and Social Disorder from the Frontier to the Inner City* (Cambridge, Mass., 1996); Daniel A. Cohen, *Pillars of Salt, Monuments of Grace: New England Crime Literature and the Origins of American Popular Culture, 1674–1860* (New York, 1993); Patricia Cline Cohen, *The Murder of Helen Jewett: The Life and Death of a Prostitute in Nineteenth-Century New York* (New York, 1998); Karen Halttunen, *Murder Most Foul: The Killer and the American Gothic Imagination* (Boston, 1998); Donna Merwick, *Death of a Notary: Conquest and Change in Colonial New York* (Ithaca, N.Y., 1999); Peter G. Filene, *In the Arms of Others: A Cultural History of the Right-to-Die in America* (Chicago, 1998).

Chapter 1. The Christian Origins of the Vanishing Indian

1. Many scholars have commented on the racist dynamics of the United States' nostalgic attachment to American Indians. Peter Matthiessen, *In the Spirit of Crazy Horse* (1980; New York, 1991), has written, "American hearts respond with emotion to . . . modern films and television dramas in which the nineteenth-century Indian is portrayed as the tragic victim of Manifest Destiny; we honor his sun dances and

thunderbirds in the names of our automobiles and our motels. Our nostalgia comes easily, since those stirring peoples are safely in the past, and the abuse of their proud character . . . can be blamed on our roughshod frontier forebears" (xxii). Daniel R. Mandell has shown that many more Indians lived within eighteenth-century English territories than we usually think. The United States' cultural attachment to visions of dying Indians has, until recently, precluded extensive studies of Indian assimilation and survival. *Behind the Frontier: Indians in Eighteenth-Century Eastern Massachusetts* (Lincoln, Neb., 1996). On this topic, see also Colin G. Calloway, ed., *After King Philip's War: Presence and Persistence in Indian New England* (Hanover, N.H., 1997). Noting this conjunction between a focus on dying Indians and an ignorance of living ones, Brian Dippie has argued that "the belief in the Vanishing Indian was the ultimate cause of the Indian's vanishing." *The Vanishing American: White Attitudes and U.S. Indian Policy* (Middletown, Conn., 1972), 71, quoted in Jill Lepore, *The Name of War: King Philip's War and the Origins of American Idenity* (New York, 1998), 211. Of dying Indians in nineteenth-century frontier romances, Michelle Burnham has observed, "Central to this Jacksonian-era model of the imperialist audience is the subtraction of agency from the historical stage, so that causal aggression looks like inevitability. . . . The convenient elision of agency allows mourning to be free of responsibility." *Captivity and Sentiment: Cultural Exchange in American Literature, 1682–1861* (Hanover, N.H., 1997), 94.

2. Michael P. Rogin, "Liberal Society and the Indian Question," in *"Ronald Reagan," the Movie, and Other Episodes of Political Demonology* (Berkeley, Calif., 1987), 137–38. See also Richard Slotkin, *Regeneration Through Violence: The Mythology of the American Frontier, 1600–1860* (Middletown, Conn., 1973). Along similar lines, Jill Lepore observes, "For Indians' role in American history (even as wartime enemies) to be cherished, romanticized, and fetishized, Indians themselves must exist only in the past, mute memorials, silent as rock." *The Name of War,* 224.

3. Of Jackson's speech in 1830 on the removal of indigenous peoples, Roy Harvey Pearce has noted, "Concern for the Indian's sad state was as deep and honest as certainty of his inevitable destruction. Jackson's . . . rhetoric amounts to formal public expression of American regret in the face of the tragic and triumphant progress of civilization over savagism." *The Savages of America: A Study of the Indian and the Idea of Civilization* (Baltimore, 1953), 58.

4. Andrew Burstein, *Sentimental Democracy: The Evolution of America's Romantic Self-Image* (New York, 1999), xiii, xx.

5. Renato Rosaldo, "Imperialist Nostalgia," in *Culture and Truth: The Remaking of Social Analysis* (1989; Boston, 1993), 69–70.

6. Of vanishing Indians in poems of the early republic, for example, Julie Ellison has noted, "The structural convenience of this device, of course, lies in the way North America depopulates itself to make room for white settlement." *Cato's Tears and the Making of Anglo-American Emotion* (Chicago, 1999), 140

7. *Natural Born Killers,* prod. by Jane Hamsher, Don Murphy, and Clayton Townsend, dir. by Oliver Stone, Warner Brothers, 1985, videocassette. In an interview from prison, Mickey says that the Indian is the only person he regrets killing. The film also suggests a biblical fall through the Indian's death; the shaman's rattlesnakes bite Mickey and Mallory just after he is killed, debilitating them so that the police can catch them.

8. *Poltergeist,* prod. by Steven Spielberg and Frank Marshall, dir. by Tobe Hooper, Metro-Goldwyn-Mayer, 1982, videocassette; Philip Freneau, "The Indian Burial Ground," in Fred Lewis Pattee, *The Poems of Philip Freneau, Poet of the American Revolution,* 3 vols. (Princeton, N.J., 1903), 2:369.

9. Roy Harvey Pearce has suggested connections between missionaries and dying Indians; he describes, for example, a belated burst of Puritan missionary interest in the early eighteenth century: "Essentially an evangelical hope of saving a dying Indian for God, it rose as part of the last ditch efforts of some Puritans to remain Puritans." *The Savages of America,* 31. Julie Ellison has noted, "The Indian death song thrived among British and Euro-American poets in the late eighteenth century, and a rigorous study of the genre's origins in response to early ethnographic feedback from traders and missionaries would certainly yield even earlier examples." *Cato's Tears,* 98. See also David Murray's reading of John Eliot's collecting of dying Indian speeches. *Forked Tongues: Speech, Writing, and Representation in North American Indian Texts* (Bloomington, Ind., 1991), 34–39.

10. Thoroughgood Moore to John Chamberlayne, Secretary, November 13, 1705, no. 122, Letterbook A2, United Society for the Propagation of the Gospel in Foreign Parts [S.P.G.] Archives, Rhodes House Library, Oxford, UK. The S.P.G. often paraphrased this line in its published texts. See, e.g., *An Account of the Society for Propagating the Gospel in Foreign Parts* (London, 1706), 53. See also H. P. Thompson, *Into All Lands: The History of the Society for the Propagation of the Gospel in Foreign Parts 1701–1950* (London, 1951), 44–45; Richmond T. Bond, *Queen Anne's American Kings* (Oxford, 1952), 56–57.

11. In *Colonial Writing and the New World, 1583–1671* (Cambridge, 1999), 19–28, Thomas Scanlan interprets these translations against the backdrop of broader English colonial propaganda.

12. On the Black Legend, see Charles Gibson, *The Black Legend: Anti-Spanish Attitudes in the Old World and the New* (New York, 1971).

13. My emphasis here is not so much on the object that is depleted of value or inherently worthless, but on the object whose potential value has been neglected or discarded. I stress a value that could have been but is not, rather than a value that is no longer, or a value that never existed. I focus on this understanding of waste because it elicits both the elegaic response and the fear of loss that I think were present in missionary and in sentimental English treatments of dying Indians. In developing this understanding I have learned much from, but have not adopted, Michael Thompson's formulations of rubbish in *Rubbish Theory: The Creation and Destruction of Value* (Oxford, 1979), which incline toward the former definitions I presented. Rather, I have drawn some of my ideas from Georges Baitaille's theories of waste as unnecessary, heedless expenditure or consumption of resources, ranging from food and capital to human beings. This formulation informs Baitaille's "notion of 'a general economy' in which the 'expenditure' (the 'consumption') of wealth, rather than the production, was the primary object." *The Accursed Share: An Essay on General Economy,* vol. 1, in *Consumption,* trans. Robert Hurley (New York, 1991), 9.

14. Bartolomé de Las Casas, *The Tears of the Indians: Being an Historical and True Account of the Cruel Massacres and Slaughters of above Twenty Millions of Innocent People; Committed by the Spaniards in the Islands of Hispaniola, Cuba, Jamaica, &c. As also, in the Continent of Mexico, Peru, & other Places of the West-Indies, To the Total Destruction of those Countries,* trans. J. Phillips (London, 1656), 20.

15. Jonathan Field, " 'Peculiar Manuerance': Puritans, Indians, and the Rhetoric of Agriculture, 1629–1654," *Annual Proceedings of the Dublin Seminar for New England Folklife* 20 (1995): 12–24.

16. This assumption extended well past the seventeenth century, guiding missionaries such as John Sergeant who worked in Stockbridge, Massachusetts, through the 1740s. Noting that the local indigenous population had fallen over

several years, Sergeant attributed this population decline to "Their Intemperance. . . . Their great Irregularity in Diet. . . . When they are sick, they take little or no Care of themselves. . . . And in the mean Time they make use of few, or no Means to help the Sick. It is a Wonder therefore that they be not all sick, and that any recover when they are so!" Samuel Hopkins, *Historical Memoirs, Relating to the Housatunnuk Indians: Or, an Account of the Methods Used, and Pains Taken, for the Propagation of the Gospel among that Heathenish-Tribe, and the Success thereof, under the Ministry of the Late Reverend Mr. John Sergeant* (Boston, 1753), 82.

17. On the "deuteronomic" vision (relating, of course, to the Book of Deuteronomy and the chronologically linked Books of Joshua and Judges), see Alfred C. Cave, *The Pequot War* (Amherst, Mass., 1996), 171.

18. On these tracts and on the New England Company, the missionary society responsible for publishing some of these texts, see George Parker Winship, *The Eliot Indian Tracts* (Cambridge, Mass., 1925); William Kellaway, *The New England Company, 1649–1776: Missionary Society to the American Indians* (London, 1961).

19. *New England's First Fruits; In Respect, First of the Conversion of Some, Conviction of Divers, Preparation of Sundry of the Indians. 2. Of the Progress of Learning, in the Colledge at Cambridge in Massachusetts Bay* (London, 1643), 1, 8, 19.

20. Ibid., 20–21.

21. Cave, *Pequot War,* 19; *New England's First Fruits,* 18.

22. Elaine Scarry, *The Body in Pain: The Making and Unmaking of the World* (New York, 1985), 124, 128.

23. Ibid., 77.

24. Cotton Mather, *Days of Humiliation, Times of Affliction and Disaster: Nine Sermons for Restoring Favor with an Angry God* (Gainesville, Fla., 1970), 132–33.

25. Mather, *Humiliation,* 133.

26. In *The Curse of Cain: The Violent Legacy of Monotheism* (Chicago, 1997), Regina M. Schwartz confronts the problem of identity formation through violence in the Bible, criticizing the varied political ends for which the covenantal relationship has been invoked. My theory of waste coincides with her argument that violence emerges from the sense of scarcity that pervades the Bible—the sense, that is, that humans exist in fierce competition for land, for wealth, for God's favor, and for identity. If violence is the response to scarcity, perceived or real, so also is the effort to dole out violence in less destructive forms.

27. John W. Ford, ed., *Some Correspondence Between the Governors and Treasurers of the New England Company in London and the Commissioners of the United Colonies in America, the Missionaries of the Company and Others Between the Years 1657 and 1712 to which are Added the Journals of the Rev. Experience Mayhew in 1713 and 1714* (London, 1896), 84.

28. Eleazar Wheelock to Nathaniel Whitaker, December 21, 1766, Lebanon, Conn., in Leon Burr Richardson, ed., *An Indian Preacher in England: Being Letters and Diaries Relating to the Mission of the Reverend Samson Occom and the Reverend Nathaniel Whitaker to Collect Funds for the Benefit of Eleazar Wheelock's Indian Charity School, from Which Grew Dartmouth College* (Hanover, N.H., 1932), 193.

29. Wheelock, *A Continuation of the Narrative of the Indian Charity-School* (1771), 24.

30. See, e.g., John Eliot to Robert Boyle and the Commissioners of the New England Company, October 17, 1675, in Ford, *Some Correspondence,* 54–55. On the treatment of Christian Indians during this war, see Lepore, *Name of War,* esp. 21–47, 140, and Jenny Hale Pulsipher, "Massacre at Hurtleberry Hill: Christian Indians and English Authority in Metacom's War," *William and Mary Quarterly,* 3d ser., 53 (1996): 459–86. On Gookin's attitudes to the Praying Indians, see James Drake,

"Restraining Atrocity: The Conduct of King Philip's War," *New England Quarterly* 70 (1997): 33–56.

31. John Heckewelder, *A Narrative of the Mission of the United Brethren Among the Delaware and Mohegan Indians From Its Commencement in the Year 1740 to the Close of the Year 1808,* ed. William Elsey Connelley (Cleveland, Ohio, 1907), 427.

32. Daniel Gookin, *Historical Collections of the Indians in New England* (Boston, 1792); John Eliot, *The Dying Speeches of Several Indians* (Cambridge, 1685); John Cripps, ed., *A True Account of the Dying Words of Ockanickon, an Indian King, Spoken to Jakhursoe, His Brother's Son, Whom He Appointed King After Him* (London, 1682); Experience Mayhew, *Indian Converts: or, some Account of the Lives and Dying Speeches of a Considerable Number of the Christianized Indians of Martha's Vineyard, in New-England* (London, 1727).

33. See L. M. Beier, "The Good Death in Seventeenth-Century England," in Ralph Houlbrooke, ed., *Death, Ritual, and Bereavement* (London, 1989), 43–61; Philip Morgan, "Of Worms and War, 1380–1558," Clare Gittings, "Sacred and Secular, 1558–1660," and Ralph Houlbrooke, "The Age of Decency, 1660–1760," in Peter C. Jupp and Clare Gittings, eds., *Death in England: An Illustrated History* (New Brunswick, N.J., 1999), 119–74.

34. Erik R. Seeman, "Reading Indians' Deathbed Scenes: Ethnohistorical and Representational Approaches," *Journal of American History* 88 (2001): 17–47.

35. Mayhew, *Indian Converts,* 20.

36. *The Rule and Exercises of Holy Dying. In which are Described the Means and Instruments of Preparing Our Selves, and Others Respectively, for a Blessed Death* (London, 1651), 178–81; Mayhew, *Indian Converts,* 20.

37. As David Murray has said, these dying narratives "fix[ed] [Indians] in a certain safe and comforting role for a white readership." *Forked Tongues,* 35.

38. *New England's First Fruits,* 2; Cave, *Pequot War,* 120.

39. *New England's First Fruits,* 15. Roger Williams's very different account of Wequash's death is in the introduction to *A Key into the Language of America,* ed. John J. Teunissen and Evelyn J. Hinz (1643; Detroit, 1973), 88. As New England's first and most famous exile, Williams expressed uncertainty about Wequash's conversion and skepticism about the missionary work undertaken by the Massachusetts Bay Company. His religious beliefs along with his desire to secure a charter for his rival colony of Providence no doubt informed this uncertainty.

40. Michel Foucault, *Discipline and Punish: The Birth of the Prison,* trans. Alan Sheridan, 2d ed. (New York, 1995), 7.

41. Gittings, "Sacred and Secular," 153.

42. On Mayhew's text and on the Christian Wampanoag community of Martha's Vineyard, see Hilary E. Wyss, *Writing Indians: Literacy, Christianity, and Native Community in Early America* (Amherst, Mass., 2000).

43. John Foxe, *Acts and Monuments of these Latter and Perilous Days . . .* (London, 1563). This text is commonly called *The Book of Martyrs.*

44. Mayhew, *Indian Converts,* 101.

45. Timothy Horsfield to Gov. Denny, January 21, 1757, no. 353, Horsfield Papers, American Philosophical Society, Philadelphia, Pa.

46. Timothy Horsfield to Benjamin Franklin and others, January 21, 1757, no. 351, Horsfield Papers.

47. Fred Anderson, *Crucible of War: The Seven Years' War and the Fate of Empire in British North America, 1754–1766* (New York, 2000), 162.

48. Hugh Henry Brackenridge and Philip Freneau, *The Rising Glory of America,* in *The Poems of Philip Freneau* (Princeton, N.J., 1902), 1:49–50.

49. Ellison, *Cato's Tears,* 143.

Chapter 2. Blood Will Out

I would like to thank Elizabeth Bussiere, Morris L. Cohen, and the participants in the Mortal Remains conference for their helpful suggestions. Special thanks are due to Nancy Isenberg and Andrew Burstein for inviting me to Tulsa. I am also grateful to Florida International University for its support of my scholarship and to FIU's Instructional Photography and Graphics staff for their help with most of the illustrations that appear in this essay.

1. For overviews of early American crime literature, see Daniel A. Cohen, *Pillars of Salt, Monuments of Grace: New England Crime Literature and the Origins of American Popular Culture, 1674–1860* (New York, 1993); Karen Halttunen, *Murder Most Foul: The Killer and the American Gothic Imagination* (Cambridge, Mass., 1998); Halttunen, "Early American Murder Narratives: The Birth of Horror," in Richard Wightman Fox and T. J. Jackson Lears, eds., *The Power of Culture: Critical Essays in American History* (Chicago, 1993), 66–101; Daniel E. Williams, *Pillars of Salt: An Anthology of Early American Criminal Narratives* (Madison, Wis., 1993), 1–63; D. E. Williams, "Rogues, Rascals, and Scoundrels: The Underworld Literature of Early America," *American Studies* 24 (1983): 5–19; David Ray Papke, *Framing the Criminal: Crime, Cultural Work, and the Loss of Critical Perspective, 1830–1900* (Hamden, Conn., 1987). For helpful bibliographies, see Morris L. Cohen, *Bibliography of Early American Law,* 6 vols. (Buffalo, N.Y., 1998); Wilfred J. Ritz, comp., *American Judicial Proceedings First Printed Before 1801* (Westport, Conn., 1984); Thomas M. McDade, comp., *The Annals of Murder: A Bibliography of Books and Pamphlets on American Murders from Colonial Times to 1900* (Norman, Okla., 1961).

2. See Halttunen, *Murder Most Foul,* 2, 35–43, 59, 62–63, 73–75, 84–87, 120–23, 239. With respect to domestic murders and murders involving claims of insanity, see her chapters 5, 6, and 7, respectively. I place Halttunen's concept of the "Gothic" in quotation marks throughout this chapter, because I believe it to be a somewhat misleading designation for American murder publications of the early republic, both for reasons explored in this essay and for reasons not broached here.

3. See Halttunen, *Murder Most Foul,* 4–5, 35–90, passim, 239–40.

4. In her own brief discussion of early modern English crime publications, Halttunen emphasizes two narrative patterns: "the picaresque tale of criminality" (often narratives of "roguish" highwaymen) and "the spiritual biography of the criminal-as-sinner." See Halttunen, *Murder Most Foul,* 10–11, 254 n. 5. That formulation appears to be largely drawn from the work of Lincoln B. Faller, which focuses on criminal biographies of the late seventeenth through early eighteenth centuries; see Faller, *Turned to Account: The Forms and Functions of Criminal Biography in Late Seventeenth- and Early Eighteenth-Century England* (Cambridge, 1987). Neither Halttunen nor Faller takes much account of the sorts of sensationalistic motifs found in early English crime publications and emphasized in my discussion.

5. Much of my discussion here of early modern English murder publications is new. However, my account of the transformation of early New England crime literature toward the end of this chapter tends to follow evidence and arguments already made in *Pillars of Salt, Monuments of Grace* (1993). While Halttunen occasionally cites *Pillars of Salt, Monuments of Grace* in the endnotes of *Murder Most Foul,* she never explicitly discusses my findings, either to clarify for readers where her evidence and arguments follow mine—or where they diverge. There are in fact two important differences in the coverage of our respective studies: 1. She focuses exclusively on publications dealing with murder cases, whereas I examine publications dealing with other crimes as well (e.g., piracy, rape, arson, robbery, etc.); 2. I focus on

crime literature published in New England, whereas she examines murder publications throughout colonial British America and the United States. Nevertheless, the overlap between our two studies is substantial, as a high percentage of early American crime publications dealt with murder cases (particularly during the seventeenth and nineteenth centuries), and a high percentage of seventeenth- and eighteenth-century murder publications appeared in New England.

6. Joseph H. Marshburn, *Murder and Witchcraft in England, 1550–1640 As Recounted in Pamphlets, Ballads, Broadsides, and Plays* (Norman, Okla., 1971).

7. Marshburn, *Murder and Witchcraft in England*, 3–22, 35–38, 72–81, 85–92, 103–19, 132–44, 154–73, 179–82, 198–200, 222–33. About ten of the fifty or so criminal cases that Marshburn examines in detail are identified primarily as witchcraft cases. In addition to his main corpus of cases, Marshburn appends a supplementary list of crime publications of the same period; these depict a similar profusion of domestic or sex-related homicides; see Marshburn, *Murder and Witchcraft in England*, 241, 252–53, 258–69, 271–72. It should also be noted that the popular preoccupation with cases of domestic homicide documented by Marshburn did not disappear after 1640—the terminal date of his bibliography. To the contrary, in a more recent study, *Dangerous Familiars: Representations of Domestic Crime in England, 1550–1700* (Ithaca, N.Y., 1994), Frances E. Dolan identifies a shift after about 1640 in the particular mix of domestic homicide cases treated in popular English crime publications—"from insubordinate dependents [mostly wives and servants] to the murderous husband"—but confirms that the broad interest in domestic murders as a literary subject remained strong during the second half of the seventeenth century (see Dolan, *Dangerous Familiars*, quotation 13, 20–120). For an excellent comparative study of similar publications, see Joy Wiltenburg, *Disorderly Women and Female Power in the Street Literature of Early Modern England and Germany* (Charlottesville, Va., 1992).

8. *Two Horrible and Inhumane Murders Done in Lincolnshire, by Two Husbands Upon Their Wiues* . . . (London, 1607), t.p.; Marshburn, *Murder and Witchcraft in England*, 116–18 and unpaginated illustration. For Halttunen's terminology, see *Murder Most Foul*, 38, 40–43, 73–75, 86, 120–21, and caption in illustration cluster after 32.

9. Marshburn, *Murder and Witchcraft in England*, 201–4, 222–27.

10. H[enry] G[oodcole], *Heavens Speedie Hue and Cry Sent After Lust and Murther* . . . (London, 1635), unpaginated; Marshburn, *Murder and Witchcraft in England*, 228–33; on Goodcole, see Sir Leslie Stephen and Sir Sidney Lee, eds., *The Dictionary of National Biography*, 22 vols. (1921–22; rpt. Oxford, 1967–68), 8:119 (cited hereafter as *DNB*). The image of the "Trunchin, or Bastinado" that appears twice in this seventeenth-century English murder pamphlet is quite similar to the image of the "bludgeon" that illustrates a published report of the trial of John Francis Knapp for the murder of Captain Joseph White in Salem, Massachusetts in 1830; image reproduced and discussed in Halttunen, *Murder Most Foul*, 120 and illustration cluster after 90. On nineteenth-century "urban exposés" or "urban mysteries," see Ronald J. Zboray and Mary Saracino Zboray, "The Mysteries of New England: Eugène Sue's American 'Imitators,' 1844," *Nineteenth-Century Contexts* 22 (2000): 457–92; Halttunen, *Murder Most Foul*, 123–26; Cohen, *Pillars of Salt, Monuments of Grace*, 213–15; David S. Reynolds, *Beneath the American Renaissance: The Subversive Imagination in the Age of Emerson and Melville* (Cambridge, Mass., 1988), 82–84, 208–9; Adrienne Siegel, *The Image of the American City in Popular Literature, 1820–1870* (Port Washington, N.Y., 1981), 36–46; Michael Denning, *Mechanic Accents: Dime Novels and Working-Class Culture in America* (London, 1987), 85–117; Louis James, *Fiction for the Working Man, 1830–1850* (London, 1963), 140–41, 165.

11. [Henry Goodcole], *Natures Cruell Step-Dames: Or, Matchless Monsters of the*

Female Sex; Elizabeth Barnes, and Anne Willis . . . (London, 1637), t.p., 1–3; on Halttunen's characterizations of the later "Gothic" mode, see notes 2 and 3 above.

12. Iohn Taylor, *The Unnatural Father: Or, A Cruell Murther committed by one Iohn Rouuse . . . Upon two of his owne Children* (London, 1621), reprinted in Charles Hindley, ed., *The Book Collector's Miscellany: Or, a Collection of Readable Reprints of Literary Rarities . . .* , vol. 4 (London, 1873); Marshburn, *Murder and Witchcraft in England,* 172–73, 198–200, 267–69; *Deeds Against Nature, and Monsters by Kinde . . .* (London, 1614), t.p.; [Goodcole], *Natures Cruell Step-Dames,* t.p. and 2; G[oodcole], *Heavens Speedie Hue and Cry,* unpaginated; for Halttunen's discussion of the characterization of later American murderers as unnatural or subhuman "monsters," see Halttunen, *Murder Most Foul,* 4–6, 46–49, 56–57, 136, 144, 236–40, 244, 248–50; see also Halttunen, "Early American Murder Narratives," 83–85, 91–94.

13. [James Cranford?], *The Teares of Ireland Wherein is Lively Presented as in a Map, a List of the Unheard Off Cruelties and Perfidious Treacheries of Bloud-thirsty Jesuits and the Popish Faction . . .* (London, 1642), unpaginated preliminary leaves, 4, 10, 23, 26, 28–32, 40–47, 55–56, 62, 73, 75, 80, and passim; on Cranford and the attribution of this pamphlet to him, see *DNB,* 5:16–17; on the similar characterizations of murderers as monsters or beasts in American crime pamphlets of the early republic, see citations of Halttunen in note 12 above; also D. A. Cohen, "Social Injustice, Sexual Violence, Spiritual Transcendence: Constructions of Interracial Rape in Early American Crime Literature, 1767–1817," *William and Mary Quarterly,* 3d ser., 56 (July 1999): 510, 512, 517.

14. John Reynolds, *The Triumphs of Gods Revenge Against the Crying and Execrable Sinne of (Wilful and Premeditated) Murther,* 5th ed. (London, 1670), t.p., preliminary leaf "a a 3," and passim; on Reynolds, see *DNB,* 16:933; for the various seventeenth-century editions of his popular compilation, see A. W. Pollard and G. R. Redgrave, comps., *A Short-Title Catalogue of Books Printed in England, Scotland, and Ireland and of English Books Printed Abroad 1475–1640,* 2d ed., rev. and enl. (London, 1976), 2:274; Donald Wing, comp., *Short-Title Catalogue of Brooks Printed in England, Scotland, Ireland, Wales, and British America and of English Books Printed in Other Countries 1641–1700,* rev. ed., 3 vols. (New York, 1988–94), 3:202.

15. For the edition that includes several nonfiction English murder cases, see Reynolds, *Blood for Blood, or Murthers Revenged . . . to Which are Added Five More, Being the Sad Product of Our Times* (Oxford, 1661) (cited in Marshburn, *Murder and Witchcraft in England,* 166); for an example of the sequential "action" engravings, see Figure 2.5b; for the characterizations of murderers as "monsters," see Reynolds, *Triumphs of Gods Revenge* (London, 1670), 44, 45, 104, 280, 317, 334, 344, 345, 376, 467; for the edition of 1778, which includes additional material not by Reynolds, see *God's Revenge Against Murder and Adultery* (London, 1778).

16. See the various seventeenth-century pamphlets already cited; also see Henry Goodcole, *A True Declaration of the Happy Conversion, Contrition, and Christian Preparation of Francis Robinson . . .* (London, 1618); J[ohn] Q[uick], Minister of the Gospel, *Hell Open'd, or, The Infernal Sin of Murther Punished, Being a True Relation of the Poysoning of a Whole Family in Plymouth . . . With An Account of the Several Discourses and Religious Means Used by Divers Godly Ministers to Bring Them to Repentance* (London, 1676). For more on the religious content of early modern English and European crime publications, see Cohen, *Pillars of Salt, Monuments of Grace,* 42–46; Faller, *Turned to Account,* 21–116. On the role of Calvinists, in particular, in producing late seventeenth-century English crime pamphlets, see Faller, *Turned to Account,* 246–47 n. 15, but cf. Cohen, *Pillars of Salt, Monuments of Grace,* 282 n. 23. It should be noted that the second half of the seventeenth century, when English murder

pamphlets tended to become somewhat more religious in content, also saw the emergence of the execution sermon genre in New England.

17. See John H. Langbein, "The Criminal Trial Before the Lawyers," *University of Chicago Law Review* 45 (Winter 1978): 263–316; J. M. Beattie, *Crime and the Courts in England, 1660–1800* (Princeton, N.J., 1986); Halttunen, *Murder Most Foul,* 92–96.

18. [Robert Ferguson], *An Enquiry Into, and Detection of the Barbarous Murther of the Late Earl of Essex* (1684; rpt. London, 1689), 15, 19 (all subsequent citations to the 1689 edition). On Ferguson, see *DNB,* 6:1214–17. the biography of Arthur Capel, Earl of Essex, in *DNB* concludes that the claim that the Earl of Essex was murdered "is utterly without antecedent probability, and is unsupported by trustworthy evidence"; see *DNB,* 3:921–26, quotation 925.

19. [Ferguson], *Enquiry,* 3, 8, 26–40, 43–45, 47–71, passim. The summary in this paragraph is not exhaustive; Ferguson cited other evidence and made other arguments as well.

20. For references to the case as a "mystery," see Ferguson, *Enquiry,* 8, 28, 36, 57, 72.

21. *Tryal of Spencer Cowper, Esq; John Marson, Ellis Stevens, and William Rogers, Gent. Upon an Indictment for the Murther of Mrs. Sarah Stout, a Quaker* (London, 1699). The biographer of Spencer Cowper in *DNB* argues that the "innocence" of the defendants in this case was "beyond a doubt, as was admitted by impartial people at the time"; the author further suggests that the prosecution was instigated by Cowper's political enemies and by Quakers who wanted to clear the victim, and hence their denomination, of "the reproach of suicide" (*DNB,* 4:1311–12).

22. *Tryal of Spencer Cowper,* 3–17, 28–31, quotation 4. For Halttunen's discussion of forensic testimony in murder pamphlets of the early republic, see *Murder Most Foul,* 77–78, 165–66, 172–98, passim.

23. *Tryal of Spencer Cowper,* 17–37, quotation 26–27, 32, and 35; the phrase "Love-fit" (35) was the prosecutor's characterization of Cowper's claim.

24. Estelle Fox Kleiger, *The Trial of Levi Weeks or the Manhattan Well Mystery* (New York, 1989), 1–3, 51; D. A. Cohen, "Pillars of Salt: The Transformation of New England Crime Literature, 1674–1860" (Ph.D. diss. Brandeis University, 1989), 353–55.

25. Kleiger, *The Trial of Levi Weeks or The Manhattan Well Mystery,* quotations 115, 130, 146, 168; Cohen, "Pillars of Salt: The Transformation of New England Crime Literature, 1674–1860" 355, 357–58, 364, 366–73. Subsequent examples of sex-related homicides of the early republic in which defense lawyers assailed the character of the female victim include the cases of Avery/Cornell (1832–33), Jewett/Robinson (1836), and Tirrell/Bickford (1845–47). I discuss crimes of sexual violence and their literary depiction in "Heroic Women Found: Transgressive Feminism, Popular Biography, and the 'Tragical Deaths of Beautiful Females,'" *Proceedings of the American Antiquarian Society* 109 (October 1999): 51–97; "Social Injustice, Sexual Violence, Spiritual Transcendence," 481–526; "The Beautiful Female Murder Victim: Literary Genres and Courtship Practices in the Origins of a Cultural Motif, 1590–1850," *Journal of Social History* 31 (Winter 1997): 277–306; *Pillars of Salt, Monuments of Grace,* 167–248. See also Halttunen, *Murder Most Foul,* 172–207; Halttunen, "'Domestic Differences': Competing Narratives of Womanhood in the Murder Trial of Lucretia Chapman," in Shirley Samuels, ed., *The Culture of Sentiment: Race, Gender, and Sentimentality in Nineteenth-Century America* (New York, 1992), 39–57; Patricia Cline Cohen, *The Murder of Helen Jewett: The Life and Death of a Prostitute in Nineteenth-Century New York* (New York, 1998); P. C. Cohen, "The Mystery of Helen Jewett: Romantic Fiction and the Eroticization of Violence," *Legal Studies Forum* 17:2 (1993): 133–45; David Anthony, "The Helen Jewett Panic:

Tabloids, Men, and the Sensational Public Sphere in Antebellum New York," *American Literature* 69 (September 1997): 487–514; Amy Gilman Srebnick, *The Mysterious Death of Mary Rogers: Sex and Culture in Nineteenth-Century New York* (New York, 1995); Andie Tucher, *Froth and Scum: Truth, Beauty, Goodness, and the Ax Murder in America's First Mass Medium* (Chapel Hill, N.C., 1994), 21–96; David Richard Kasserman, *Fall River Outrage: Life, Murder, and Justice in Early Industrial New England* (Philadelphia, 1986); William G. McLoughlin, "Untangling the Tiverton Tragedy: The Social Meaning of the Terrible Haystack Murder of 1833," *Journal of American Culture* 7 (Winter 1984): 75–84.

26. [Rev. Paul Williams?], *The Vain Prodigal Life, and Tragical Penitent Death of Thomas Hellier* (London, 1680), 1–2 and passim; for more on this case and publication, see T. H. Breen, James H. Lewis, and Keith Schlesinger, "Motive for Murder: A Servant's Life in Virginia, 1678," *William and Mary Quarterly*, 3d ser., 40 (January 1983): 106–20.

27. *Blood Will Out, Or, An Example of Justice in the Tryal, Condemnation, Confession, and Execution of Thomas Lutherland . . .* (Philadelphia, 1692), 16 and passim. This pamphlet is reproduced, with some scholarly annotations relating to the history and practice of "Bier Right" or the blood test, in Joseph S. Sickler, ed., *Rex Et Regina vs Lutherland . . .* (Woodstown, N.J., 1948). For the phrase quoted from Halttunen, see *Murder Most Foul*, 38.

28. Cohen, *Pillars of Salt, Monuments of Grace*, 3–24. For Halttunen's somewhat different chronology, see *Murder Most Foul*, 2, 35–37; "Early American Murder Narratives," 67–68, 76–78.

29. For more details and documentation, see Cohen, *Pillars of Salt, Monuments of Grace*, 7–13, 66–69, 249. For the sensationalistic quotation from a sermon volume of the 1720s, see Benjamin Colman, *It is a Fearful Thing to Fall Into the Hands of the Living God . . .* (Boston, 1726), 30; for similar salty dialogue, see [Cotton Mather], *The Vial Poured Out Upon the Sea . . .* (Boston, 1726), 3 and passim.

30. For more on execution broadsides and the other eighteenth-century crime genres referred to here, see Cohen, *Pillars of Salt, Monuments of Grace*, 13–25, 117–63, 249–50.

31. For more detailed documentation (and appropriate qualifications) of this summary, see Cohen, *Pillars of Salt, Monuments of Grace*, 26–38, 167–253; for other accounts of the nineteenth-century literature, see Halttunen, *Murder Most Foul*, 33–240, and the various books and articles cited in notes 1 and 25 above.

32. Halttunen, *Murder Most Foul*, 55–56, 116, 123–71, 208–40; Cohen, *Pillars of Salt, Monuments of Grace*, 26–36, 147–49, 161–246.

33. While not the deus ex machina implied by Halttunen, Enlightenment ideas did sometimes influence the content of early American crime publications, including execution sermons. Aside from Puritan cultural dominance, another early obstacle to "sensationalistic" images of crime and punishment was the apparent inability of many early American printers to produce or otherwise obtain illustrations for their publications, a technical barrier that was only gradually overcome over the century 1730–1830. Halttunen also emphasizes the impact of the new trial system.

Chapter 3. A Tale of Two Cities

1. John Donne, Meditation 17.
2. A good introduction to the rituals of death may be found in Richard Hunting-

ton and Peter Metcalf, *Celebrations of Death: The Anthropology of Mortuary Ritual* (Cambridge, 1979).

3. Thucydides, "Plague of Athens" in *the History of the Peloponnesian War,* Edgar Allen Poe, "The Masque of the Red Death"; Albert Camus, *La Peste* (Paris, 1947). Other authors who have written about the distorting effects of epidemics include Giovanni Boccaccio, *The Decameron* (bubonic plague, Florence, 1348); Daniel Defoe, *A Journal of the Plague Year* (bubonic plague, London, 1665); Katherine Anne Porter, "Pale Horse, Pale Rider" (influenza, 1918); and Michael Crichton, *The Andromeda Strain* (New York, 1969) (science fiction).

4. For an overview of epidemics in early America, see John Duffy, *Epidemics in Colonial America* (Baton Rouge, La., 1953).

5. Elizabeth Drinker, *The Diary of Elizabeth Drinker,* ed. by Elaine F. Crane, 3 vols. (Boston, 1991). The diary runs from 1758 to 1807; Cotton Mather, *The Diary of Cotton Mather,* ed. by Worthington C. Ford, 2 vols., Massachusetts Historical Society Collections, 7th ser., vols. 7 and 8 (Boston, 1911–12). In most of what follows, I will refer to the dates of the entries, often in the text, rather than provide a long series of page numbers. Moreover, I will modernize spelling and punctuation, as both have somewhat different styles, and there is little to be gained in struggling with their vagaries.

6. Fischer's four deathways are (1) Puritan Massachusetts (greater New England); (2) Anglican Virginia (Tidewater South); (3) Quaker Delaware Valley (New Jersey, Pennsylvania, Delaware, Northern Maryland); and (4) backcountry Southern Highlands. See David H. Fischer, *Albion's Seed: Four British Folkways in America* (New York, 1989), 111–16, 326–32, 517–22, 697–702, 813.

7. I have described nine stages in the rituals of death which were common in English America over several centuries and which have deep roots in European Christian tradition in Robert V. Wells, *Facing the "King of Terrors": Death and Society in an American Community, 1750–1990* (New York, 2000), 15 and passim.

8. Drinker, *Diary,* 2: 1022–39.

9. Ibid., 3: 2079–82.

10. Ibid., 1: 386.

11. For discussions of these two epidemics in a different context, see Kenneth Silverman, *The Life and Times of Cotton Mather* (New York, 1984), 261–75, 335–63. On Mather's role in the introduction of inoculation, see Otho T. Beall, Jr., "Cotton Mather, the First Significant Figure in American Medicine," *Bulletin of the History of Medicine* 26 (1952): 103–66. Although most Bostonians accepted inoculation by 1752, the initial response was hostile, which, with reciprocal anger on Mather's part, left him isolated from much of his community. No doubt a greater number of fatalities (850 from smallpox; 160 from measles), a longer presence in town (twelve as opposed to two months), and a more loathsome physical appearance enhanced the social tensions that resulted during the 1721 epidemic. For one of the first pieces of statistical proof of the efficacy of a treatment, see the table on the adoption of inoculation in Boston published in 1794 in the Massachusetts Historical Society *Collections,* 1st ser., vol. 3 (Boston, 1794), 292. I have reprinted this table in Robert V. Wells, *Revolutions in Americans' Lives* (Westport, Conn., 1982), 36. Silverman, *Cotton Mather,* 269, 359, provides statistics at slight variance from the totals in the 1794 account.

12. Mather, *Diary,* 2: 248–72, contains the entries on the measles epidemic.

13. Ibid., October 24, 27, and 30.

14. Ibid., October 27–29; November 4

15. Ibid., November 7 and 8.

16. Ibid., November 9, 11, and 14.

17. Ibid., November 20 and 21.

18. Ibid., November 22.

19. Ibid., December 5.

20. Ibid., 290. Following this summary Mather wrote a Latin phrase that can be translated as follows: "These are the sons and daughters whom God gave [to me] as a most underserved source of woe." There is, here, a double meaning in that "underserved" can refer both to his own personal sense of not deserving such trials and to his desire that his children should be a source of happiness and not woe. The Latin phrase is *Quos nubi Indignissimo Deus dedit Fillii Filiaeque.* My colleagues Jeannette and Steven Sargent, a classicist and medievalist respectively, have rendered the probable meaning.

21. Ibid., 618–70 includes his discussions of this epidemic.

22. Ibid., May 28.

23. Ibid., June 22 and 24.

24. Ibid., July 16. Data published in 1794 indicate 247 were inoculated out of 6,000 who contracted the disease; see Wells, *Revolutions,* 36. For Boylston's activities, see Silverman, *Cotton Mather,* 341–43, 349.

25. Mather *Diary,* July 18.

26. Ibid., July 16, 18, 27, 30; August 6, 18, 22, 24, 27, 28; September 4.

27. Ibid., September 29.

28. Ibid., September 23; October 7, 15, and 28.

29. Ibid., October 18 and 25.

30. Ibid., October 29, November 3 and 4.

31. Ibid., November 14, 658 n. 1.

32. Ibid., November 19.

33. Ibid., November 23, 24, and 30; December 4 and 14.

34. Ibid., December 3 and 9. The printer was Benjamin Franklin's older brother, James, who linked Mather's advocacy of inoculation with his support for the witchcraft trials in Salem thirty years earlier.

35. Ibid., December 16 and 20; January 4.

36. This epidemic has received a great deal of attention from historians. The best-known account is J. M. Powell, *Bring Out Your Dead: The Great Plague of Yellow Fever in Philadelphia in 1793* (Philadelphia, 1949; rpt. 1993). A recent collection of essays on the topic, none of which discuss the rituals of death, is J. Worth Estes and Billy G. Smith, eds., *A Melancholy Scene of Devastation: The Public Response to the 1793 Philadelphia Yellow Fever Epidemic* (Philadelphia, 1997).

37. Drinker, *Diary,* 1:96.

38. Susan Klepp, " 'How Many Precious Souls Are Fled'? The Magnitude of the 1793 Yellow Fever Epidemic," in Estes and Smith, *Melancholy Scene,* 166–73. Five years after the epidemic, Charles Brockden Brown set his novel, *Arthur Mervyn, or Memoirs of the Year 1793,* in and around Philadelphia during the height of the crisis. See esp. chapters 13–21, part 1.

39. Drinker, *Diary,* 1:488 n. 7.

40. In all, Drinker listed 414 names of victims. On October 29, she mentioned that a newspaper had reported a total of 2,730 deaths.

41. See August 23, 25, 27, and 31 for possible causes. Although it would be a century before mosquitoes were identified as the transmitters of the infection, Drinker twice made observations that could have led to that conclusion. On October 5, she remarked that the weather had been cool several times when the epidemic seemed to be abating. On October 26, she observed that no one in Germantown had been infected by any of those who had arrived from the city already sick. One either had

the disease from exposure in the city or was spared. No doubt mosquitoes were present in Germantown, and no one would have observed that they were not the dangerous *aedes aegypti* to be found near the wharves.

42. Ibid., September 1, 4, and 16.

43. Ibid., September 3, 24.

44. Ibid., September 4, 6, 9, 10, 12, 14, and 30.

45. Ibid., September 23, 24, and 28.

46. Ibid., September 30; October 4.

47. See ibid., October 5, 11, 16, and 17. Brown, *Arthur Mervyn,* chapters 15 and 17, part 1, refers to the dangers of being buried alive by careless attendants.

48. Ibid., October 9. For returning to normal rituals, see November 7 and 24.

49. Ibid., November 19–23.

Chapter 4. Death and Satire

1. No. 63. (Saturday, May 12, 1711), in *The Spectator* (London, 1898), 1:334.

2. Karl S. Guthke, *The Gender of Death: A Cultural History of Art and Literature* (Cambridge, 1999), 44, 103–4. For Manuel's roles as Protestant humorist, see Carlos M. N. Eire, *War Against Idols: The Reformation of Worship from Erasmus to Calvin* (Cambridge, 1986), 108.

3. E. McClung Fleming, "The American Image As Indian Princess, 1765–1783," *Winterthur Portfolio* 2 (1965): 65, 67. Fleming establishes the Indian Queen as antecedent of the Indian princess, who symbolizes America's position in the British political family as a daughter. The queen referred to America as a continent, while the princess compared America to a subordinate colony.

4. Rachel Doggett with Monique Hulvey and Julie Ainsworth, eds., *New World of Wonders: European Images of the Americas, 1492–1700* (Seattle, 1992), 37; and Anne McClintock, *Imperial Leather: Race, Gender, and Sexuality in the Colonial Contest* (New York, 1995), 25.

5. Alden T. Vaughan, "People of Wonder: England Encounters the New World's Natives," in *New World of Wonders,* 15–16; and McClintock, *Imperial Leather,* 26–27.

6. Jonathan Sawday, *The Body Emblazoned: Dissection and the Human Body in Renaissance Culture* (London, 1995), 23, 27–28.

7. The *O.E.D.* identifies the first usage of Britannia as occurring in 893 A.D., but the earliest coin with the female Britannia figure is the copper halfpenny of 1672; see the *Compact Edition of the Oxford English Dictionary,* 118.

8. For a discussion the Woman Warrior (and its variations, such as the Female Volunteer), see Dianne Dugaw, *Warrior Women and Popular Balladry, 1650–1850* (Chicago, 1996).

9. For Franklin as a prolific propagandist, see J. A. Leo Lemay, "Benjamin Franklin," in Everett Emerson, ed. *Major Writers of Early American Literature* (Madison, Wis., 1972), 226. For the printing and distribution of the notecards, see Edwin Wolf II, "Benjamin Franklin's Stamp Act Cartoon," *Proceedings of the American Philosophical Society* 99 (December 1955): 390, 392; also see Vernon Crane, "Benjamin Franklin and the Stamp Act," Colonial Society of Massachusetts, *Transactions* 32 (1933–37): 56–77; Lester C. Olsen, "Benjamin Franklin's Pictorial Representation of the British Colonies in America: A Study in Rhetorical Iconology," *Journal of Speech* 73 (February 1987): 29–31.

10. Karen Severud Cook, "Benjamin Franklin and the Snake That Would Not Die," *British Library Journal* 22 (1996): 88–90.

11. Franklin also used an organic or human trope to describe the national body

in 1761. In his extract, "The Jesuit Campanella's Means of Disposing the Enemy to Peace," *London Chronicle*, August 13, 1761, taken from a 1629 edition of Campanella's discourses, he quotes a relevant passage. Campanella uses "cut off" and "smaller limbes and members" in reference to colonies severed through economic competition; he suggests that the limbs supply nourishment to the body, and, if weakened, the nation suffers. See J. A. Leo Lemay, ed., *Benjamin Franklin: Writings* (New York, 1987), 535–36. One of the most popular British pamphlets, Samuel Johnson's *Taxation No Tyranny*, later capitalizes on this same theme by linking the colonies with amputation. Johnson stated that just as infected limbs were removed from the body, so, too, could the colonies be cut from the empire. The pamphlet's full title was *Taxation No Tyranny; An Answer to the Resolution and Address of the American Congress* (London, 1775). See Lester C. Olsen, *Emblems of American Community in the Revolutionary Era: A Study in Rhetorical Iconology* (Washington, D.C., 1991), 207.

12. Both the Hogarth print and *The Conduct of the Two B[utche]rs* are a response to the Murder Act. This law was framed in 1749 in response to the Penlez riots, which were provoked by the Company of Surgeons taking bodies for dissection. It was not passed until 1752, and it specifically designated that criminals who were convicted for murder would be dissected. See Ronald Paulson, *Popular and Polite Art in the Age of Hogarth and Fielding* (South Bend, Ind., 1979), 7–8.

13. For the earlier print, see Leonard W. Labaree, ed., *The Papers of Benjamin Franklin* (New Haven, Conn., 1969), 13:455–56; Cook, "Benjamin Franklin," 97. Hogarth's print appeared February 1, 1751. See *Catalogue of Prints and Drawings in the British Museum*, Division I, *Political and Personal Satires*, prepared by Edward Hawkins (London, 1870–83), 1:835.

14. While there is no written record that Franklin saw a dissection, Dr. Brian Owen-Smith, president of the Hunterian Society, agrees that it is "inconceivable" that Franklin did not observe dissection through his connection with the Hunter brothers or William Hewson. For the nature of the professional and personal relationships among Hunter, Hewson, and Franklin, see Garland Howard Bailey, "William Hewson, F.R.S.," *Annals of Medical History* 5 (1923): 210–12, 214, 218–19.

15. The same interest in dissection made its way to the colonies. The physician William Shippen built the first anatomical theater in Philadelphia in the 1760s. In 1763, Samuel Clossy, an Irish anatomist, gave a course of lectures in New York. See Michael Sappol, "The Cultural Politics of Anatomy in Nineteenth-Century America: Death, Dissection, and Embodied Social Identity" (Ph.D. diss., Columbia University, 1997), 71–72, 141–42; and Ruth Richardson, *Death, Dissection, and the Destitute* (Chicago, 2000), 37, 64.

16. See L. J. Jordanova, "Gender, Generation, and Science: William Hunter's Obstetrical Atlas," in *William Hunter and the Eighteenth-Century Medical World* (Cambridge, 1985), 388, 395. For information on Hunter's engravings before their official publication in 1774, see C. Helen Brock, *Calendar of the Correspondence of Dr. William Hunter 1740–1783* (Cambridge, 1996), esp. 6, 9, 31, 33; and John L. Thorton, F.L.A., *Jan Van Rymskyk: Medical Artist of the Eighteenth Century* (Cambridge, 1982), 22, 29.

17. The *New York Gazette* published a harangue against Clossy's public dissections, describing the single corpse as a "raw head and bloody bones," which had been hacked to pieces by a 'tribe of dissectors." See Steven R. Wilf, "Anatomy and Punishment in Late Eighteenth-Century New York," *Journal of Social History* 22 (1989): 510. For dissections of women hung for murder and infanticide in the seventeenth century, as well as the desire of surgeons to find female subjects of childbearing age, see Sawday, *Body Emblazoned*, 61, 220–21; also see Richardson, *Death, Dissection* 27–30, 32, 35–37; and Sappol, "Cultural Politics," 141. As another scholar has ar-

gued, between 1760 and 1915, social outcasts, black people, the very poor, criminals, prostitutes, Indians, the Irish and recent immigrants, made up the great proportion of anatomical subjects. See David C. Humphrey, "Dissection and Discrimination: The Social Origins of Cadavers in America, 1760–1915," *Transactions of the New York Academy of Medicine* 49 (1973): 819–27.

18. Hawkins, *Catalogue of Prints and Drawings*, 1:835.

19. If Belisarius represented the fallen man, then an extract from Machiavelli's *Discourses on Livy* offered Franklin his ideal image of manhood. He sent this extract to the *London Chronicle*, along with instructions adopted by the Boston town meeting (September 18, 1765) and the Braintree meeting (September 24). The instructions and extract were printed January 7–9, 1766. The extract recounts the appearance of the chiefs of the rebellious Privernates for sentencing at the Roman Senate. Because the Senate was impressed that one of the leaders had spoken "like a Man and like a Freeman," it pardoned the rebels and granted them citizenship, declaring "that they deserved to be Romans, whose liberty was the greatest part of their care." See *Papers of Benjamin Franklin*, 13:26–28.

20. Cook, "Benjamin Franklin," 90–91. The original broadside of the later Stamp Act print is in the Graphic Collection of the Library Company of Philadelphia.

21. *Papers of Benjamin Franklin*, 13:170, 189.

22. Ibid., 47–48.

23. Samuel Johnson, *Dictionary of the English Language* (Philadelphia, 1813), folio edition, part II, pp. 2, 132.

24. Olsen suggests that Franklin's print portrays Britannia's suicide, especially because her own spear is pointed at her breast. Yet it is just as likely that Franklin regards British officials and their laws (backed by brute force), to be inflicting wounds on the nation—Britannia. This view of the law can be found in Franklin's earlier satire, "The Speech of Miss Polly Baker" (1747), in which a young woman, charged with fornication, pleads her case before a judge. She argues that the law is wrong (like the Stamp Act) and should be repealed because it generates greater harm by forcing many women to acts of infanticide and abortion. Abortion is another form of self-mutilation. Franklin's decision to portray Britannia displaying her injuries (there is no perpetrator in the picture) also invokes the commonly used image of self-dissection, in which the subject lifts his or her skin and reveals the internal organs to the audience. As Sawday points out, self-dissection images drew on images of the wounded Christ. As a wounded victim, Christ was feminized by the "willingness" of the divine victim to subject himself to the penetration of the crucifixion—the thorns, nails, and the soldier's spear—thus associating the violence of passion with a feminine erotic response to suffering. See Olsen, *Emblems of American Community*, 204. For a discussion of "The Speech of Miss Polly Baker" and unjust laws, see Linda Kay Bates, "Toward the Heart of Darkness: Benjamin Franklin's Satires (Ph.D. diss., University of California, Davis, 1981), 100–101; and for self-dissection, see Sawday, *Body Emblazoned*, 110–12, 121.

25. J. R. Hale, "Women and War in the Visual Arts of the Renaissance," in J. R. Mulryne and Margaret Shewring, eds., *War, Literature and the Arts in Sixteenth-Century Europe* (New York, 1989), 48–49.

26. See *The Colonies Reduced, Its Companion* [1768], in Joan D. Dolmetsch, *Rebellion and Reconciliation: Satirical Prints on the Revolution at Williamsburg* (Williamsburg, Va., 1976), 43.

27. The color version of the Dutch print, *Great Britain Mutilated*, can be found in the collection of political cartoons, *Dutch Caricatures of the American War* (177–1780) in the John Carter Brown Library, Providence, R.I. In the *Connecticut Gazette*, June 21, 1755, a report described how a master tied his eloping servant to his horse's tale.

"The horse took fright, flung the master off, and ran several miles, tearing the woman, 'the poor Creature Limb from Limb.' When the horse was recaptured, nothing was found hanging to his tail but her two hands and part of her arms." See Cornelia Hughes Dayton, "Satire and Sensationalism: The Emergence of Misogyny in Mid-Eighteenth-Century Newspapers and Almanacs" (Paper presented at the New England Seminar at the American Antiquarian Society, Worcester, Mass., November 15, 1991), 15, 18–19. For similar stories of "mangled" bodies of women, see Susan Dion, "Women in the *Boston Gazette*, 1755–1775," *Historical Journal of Massachusetts* 14 (June 1986): 94.

28. Andromeda means "ruler of men," and she was an appropriate allegorical reference for Britannia. In the tale, Andromeda is chained to the rock by her parents, and about to be eaten by a monster, until she is saved by Perseus. She has no voice in her fate; she neither defies the gods nor her parents, and she does not choose her mate. See Adrienne Auslander Munich, *Andromeda's Chains: Gender and Interpretation in Victorian Literature and Art* (New York, 1989), 12–13, 16, 30.

29. Revere's engraving appeared in the *Royal American Magazine*, March 1775. See William H. Helfand, *Medical and Pharmacy in American Political Prints (1765–1870)* (Madison, Wis., 1978), 35.

30. Hopkinson's poem was printed in the *Pennsylvania Packet*, April 22, 1778. See Bruce Ingram Granger, *Political Satire in the American Revolution, 1763–1783* (Ithaca, N.Y., 1960), 96.

31. Dolmetsch, *Rebellion and Reconciliation*, 174–75, 190–91.

32. Jordanova, "Gender, Generation," 385. Surgeons eagerly sought pregnant women (or those of childbearing age) for dissection, prizing such corpses. Dissection (and grave robbing) were acts compared to rape, seen as an unnatural violation of the body. See Sawday, *Body Emblazoned*, 220–21; Sappol, "Cultural Politics," 116. It was common for women to die in childbirth, especially from puerperal or childbirth fever. Eighteenth-century physicians and midwives described puerperal fever as a "fierce and untamed enemy," "a secret revengeful foe," using the analogy of an internal conspiracy and rebellion to explain the disease. See Jo Murphy-Lawless, *Reading Birth and Death: A History of Obstetric Thinking* (Bloomington, 1998), 105.

33. See Franklin's *Observations concerning the Increase of Mankind, Peopling of Countries, etc.* (1755). In this text as well, Franklin compared Britain to the nourishing mother who would not restrain growth. He wrote, "A wise and good mother would not do it. To distress is to weaken, and weakening the children weakens the whole family." See Carl Van Doren, *Benjamin Franklin* (New York, 1938), 216–17. It is important to remember that Franklin equated abortion with self-mutilation, thus contrasting the harsh rule of law (fornication laws) with natural increase. He did so in his satire "The Speech of Miss Polly Baker" (1747); see n. 24 above for a more detailed summary of this point.

34. See David A. Wilson, ed., *Peter Porcupine in America: Pamphlets on Republicanism and Revolution* (Ithaca, N.Y., 1994), 2, 8, 10; and Karen List, "The Role of William Cobbett in Philadelphia Party Press, 1794–1799," *Journalism Monographs* 82 (1993): 1, 23.

35. Abigail Adams to Mary Cranch, May 7, 1798, in Stewart Mitchell, ed., "New Letters of Abigail Adams," *Proceedings of the American Antiquarian Society* 55 (April-October, 1945): 347.

36. Wilson, *Peter Porcupine in America*, 23; List, "The Role of William Cobbett," 7; James Morton Smith, *Freedom's Fetters: The Alien and Sedition Laws and American Civil Liberties* (Ithaca, N.Y., 1956), 7.

37. Marie Hélèn Huet, *Mourning Glory: The Will of the French Revolution* (Philadelphia, 1997), 34.

38. Print Collection of the New York Historical Society, New York, N.Y., negative 2737.

39. Gallatin was one of Cobbett's frequent targets. He published a cartoon of Gallatin in 1796, with the guillotine in the background, the pun on Gallatin's name, and a slight variation on the tag line: "Stop de Wheels of the Government." See Wilson, *Peter Porcupine in America,* 237.

40. Washington had retired from the presidency and had been appointed lieutenant general by Adams in preparation for a war with France. See Noble E. Cunningham, *Popular Images of the Presidency from Washington to Lincoln* (Columbia, Mo., 1991), 181.

41. List, "The Role of William Cobbett," 7. The term "savage speech" comes from Sandra M. Gustafson, *Eloquence Is Power: Oratory and Performance in Early America* (Chapel Hill, N.C., 2000). Bache died in 1798, but in 1799, Federalist William Pickering sent Adams a copy of the *Aurora,* and he agreed that William Duane, Bache's successor, deserved prosecution under the Alien and Sedition Acts. See Walt Brown, *John Adams and the American Press: Politics and Journalism at the Birth of the Republic* (Jefferson, N.C., 1995), 102.

42. This print imitates a device developed in older satirical prints. Hogarth specifically used the dog to express contempt. He shows a dog urinating on Charles Churchill's *Epistle to William Hogarth,* a work that was a vicious personal attack on Hogarth. See Paulson, *Popular and Polite Art,* 51, 56.

43. As Hannah Arendt contended, theories of the public sphere are premised on the idea that "sheer violence is mute." See Arendt, *The Human Condition* (Chicago, 1958), 26.

44. The words of French radical Vergniaud, spoken in 1793, were "The revolution devours its own children." See Paulson, *Popular and Polite Art,* 24; also P. Viola, "The Rites of Cannibalism and the French Revolution," *Quaderno,* 3 (1992): 157–74; and D. Binderman, "Revolution Soup, dished up with human flesh and French pot herbs': Burke's Reflections and the Visual Culture of Late Eighteenth-Century England," in G. Sutherland, ed., *British Art 1740–1820: Essays in Honor of Robert R. Wark* (San Marino, Calif., 1995), 125–43.

45. For a discussion of "overkill"—the pattern of stabbing and mutilating bodies even after the victim is fatally shot, which is still common in homosexual murders, see Kendall Thomas, "Beyond the Privacy Principle," *Columbia Law Review* 92 (1992): 1466. Cobbett also published a German translation of an account of the French invasion of Germany that characterized the French in the same manner as uncivilized brutes and murdering savages. See Anthony Aufrere, *The Cannibal's Progress: Or, The Dreadful Horrors of French Invasion, as Displayed by the Republican Officers and Soldiers, in their Perfidy, Rapacity, Ferociousness, and Brutality, exercised towards the Innocent Inhabitants of Germany. Translated from the German, by Anthony Aufrer, [sic] Esq.* (Philadelphia, 1798).

46. Peter Porcupine [William Cobbett], *The Bloody Buoy, thrown out as a warning to the Political Pilots of all Nations, or a Faithful Relation of the Multitude of Acts of Horrid Barbarity, such as the Eye Never Witnessed, the tongue never expressed, or the Imagination conceived, until the Commencement of the French Revolution, to which is added, as instructive essay, tracing the dreadful effects to the real causes* (Philadelphia, 1797), 206, 107, 116, 130, 207. I use two versions of *The Bloody Buoy* in this chapter, one is a longer, book-length narrative, the other a pamphlet. Hereafter the book is identified as Cobbett, *The Bloody Buoy,* and the pamphlet as Cobbett, "The Bloody Buoy," in Wilson, *Peter Porcupine in America.*

47. Huet asserts that the post Thermidorian caricatures in France "portrayed a

feminized Terror, closely associating the disorder of revolutionary history with the fury of women." See Huet, *Mourning Glory,* 177.

48. Cobbett called the French Republic a "many-headed hydra," and he feminized France as a "whore," "guilty of polygamy," indicating unquenchable sexual desire. The horror and atrocities, he claimed, had turned France into "a gloomy wilderness with rivers of human blood." Here, again, he implied a blood lust, or unending flow of human blood. See Wilson, *Peter Porcupine in America,* 27–29, 154.

49. For Fisher Ames's quotation, see his *An Oration on the Sublime Virtues of George Washington . . .* (Dedham, Mass., 1800) cited in Gustafson, *Eloquence Is Power,* 240. The reference to "the furies of hell," in the "shape of the vilest of women," comes from Edmund Burke, *Reflections on the Revolution in France,* ed. Conor Cruise O'Brien (Baltimore, 1968), 165.

50. Cobbett, "A Bone to Gnaw," in Wilson, *Peter Porcupine in America,* 104, 113.

51. For "fiery Frenchified Dames," see *Porcupine's Gazette,* July 27, 1798, quoted in Karen List, "Two Party's Papers' Political Coverage of Women in the New Republic," *Critical Studies in Mass Communication* 2 (1995): 156–57; also see Susan Branson, *These Fiery Frenchfield Dames: Women and Political Culture in Early National Philadelphia* (Philadelphia, 2001), 73; and for the "terrible termagants," see "A Bone to Gnaw," in Wilson, *Peter Porcupine in America,* 112–13. For the importance of the sexual style of party rhetoric, see David Waldstreicher, "Federalism, the Styles of Politics, and the Politics of Style," in Doron Ben-Atar and Barbara B. Oberg, eds., *Federalism Reconsidered* (Charlottesville, Va., 1998), 108, 115–17.

52. As Daniel Cohen shows in his chapter in this volume, domesticated violence (here meaning violence enacted in a domestic setting) can be traced back to the early modern period. The Catholic uprising in Ireland was portrayed in Puritan propaganda in similar ways: a woman's fetus was ripped from her womb, cannibalism flourished, and parents were forced to watch their children murdered. The connection (as explained in the introduction) is English anti-Catholicism that surfaced in propaganda against the Irish and French, and the fear that domestic uprisings (like slave rebellions) were more violent than normal warfare. As Simon Newman persuasively contends, Federalists (and Cobbett) blamed actual rebellions (Gabriel's slave rebellion in Virginia in 1800 and Fries' rebellion in Pennsylvania in 1798) on the "contagion of liberty" spread by the French Revolution. See Newman, "The World Turned Upside Down: Revolutionary Politics, Fries' and Gabriel's Rebellions, and the Fears of the Federalists," *Pennsylvania History* 67 (2000): 5–20.

53. "The Bloody Buoy," in Wilson, *Peter Porcupine in America,* 144.

54. Cobbett, *The Bloody Buoy,* 6.

55. "The Bloody Buoy," in Wilson, *Peter Porcupine in America,* 152.

56. "Unexampled Cruelty: A Fragment of the Reign of Robespierre," *Philadelphia Minerva,* June 11, 1796, cited in Patricia Leigh Riley Dunlap, "Constructing the Republican Woman: American Periodical Response to the Women of the French Revolution, 1789–1844" (Ph.D. diss., George Mason University, 1999), 111.

57. "The Crimes committed during the French Revolution," *The New Star; A Republican, Miscellaneous, Literary Paper* (September 26, 1797), 194, cited in Dunlap, "Constructing the Republican Woman," 117.

58. Princess de Lambelle was mutilated and killed in the September massacres of 1793. She was a close friend of the queen. She was beheaded, the corpse was raped, the genitalia excised, and the head paraded on a pike before the prison where the king and queen were held. See Camille Naish, *Death Comes to the Maiden: Sex and Execution, 1431–1933* (London, 1991), 128.

59. Ibid., 77–78, 104–9.

60. The article in the *National Gazette* appeared April 13, 1793; see Branson, *These*

Fiery Frenchified Dames, 67. An engraving entitled *The Guillotine* was published in the *Massachusetts Magazine,* January 1794.

61. An advertisement appeared in the *Aurora* in 1794. See Branson, *These Fiery Frenchified Dames,* 67.

62. This reaction was reported by John De Peyster to Charles Willson Peale. See Ellen Fernandez Sacco, "Spectacular Masculinities: The Museums of Peale, Baker, and Bowen in the Early Republic" (Ph.D. diss., University of California, Los Angeles, 1998), 25–26.

63. Wilson, *Peter Porcupine in America,* 97–98, 198–200.

64. Anonymous artist, *Cinqué Tetes, or the Paris Monster,* print at the Henry E. Huntington Library, San Marino, Calif.

65. For Cobbett's satire on the sexual dealings in the XYZ affair, see [William Cobbett], *French Arrogance; or, "The Cate Let Out of the Bag"; A Poetical Dialogue Between the Envoys of America, and X, Y, Z and the Lady* (Philadelphia, 1798); also see Alexander DeConde, *The Quasi-War: The Politics and Diplomacy of the Undeclared War with France 1797–1801* (New York, 1966), 46, 48, 51.

66. Pascal Dupay describes the figure as "Liberty, fallen from grace in tatters," but fails to mention the Medusa-like head. See "The French Revolution in American Satirical Prints," *Print Quarterly* 15 (December 1998): 379.

67. The medusa head imagery came from Britain. A 1792 print, called *The Contrast,* compared Britannia (symbolizing prosperity, happiness, and morality) to French Liberty (symbolizing anarchy, murder, equality, madness, and cruelty). The French emblem is a woman with wild, snake-like hair, carrying a head on a pike, and standing on the headless trunk of a man. See Neil Hertz, "Medusa's Head: Male Hysteria Under Political Pressure," *Representations* 4 (Autumn 1983): 27–28.

68. For a description of this print, see William Murrell, *A History of Graphic Humor,* vol. 1 (1747–1865) (New York, 1933), 39.

69. In an article published in the United States, "Anecdotes: Marat," *Universal Magazine* (February 20, 1797), 240, Charlotte Corday, the decapitated assassin of Marat, was called "the Medusa's head of the revolution." See Dunlap, "Constructing the Republican Woman," 118.

70. *The Suppressed History of the Administration of John Adams, from 1797 to 1801 as printed and suppressed in 1802 by John Woods; now published with Notes, an Appendix by John Henry Sherburne* (Philadelphia, 1846).

71. Wilson, *Peter Porcupine in America,* 41; List, "The Role of William Cobbett," 27–28.

72. *The Last Confession and Dying Speech of Peter Porcupine, with an Account of his Dissection* (Philadelphia, 1797), 27–33.

Chapter 5. Immortalizing the Founding Fathers

1. "Democracy" was most often regarded in the early post-Revolutionary era as the tool of unscrupulous demagogues inviting popular unrest. It was a word that connoted a society out of control. A general quality of "liberty" most commonly distinguished the newness of America's political culture from Old World monarchical and aristocratic systems. Today, of course, "democratic republic" and "representative democracy" are freely used to describe America's politically stable government, but in the late eighteenth and early nineteenth centuries a "democracy," when not disparaged, was more readily associated with the ancient world.

2. On myth as depoliticized speech, see Roland Barthes, *A Barthes Reader,* ed. Susan Sontag (New York, 1973–82), 130–34.

3. William Wirt, *The Life of Patrick Henry* (1817; rpt. Hartford, Conn., 1832), 91, 395, 432.

4. Andrew Burstein, *America's Jubilee* (New York, 2001), chap. 2. Wirt confessed his romanticization of history in a letter to his close friend Dabney Carr: "the style of the narrative, fettered by a scrupulous regard to real facts, is to me the most difficult in the world. It is like attempting to run, tied up in a bag. My pen wants perpetually to career and frolic it away." Ibid., p. 35. Mason Weems's 1800 biography of George Washington is probably the best-known example of the extravagance of published accounts about the purity and unsullied purposes of the founders. See also Lester H. Cohen, *The Revolutionary Histories: Contemporary Narratives of the American Revolution* (Ithaca, N.Y., 1980); Peter Charles Hoffer, *Revolution and Regeneration: Life Cycle and the Historical Vision of the Generation of 1776* (Athens, Ga., 1983). On religious imagery and providential expectations in the Revolutionary era, see esp. Ruth H. Bloch, *Visionary Republic: Millennial Themes in American Thought, 1756–1800* (Cambridge, 1985); John F. Berens, *Providence and Patriotism in Early America, 1640–1815* (Charlottesville, Va., 1978); Nathan O. Hatch, *The Sacred Cause of Liberty: Republican Thought and the Millennium in Revolutionary New England* (New Haven, Conn., 1989).

5. John E. Ferling, *The First of Men: A Life of George Washington* (Knoxville, Tenn., 1988), 253, 260–61; Benjamin Rush to John Adams, February 12, 1812; Adams to Rush, April 22, 1812 and June 12, 1812, in John A. Schutz and Douglas Adair, eds., *The Spur of Fame: Dialogues of John Adams and Benjamin Rush, 1805–1813* (San Marino, Calif., 1966), 209, 213, 225–26; *The Journal of William Maclay* (1890; rpt., New York, 1965); Jeffrey L. Pasley, *"The Tyranny of Printers": Newspaper Politics in the Early American Republic* (Charlottesville, Va., 2001), 87–88.

6. William Smith, *Eulogium on Benjamin Franklin* (Philadelphia, 1792), unnumbered page following the title page.

7. Ibid., pp. 1–3.

8. Ibid., 7–9.

9. Ibid., 38–40.

10. Joseph Story, *An Eulogy on General George Washington* (Salem, Mass., 1800), 3, 11–12; Fisher Ames, *An Oration on the Sublime Virtues of General George Washington* (Boston, 1800).

11. Henry Holcombe, *A Sermon, Occasioned by the Death of Lieutenant-General George Washington, Late President of the United States of America* (Savannah, Ga., 1800), 9, 12, 14. It was not only men of religious training who evoked Jesus. Revolutionary historian and medical doctor David Ramsay advocated in his eulogy that the model character of Washington, like that of Jesus, should be held up for ensuing generations: "Rehearse to your children, and instruct them to rehearse to theirs, the noble deeds of your common father, and inspire them with a holy resolution to go and do likewise." See Ramsay, "An Oration on the Death of Lieutenant-General George Washington, Late President of the United States," in *Eulogies and Orations on the Life and Death of General George Washington, First President of the United States of America* (Boston, 1800), 95. Connecticut Baptist Thomas Baldwin's eulogy makes the same comparison, but puts it in perspective: Washington was "destined by Heaven to be the instrumental Saviour of his country," yet his death was of "trifling" meaning in comparison to that of Jesus. See Barry Schwartz, *George Washington: The Making of an American Symbol* (New York, 1987), 99; more generally on Washington's Christlike symbolism and paternal character, see Jay Fliegelman, *Prodigals and Pilgrims: The American Revolution Against Patriarchal Authority* (Cambridge, 1982), chap. 7.

12. Steven C. Bullock, *Revolutionary Brotherhood: Freemasonry and the Transformation of the American Social Order, 1730–1830* (Chapel Hill, N.C., 1996), 178–79.

13. Ibid., 115, 124, 133, 137.

14. Many of the Masons' visual symbols were paraphernalia associated with literal construction—such as the level, square, plumb, and compass. With Washington's death, "the noise of the busy hammer suspended," according to Brother George Blake who beseeched "the *Grand Architect* in heaven" to give guidance, now that the "fairest *column* of thy earthly *temple* is broken." See Blake, "A Masonic Euolgy," in *Eulogies and Orations*, 97–99. As for the conjunction of Masonry and patriarchy, Brother Ezekiel L. Bascom described the brotherhood's leaders as "real men," while conventionally ridiculing the idea of female Masonry as an ambition "unsuitable to their tenderer sex." See Bascom, *An Address, Delivered at Leicester (Mass.), Before King Solomon's R.A. Chapter* (Leicester, Mass., 1817).

15. Blake, "A Masonic Euolgy," 105–7.

16. Ezra Stiles, *The United States Elevated to Glory and Honour* (Worcester, Mass., 1785), 9, 70–71.

17. Titus Theodore Barton, *A Sermon Preached at Tewksbury, February 22, 1800, on Account of the Death of General George Washington* (Medford, Mass., 1800), 6–7; Ramsay, "An Oration," 78.

18. Josiah Bartlett, *An Oration on the Death of General George Washington* (Charlestown, Mass., 1800), 6; Albert Furtwangler, *American Silhouettes: Rhetorical Identities of the Founders* (New Haven, Conn., 1987), 110–14.

19. Henry Lee, "Funeral Oration on the Death of General Washington," in *Eulogies and Orations*, 12, 17.

20. James H. Hutson, ed., *Letters from a Distinguished American: Twelve Essays by John Adams on American Foreign Policy,* (Washington, D.C., 1978), letter 12, 47–48; William Wirt, *The Letters of the British Spy* (1803; rpt. Chapel Hill, N.C., 1970), 143.

21. Lee, "Funeral Oration on the Death of General Washington," in *Eulogies and Orations*, 10.

22. Ibid., 16–17.

23. *American Citizen,* April 19, 1804.

24. Elizabeth G. Wirt to William Wirt, July 6, 1826, in William Wirt Papers, Maryland Historical Society; Burstein, *America's Jubilee*, 274–77.

25. Burstein, *America's Jubilee*, 267–73; on the concept of virtuous speech and its varied uses, see esp. Andrew W. Robertson, *The Language of Democracy: Political Rhetoric in the United States and Britain, 1790–1900* (Ithaca, N.Y., 1995), and Michael P. Kramer, *Imagining Language in America: From the Revolution to the Civil War* (Princeton, N.J., 1992).

26. William Alexander Duer, "Eulogy, Pronounced at Albany, New York, July 31st, 1826"; John A. Shaw, "Eulogy, Pronounced at Bridgewater, Massachusetts, August 2nd, 1826"; and Henry Potter, "Eulogy, Pronounced in Fayetteville, North Carolina, July 20, 1826," in *A Selection of Eulogies, Pronounced in the Several States, in Honor of Those Illustrious Patriots and Statesmen, John Adams and Thomas Jefferson* (Hartford, Conn., 1826), 128, 167, 138.

27. John Sergeant, "Eulogy, Pronounced in Philadelphia, Pennsylvania, July 24th, 1826," in *A Selection of Eulogies*, 116; Clay to J. Q. Adams, July 25, 1826, in James F. Hopkins, ed., *Papers of Henry Clay* (Lexington, Ky., 1959–91), 5: 567–68.

28. Sheldon Smith, "Eulogy, Pronounced at Buffalo, New York, July 22, 1826"; Caleb Cushing, "Eulogy, Pronounced at Newburyport, Massachusetts, July 15, 1826", and Shaw, "Eulogy . . . " in *A Selection of Eulogies*, 91, 21, 155–56, 96.

29. Reference to "benefactors" is in Samuel Smith, "Eulogy Pronounced in Baltimore, Maryland, July 20th, 1826, in *A Selection of Eulogies*, 71. Similar references in Edward Turner, "Eulogy Pronounced at Portsmouth, New-Hampshire, August 10th, 1826," and William Johnson, "Eulogy, Pronounced at Charleston, South Carolina,

August 3rd, 1826," in ibid., 287, 299; Felix Grundy, "Eulogy, Pronounced at Nashville, Tennessee, August 3rd, 1826, ibid., 296; Johnson quotation, in ibid., 300.

30. *A Selection of Eulogies*, 17, 287, 174–75.

31. Daniel Webster, "Eulogy, Pronounced in Boston, Massachusetts, August 2nd, 1826," in *A Selection of Eulogies.*, 193, 230–31.

32. Peleg Sprague, "Eulogy, Pronounced at Hallowell, Maine, July, 1826," in *A Selection of Eulogies*, 139–43.

33. Ibid., 150–51.

34. Ibid., 152–53. On the celebration of America's landscape, and its romantic equation with liberty, see in particular Albert Furtwangler, *Acts of Discovery: Visions of America in the Lewis and Clark Journals* (Urbana, Ill., 1993) and Perry Miller, "The Romantic Dilemma in American Nationalism and the Concept of Nature," *Harvard Theological Review* 48 (1955): 239–53.

35. When Jackson's longtime political nemesis Henry Clay died in 1852, his "bold and manly frankness" and personal integrity were heralded in similar fashion. In Congress, colleagues stood up to celebrate his humanity: George Jones of Iowa recalled Clay as "the guardian and director of my collegiate days"; William Henry Seward of New York stressed his honorable role as a link between the Revolutionary generation and its successors, in "regulating the constitutional freedom of political debate." Rather than court "perishable popularity," said James Brooks of New York, he exhibited "moral courage, to dare to do right." *Obituary Addresses on the Occasion of the Death of the Hon. Henry Clay* (Washington, D.C., 1852), 44–45, 51, 55, 100.

36. B. M. Dusenbery, ed., *Monument to the Memory of General Andrew Jackson* (Philadelphia, 1846), 104–5.

37. Ibid., 133, 183, 213, 316.

38. Ibid., 37, 50, 99.

39. Ibid., 50, 70–73.

40. Ibid., 85, 250.

41. John Van Buren's eulogy of Jackson states this most directly: "He had no children, and, as has been so beautifully said of General Washington, Providence denied his children, that he might be the father of his country." Ibid., 104.

42. Ibid., 210, 332.

43. Jackson to James K. Polk, May 12, 1835; to Martin Van Buren, March 30, 1837, and to Amos Kendall, May 15, 1841, in John Spencer Bassett, ed., *Correspondence of Andrew Jackson* (Washington, D.C., 1926–34), 5:345, 466–68, 6:112–13; Nancy N. Scott, ed., *A Memoir of Hugh Lawson White* (Philadelphia, 1856), 325.

44. John Davis to George Nixon Briggs, March 20, 1834, in George Nixon Briggs Correspondence, American Antiquarian Society, Worcester, Mass. On the activities of Isaac Hill, see Pasley, *"The Tyranny of Printers,"* 352–56; on caricatures, see James G. Barber, *Andrew Jackson: A Portrait Study* (Washington, D.C., 1991), chap. 6.

45. Lee, "Funeral Oration on the Death of General Washington," and Ramsay, "An Oration on the Death of Lieutenant-General George Washington," in *Eulogies and Orations on the Life and Death of General George Washington*, 13–14, 78. See also Paul K. Longmore, *The Invention of George Washington* (Berkeley, Calif., 1988).

46. See esp. William G. McLoughlin and Robert N. Bellah, eds., *Religion in America* (Boston, 1968), containing Bellah's chapter, "Civil Religion in America."

47. Schwartz, *George Washington: The Making of an American Symbol*, 88, 97; Gary Laderman, *The Sacred Remains: American Attitudes Toward Death, 1799–1883* (New Haven, Conn., 1996), 17.

48. "Sensibility" should be taken in its proper historical context, as a self-conscious public expression of humanism. In an idealized (republican) setting, and as the law

of the heart, sensibility reflected sympathy and generosity, private virtues converted into national policy. See esp. Andrew Burstein, "The Political Character of Sympathy," *Journal of the Early Republic* 21 (Winter 2001): 601–32.

Chapter 6. The Politics of Tears

1. Benjamin Franklin, *The Autobiography and Other Writings,* ed. Kenneth Silverman (New York, 1986), 111–12.

2. Charles Brockden Brown was profoundly influenced by the work—particularly the fiction—of the English political philosopher William Godwin (1756–1836), the author of *Political Justice* (1793) and husband of the pioneering feminist Mary Wollstonecraft. Godwin's finest novel, *Caleb Williams* (1794), was a gothic tale of crime, committed, hidden, detected, and misavenged across bitter class lines. He emphasizes the failure of justice in "enlightened" England, and the need for human beings to depend on rationality (rather than the power of institutions) to insure personal freedom and political liberty.

3. I am thinking here not only of those class distinctions that became a vital subject of early national fiction, but also of those racial crossings that remained unspeakable and thus could not be represented in the novels of the period. The sexual relations long rumored to have taken place between Thomas Jefferson and his mulatto slave Sally Hemings, and recently corroborated by DNA analysis performed on male relatives of both figures, might have constituted just such a story. The Jefferson-Hemings union, whispered about by Virginians and others in the early national period, became a public allegation when spurned Jefferson supporter, journalist, and scandalmonger James Callender committed it to print in 1802. See Annette Gordon-Reed, *Thomas Jefferson and Sally Hemings: An American Controversy* (Charlottesville,Va.,1997); Jan Ellen Lewis and Peter Onuf, eds., *Sally Hemings and Thomas Jefferson: History, Memory, and Civic Culture* (Charlottesville, Va.,1999); and the "Forum: Thomas Jefferson and Sally Hemings, Redux," *William and Mary Quarterly*, 3[d] ser. 52 (January 2000): 122–210.

4. One cannot resist speculation that the early American novelists knew more than they were overtly expressing about the framers, some of whom, like Jefferson, were "amalgamating" in just this "unspeakable" way. The figure in this tradition most likely to be based on a founding father is General Richman of *The Coquette,* whom I identify with George Washington in my book-length treatment of the fiction of the 1790s. See *The Plight of Feeling: Sympathy and Dissent in the Early American Novel* (Chicago, 1997), 85–87.

5. Had Jonbenet been killed at the age of ten or twelve rather than six, when she still possessed the baby teeth that made her precociously sexualized beauty-queen image all the more uncanny and perverse, she could not have served as a community fetish for Americans of all classes, races, and ethnicities. Surely development of secondary sexual characteristics would have disqualified her from the role of innocent slaughtered lamb, personification par excellence of shattered childhood innocence. There is an interesting paradox here: the living Jonbenet seems either to have been a complicit co-conspirator with or an uncomplaining accomplice to her mother Patsy's perverse ambition to see her six-year-old dominate the world of children's beauty pageants. As a failed pageant winner herself, Patsy Ramsey invested her young middle age in the "making" of Jonbenet. Ironically, both tabloid and mainstream press reports following the murder revealed that all was not perfectly clean and hygienic in the golden world of Jonbenet Ramsey. Household staff

reported that the child was a chronic bed-wetter, something that apparently angered her mother, and Jonbenet was "wiped" by an adult after using the bathroom. Despite this, she was performing complicated song and dance numbers in beauty pageants across the South.

This simultaneous infantilization and eroticization of the sentimental heroine goes back to American fiction of the 1790s. The title character of *Charlotte Temple* must be rendered helplessly childlike in order to serve the cultural purpose she was expected to perform. Though nearly sixteen years old (of marriageable age in her time), Charlotte fails to understand basic economic practices: she is baffled, for example, over the premise that tenants are obligated by landlords to pay rent even when the parties contracting the agreement have disappeared. Upon eloping to the New World with her "seducer," she carries nothing aboard ship: neither gold, nor jewels, nor exchangeable commodities. Incapable of imagining either futurity or consequences, Charlotte possesses the logical faculties of a six-year-old; in terms of sophistication; she and Jonbenet might be seen as peers.

6. Witness the practice, now an American commonplace, of photographically reproducing on milk cartons the faces of runaway, kidnapped, or otherwise missing children. Do the law enforcement agencies seeking the return of these youths strategically target as the audience of their milk carton mug-shot spectaculars the very schoolchildren who, breakfasting on cereal while surveying the lost faces, could serve, in fact, as gothic doppelgangers for those missing? While such faces are captioned by names, one is struck by the near invisibility of these young casualties in our culture.

I am indebted to Jay Grossman for reminding me that Matthew Shepard, the University of Montana undergraduate murdered by a homophobic gang of men in his home state, serves as a poster boy for gay civil rights precisely because he was young, blonde, and beautiful. The anonymous black transvestite killed on the docks of New York City, however, can fulfill no such function as he fails to telegraph the innocent beauty behind which we seek to fetishize Matthew Shepard as a representative personality. For more on this notion, see Mitchell R. Breitwieser, *Cotton Mather and Benjamin Franklin: The Price of Representative Personality* (New York, 1984).

7. See Sigmund Freud, "On Fetishism," in *Sexuality and the Psychology of Love*, intro. Philip Rieff (New York, 1963), 214–19; Louise J. Kaplan, *Female Perversions: The Temptations of Emma Bovary* (New York, 1991) 123–66. Robert Stoller notes that in fetishism, "objects take the place of narratives." See *Observing the Erotic Imagination* (New Haven, Conn., 1985), 155. See also Valerie Steele, *Fetish: Fashion, Sex, and Power* (New York, 1996), 168.

8. *"The Power of Sympathy" by William Hill Brown and "The Coquette" by Mrs. Hannah Foster*, ed. William Osborne (New Haven, Conn., 1970), 62. Hereafter cited as *The Power of Sympathy*.

9. The fact that William Hill Brown bought up all the copies of his own novel and never published another may have everything to do with its being a *roman à clef* critical of the rich and socially powerful. For the historical details of the Morton-Althorp story and its relation to *The Power of Sympathy*, see Cathy N. Davidson, *Revolution and the Word: The Rise of the Novel in America* (Oxford, 1986), 101–2.

10. Osborne, ed., *The Power of Sympathy*, 33–34.

11. Ibid., 57–58.

12. Ibid., 128.

13. Susanna Rowson, *"Charlotte Temple" and "Lucy Temple,"* ed. Ann Douglas (New York, 1991), 129. Hereafter cited as *Charlotte Temple*.

14. Following Karl Marx, Ann Douglas argues that the sort of fetishism that springs up around both Charlotte the character and *Charlotte Temple* the novel is the very dynamic that inaugurates mass culture itself. See Douglas's introduction to *"Charlotte Temple" and "Lucy Temple,"* vii–xliii, and Douglas, *The Feminization of American Culture* (New York, 1977). See also Cathy N. Davidson, "The Life and Times of *Charlotte Temple*: The Biography of a Book," in Cathy N. Davidson, ed., *Reading in America: Literature and Social History,* (Baltimore, 1989), 157–79; and Eva Cherniavsky, *That Pale Mother Rising: Sentimental Discourses and the Imitation of Motherhood in Nineteenth-Century America* (Bloomington, Ind., 1995), 28–40.

15. Hannah Webster Foster, *The Coquette,* ed. Cathy N. Davidson (New York, 1986),167.

16. Ibid., 24.

17. See Bruce Burgett's chapter "Sentimental Masochism" in *Sentimental Bodies: Sex, Gender, and Citizenship in the Early Republic* (Princeton, N.J., 1998).

18. See Ann Fairfax Witherington, *Toward a More Perfect Union: Virtue and the Formation of American Republics* (New York, 1991), 92–143.

19. Charles Brockden Brown, *Wieland; Or, the Transformation, An American Tale; and Memoirs of Carwin, the Biloquist,* ed. Jay Fliegelman (New York, 1991), 8–12.

20. Ibid., 14, 18–21.

21. Charles Brockden Brown, *Ormond; Or, the Secret Witness,* vol. 2 in Sydney J. Krause and S.W. Reid, eds., *The Novels and Related Works of Charles Brockden Brown* (Kent, Ohio, 1982), 67

22. See Michael Warner, *The Letters of the Republic: Publication and the Public Sphere in Eighteenth-Century America* (Cambridge, Mass., 1990), 176.

23. See Julie Ellison, *Cato's Tears and the Making of Anglo-American Emotion* (Chicago, 1999), 9–12.

Chapter 7. Major André's Exhumation

An earlier version of this essay was presented to the Clark Library Seminar of the UCLA Center for Seventeenth- and Eighteenth-Century Studies. I would like to thank Andrew Burstein, Nancy Isenberg, Robert Cray, Jr., and Helen Deutsch for their readings of the essay.

1. Thomas Paine, *Common Sense,* in *Collected Writings,* ed. Eric Foner (New York, 1995), 52–53.

2. Paine, *Common Sense,* 25.

3. Paine, *The American Crisis,* vol. 5, in *Collected Writings,* 152.

4. Robert Cray, Jr., "Commemorating the Prison Ship Dead: Revolutionary Memory and the Politics of Sepulture in the Early Republic, 1776–1808," *William and Mary Quarterly,* 3d ser., 56 (1999): 565–90; Ronald Hoffman, Thad W. Tate, and Peter J. Albert eds., *An Uncivil War: The Southern Backcountry in the American Revolution* (Charlottesville, Va., 1985).

5. For the story of André's mission, capture, and execution, the best account remains James Thomas Flexner, *The Traitor and the Spy: Benedict Arnold and John Andre* 2d ed. (New York, 1975), 392–93.

6. James Buchanan, "Narrative of the Exhumation of the Remains of Major André," *United Service Journal and Naval and Military Magazine,* pt. 3 (London, 1833), 307–8.

7. Ibid., 308.

8. Ibid., 305–6.

9. Ibid., 307.

10. James Thacher, "Observations Relative to the Execution of Major John André as Spy, in 1780, Correcting Errors and Refuting False Imputations," *New England Magazine* (May 1834), 353–64.

11. Buchanan, "Narrative of the Exhumation," 306.

12. Ibid., 306–7.

13. Ibid., 310.

14. Ibid., 308.

15. *Niles Weekly Register,* July 25, 1818, 371–75. For a wider discussion of Montgomery's place in the mythos of the early republic, see Charles Royster, *A Revolutionary People at War: The Continental Army and American Character, 1775–1783* (Chapel Hill, N.C., 1979), 120–26, Livingston quoted at 125.

16. Buchanan, "Narrative of the Exhumation," 303. Interestingly, editor Hezekiah Niles assumed that Buchanan's efforts had been stimulated by William Cobbett's removal of Thomas Paine's bones back to England in 1819. That Niles linked the removal of André's remains to those of Paine's suggests the complex politics of exhumation in the early republic and the ways that these ceremonies could mobilize a variety of political positions. See *Niles' Weekly Register,* August 18, 1821, 386. For a recent attempt to think through the multiple politics of exhumation and reburial, albeit in the context of the 1990s, see Katherine Verdery, *The Political Lives of Dead Bodies: Reburial and Postsocialist Change* (New York, 1999).

17. This was certainly Hezekiah Niles's understanding. *Niles' Weekly Register,* August 18, 1821, 386.

18. See Robert Cray, "Major John André and the Three Captors: Class Dynamics and Revolutionary Memory Wars in the Early Republic, 1780–1831," *Journal of the Early Republic,* 17 (1997): 371–97.

19. *Niles' Weekly Register,* January 18, 1817, 350; February 8, 1817, 386–87. For a more general discussion, see Cray, "Major John André and the Three Captors," 386–88.

20. For a provocative discussion of the circumstances surrounding the novel's creation and reception, see Wayne Franklin's introduction in his edition of James Fenimore Cooper, *The Spy,* (1821; rpt. New York, 1997), esp. x–xxiii. For a larger discussion of the political and social contexts of Cooper's fiction, especially the tensions around his aristocratic identifications, see Alan Taylor, *William Cooper's Town: Power and Persuasion on the Frontier of the Early American Republic* (New York, 1995), esp. 406–26.

21. Cooper, *The Spy,* 397–98.

22. Ibid., 383–84.

23. D. H. Lawrence, *Studies in Classic American Literature* (New York, 1923); Richard Slotkin, *Regeneration Through Violence: The Mythology of the American Frontier, 1600–1860* (Middletown, Conn., 1973).

24. This is not simply a case of, for instance, the neoroyalist predilection for referring to the 1650s as the interregnum, but of an entry into the early modern Atlantic not through its various radicalisms but through the genteel fear of those radicalisms. An entry through the pleasures of imagination instead of Great Nore, or San Domingue, or even Ireland of 1798.

25. For one particularly fine example of this newer historiography (from which I borrow the phrase "the pleasures of the imagination"), see John Brewer, *The Pleasures of the Imagination: English Culture in the Eighteenth Century* (New York, 1997).

26. Paine, *The American Crisis,* in *Collected Writings,* 152.

27. For Cobbett's efforts and the fate of Paine's remains, see Leo A. Bressler, "Pe-

ter Porcupine and the Bones of Thomas Paine," *Pennsylvania Magazine of History and Biography* 82: (1958): 176–85. Thanks to Nancy Isenberg for alerting me to this article. It is a bit of an overstatement to say that Paine's bones passed out of history, since at least some groups and individuals continue to search for their location. For one example, see the *Los Angeles Times*, April 1, 2001.

Chapter 8. Patriotic Remains

1. Philip Freneau, "The Indian Burying Ground" (1787), frequently anthologized, as in Paul Lauter, ed., *The Heath Anthology of American Literature*, 3d ed. (Boston, 1998).

2. On the controversy over Native American remains, see esp. Devon A. Mihesuah, ed., *Repatriation Reader: Who Owns American Indian Remains* (Lincoln, Neb., 2000); David Hurst Thomas, *Skull Wars: Kennewick Man, Archaeology, and the Battle for Native American Identity* (New York, 2000).

3. Paul Semonin, *American Monster: How the Nation's First Prehistoric Creature Became a Symbol of National Identity* (New York, 2000); esp. 15–40 (quotation 39–40). See also David Levin, "Giants in the Earth: Science and the Occult in Cotton Mather's Letters to the Royal Society," *William and Mary Quarterly*, 3d ser., 45 (October 1988): 751–70.

4. On relics in medieval Christianity, see Patrick J. Geary, *Living with the Dead in the Middle Ages* (Ithaca, N.Y., 1994), esp. 163–77.

5. Today, of course, we acknowledge the connections between the ancient societies that constructed the various earthworks and mounds between approximately 900 B.C.E. and 1200 C.E.—designed for burials, constructed in massive effigy shapes, or raised as colossal pedestals for temples—and those Native American people encountered in person by European colonists and United States settlers. On the "mound builders," see Roger G. Kennedy, *Hidden Cities: The Discovery and Loss of Ancient North American Civilization* (New York, 1994); Robert Silverberg, *Mound Builders of Ancient America* (Greenwich, Conn., 1968). On the ancient societies of the Southeast, see Charles M. Hudson, *The Southeastern Indians* (Knoxville, Tenn., 1976); on the Midwest, see Ronald J. Mason, *Great Lakes Archaeology* (Orlando, Fla., 1981). And see Gordon M. Sayre, "The Mound Builders and the Imagination of American Antiquity in Jefferson, Bartram, and Chateaubriand," *Early American Literature* 33 (1998): 225–49.

6. Thomas Jefferson, *Notes on the State of Virginia*, ed. William Peden, 1785; (Chapel Hill, N.C., 1954), 97–100.

7. Jeremy Belknap, *A Discourse, Intended to Commemorate the Discovery of America by Christopher Columbus* (Boston, 1792), 45. See also Bernard W. Sheehan, *Seeds of Extinction: Jeffersonian Philanthropy and the American Indians* (Chapel Hill, N.C., 1973), 48–54; Elisabeth Tooker, "History of Research," in William C. Sturtevant, general ed., *Handbook of North American Indians*, vol. 15, *Northeast*, ed. Bruce G. Trigger (Washington, D.C., 1978), 6–7; Sayre, "Mound Builders and American Antiquity." For the results of early scientific investigation of the mounds, see Caleb Atwater, "A Description of the Antiquities Discovered in the State of Ohio and Other Western States," *Transactions of the American Antiquarian Society* 9 (1820); Ephraim Squier and Edwin H. Davis, *Ancient Monuments of the Mississippi Valley, Comprising the Results of Extensive Original Surveys and Explorations, Smithsonian Contributions to Knowledge* (Washington, D.C., 1848).

8. Sayre, "Mound Builders and American Antiquity," 229.

9. William Cullen Bryant, "The Prairies" (1832), reprinted in Paul Lauter, ed., *The Heath Anthology of American Literature*, 2d ed. (Lexington, Mass., 1994), 1: 2711–14. See also Freneau, "Indian Burying Ground."

10. Jefferson, *Notes on the State of Virginia*, 98–100.

11. Philip Freneau, *The Hospital Prison-Ship*, canto 3 of *The British Prison-Ship* (1781).

12. Ibid.

13. Henry Stiles, *History of the City of Brooklyn* (New York, 1867), 1: 363–64.

14. See esp. G. Kurt Piehler, *Remembering War the American Way* (Washington, D.C., 1995), 20–23. On the reluctance to finance monuments in the United States, see also Michael Kammen, *Mystic Chords of Memory: The Transformation of Tradition in American Culture* (New York, 1991), 19, 54–55, 71. Robert E. Cray, Jr., "Commemorating the Prison Ship Dead: Revolutionary Memory and the Politics of Sepulture in the Early Republic, 1776–1808," *William and Mary Quarterly*, 3d ser., 61 (July 1999): 565–90, is a fine treatment of the subject.

15. "A Citizen," "To the Citizens of New-York," *American Citizen*, January 8, 1803.

16. "Humanitus" letter to the editors, *American Citizen*, January 11, 1803. My thanks to Nancy Isenberg for bringing this article to my attention.

17. Adams to Rush, February 25, 1808, in John A. Schutz and Douglass Adair, eds. *The Spur of Fame: Dialogues of John Adams and Benjamin Rush, 1805–1813* (San Marino, Calif., 1980), 103–5. On the celebration of Washington and erection of his birthday as a national holiday (and, more generally, on the role of public holidays in shaping American identity and nationalism), see Matthew Dennis, *Red, White, and Blue Letter Days: Identity, History, and the American Calendar* (Ithaca, N.Y., 2002).

18. See Piehler, *Remembering War the American Way;* Kirk Savage, "The Politics of Memory: Black Emancipation and the Civil War Monument," in John R. Gillis, ed., *Commemorations: The Politics of National Identity* (Princeton, N.J., 1994), 127–49; Kirk Savage, *Standing Soldiers, Kneeling Slaves: Race, War, and Monument in Nineteenth-Century America* (Princeton, N.J., 1997).

19. Tammany Society, or Columbian Order, *Account of the Internment of the Remains of 11,500 American Seamen, Soldiers, and Citizens, Who Fell Victims to the Cruelties of the British, on Board their Prison Ships at the Wallabout, during the American Revolution. With a Particular Description of the Grand & Solemn Funeral Procession, which Took Place on the 26 MAY, 1808. And an Oration, Delivered at the Tomb of the Patriots, by Benjamin De Witt, M.D., A Member of the Tammany Society or Columbian Order. Compiled by the Wallabout Committee* (New York, 1808), 8.

20. Ibid., 9–11.

21. Ibid., 18–19.

22. Ibid., 12.

23. Ibid., 20; Tammany Society, or Columbian Order, *Circular* (New York, February 11, 1808), a broadside.

24. Tammany Society, *Account of the Internment of the Remains*, 22–47.

25. Ibid., 49–60; quotation 59–60.

26. Ibid., 62–67; Tammany Society, or Columbian Order, Wallabout Committee, *Arrangement for the Grand and Solemn Procession, which is to take place on the the 25th inst. 1808* (1808), a broadside.

27. Tammany Society, *Account of the Internment of the Remains*, 67–75.

28. Ibid., 75–93.

29. Ibid., 94; Jefferson to James Madison, September 6, 1789, in Thomas Jefferson, *Writings*, ed. Merrill D. Peterson (New York, 1984), 959–64.

30. Cray, "Commemorating the Prison Ship Dead," 586–90; Stiles, *History of Brooklyn*, 371–72; Walt Whitman, "The Wallabout Martyrs" in *Leaves of Grass* (1891).

See generally David Charles Sloan, *The Last Great Necessity: Cemeteries in American History* (Baltimore, 1991).

31. Cray, "Commemorating the Prison Ship Dead," 589–90.

32. "Westward, the March of Empire Takes Its Way," *Kirwin Chief* (Kansas), February 26, 1876, quoted by Brian W. Dippie, "The Moving Finger Writes: Western Art and the Dynamics of Change," in Jules David Prown et al., *Discovered Lands, Invented Pasts: Transforming Visions of the American West* (New Haven, Conn., 1992), 97.

Chapter 9. A Peculiar Mark of Infamy

1. Benjamin Henry Latrobe diary, August 20, 1796, in Edward C. Carter, ed., *The Papers of Benjamin Henry Latrobe: Virginia Journals* (New Haven, Conn., 1977), 1:191.

2. Donald R. Wright, *African Americans in the Colonial Era: From African Origins Through the Colonial Era*, 2d ed. (Arlington Heights, Ill., 2000), 149; Elizabeth B. Pharo, ed., *Reminiscences of William Hasell Wilson* (Philadelphia, 1937), 8; Karl Bernhard, *Travels Through North America, During the Years 1825 and 1826* (Philadelphia, 1828), 2:10.

3. Edward L. Ayers, *Vengeance and Justice: Crime and Punishment in the Nineteenth-Century American South* (New York, 1984), 136.

4. Peter Linebaugh and Marcus Rediker, *The Many-Headed Hydra: Sailors, Slaves, Commoners, and the Hidden History of the Revolutionary Atlantic* (Boston, 2000), 185–86; T. J. Davis, *A Rumor of Revolt: The "Great Negro Plot" in Colonial New York* (New York, 1985), 54–55; Wright, *Colonial Era*, 170.

5. Douglas Hay, "Property, Authority, and the Criminal Law," in Douglas Hay, ed., *Albion's Fatal Tree: Crime and Society in Eighteenth Century England* (New York, 1975), 29; Frank McLynn, *Crime and Punishment in Eighteenth-Century England* (New York, 1991), 258. The Charleston workhouse became unstable and was razed following an 1886 earthquake, but photographs in the South Carolina Historical Society indicate its imposing size. In the 1850s, both the workhouse and the adjoining city jail, which still stands, were given castle-like facades and elaborate turrets. In times of slave unrest, as in 1822, when the workhouse became full, slaves awaiting execution were housed in the upper floors of the jail.

6. Peter Linebaugh, *The London Hanged: Crime and Civil Society in the Eighteenth Century* (Cambridge, 1992), 280; Norrece T. Jones, *Born a Child of Freedom, Yet a Slave: Mechanisms of Control and Strategies of Resistance in Antebellum South Carolina* (Hanover, N.H., 1990), 91; Betty Wood, " 'Until He Shall Be Dead, Dead, Dead': The Judicial Treatment of Slaves in Eighteenth-Century Georgia," *Georgia Historical Quarterly* 71 (Fall 1987): 395. On Dent, see Ayers, *Vengeance and Justice*, 136.

7. Richmond *Virginia Argus*, October 3, 1800; unidentified newspaper clipping, William Palmer Scrapbook, Virginia Historical Society, Richmond, Va.

8. John B. Adger, *My Life and Times, 1810–1899* (Richmond, Va.,1899), 52; Mary Lamboll Beach to Elizabeth Gilchrist, July 5, 1822, Beach Letters, South Carolina Historical Society, Charleston, S.C.; Martha Proctor Richardson to James Screven, July 6, 1822, Arnold and Screven Papers, University of North Carolina Library.

9. On stoicism, see Graham Russell Hodges, *Root and Branch: African Americans in New York and East Jersey, 1613–1863* (Chapel Hill, N.C., 1999), 135–36; on Coromantees, see Michael M. Craton, *Testing the Chains: Resistance to Slavery in the West Indies* (Ithaca, N.Y., 1982), 100.

10. David Barry Gaspar, *Bondmen and Rebels: A Study of Master-Slave Relations in Antigua, with Implications for Colonial British America* (Baltimore, 1985), 23.

11. Lionel Kennedy and Thomas Parker, eds., *An Official Report of the Trials of*

Sundry Negroes (Charleston, S.C., 1822), 46; Mary Lamboll Beach to Elizabeth Gilchrist, July 5, 1822, Beach Letters; notation on confession of Hammet's Bacchus, n.d., William and Benjamin Hammet Papers, Duke University Library.

12. Sylvia R. Frey and Betty Wood, *Come Shouting to Zion: African American Protestantism in the American South and British Caribbean to 1830* (Chapel Hill, N.C., 1998), 22–23.

13. Frey and Wood, *Come Shouting to Zion,* 38; David R. Roediger, "And Die in Dixie: Funerals, Death, and Heaven in the Slave Community, 1700–1865," *Massachusetts Review* 22 (1981): 167.

14. Michel Foucault, *Discipline and Punish: The Birth of the Prison,* trans. Alan Sheridan (New York, 1979), 10–11; Philip J. Schwarz, *Slave Laws in Virginia* (Athens, Ga., 1996), 26; Anthony Ashmore and Gillian Stacey, *Black Kingdoms, Black Peoples* (London, 1979), 53; Craton, *Testing the Chains,* 100.

15. Schwarz, *Slave Laws in Virginia,* 72–73; Kathryn Preyer, "Crime, the Criminal Law, and Reform in Post-Revolutionary Virginia," *Law and History Review* 1 (Spring 1983): 64.

16. Roediger, "And Die in Dixie," 167; Peter H. Wood, *Black Majority: Negroes in Colonial South Carolina from 1760 through the Stono Rebellion* (New York, 1974), 314–15.

17. Craton, *Testing the Chains,* 136, 287.

18. McLynn, *Crime and Punishment,* 273–74; Peter Linebaugh, "The Tyburn Riot Against the Surgeons," in Hay, ed., *Albion's Fatal Tree,* 76–77; Randall McGowen, "The Body and Punishment in Eighteenth-Century England," *Journal of Modern History* 59 (December 1987): 660–61.

19. *Charleston Mercury,* July 27, 1822; Charleston *City Gazette,* July 20, 1822.

20. Zephaniah Kingsley, *A Treatise on the Patriarchal, or Co-operative System of Society* (1829; rpt. New York, 1970), 13; Kennedy and Parker, eds., *Official Record,* 47.

21. Eugene D. Genovese, *Roll, Jordan, Roll: The World the Slaves Made* (New York, 1972), 203; Roediger, "And Die in Dixie," 167–68.

22. Mechal Sobel, *The World They Made Together: Black and White Values in Eighteenth-Century Virginia* (Princeton, N.J., 1987), 174–175; Margaret Washington, *"A Peculiar People": Slave Religion and Community-Culture Among the Gullah* (New York, 1988), 54–55; Frey and Wood, *Come Shouting to Zion,* 23.

23. Josephine A. Beoku-Betts, " 'She Make Funny Flat Cake She Call Saraka': Gullah Women and Food Practices Under Slavery," in Larry Hudson, ed., *Working Toward Freedom: Slave Society and Domestic Economy in the American South* (Rochester, N.Y., 1994), 220; Roediger, "And Die in Dixie," 169.

24. Interview with Cordelia Thomas, n.d., in George P. Rawick, ed., *The American Slave: A Composite Autobiography* (Westport, Conn., 1972), 13:4:20; interview with Julia Larken, n.d., ibid., 13:3:42–43; interview with Robert Shepherd, n.d., ibid., 13:3:251–52.

25. Roediger, "And Die in Dixie," 166; interview with Caleb Craig, n.d., in Rawick, ed., *American Slave,* 2:1:231; Betty Wood, *Women's Work, Men's Work: The Informal Slave Economies of Lowcountry Georgia* (Athens, Ga., 1995), 167–68.

26. Interview with Emmaline Heard, December 8, 1936, in Rawick, ed., *American Slave,* 13:4:250; Genovese, *Roll, Jordan, Roll,* 197–98.

27. Sterling Stuckey, *Slave Culture: Nationalist Theory and the Foundations of Black America* (New York, 1987), 108–9; Sylvia R. Frey, *Water from the Rock: Black Resistance in a Revolutionary Age* (Princeton, N.J., 1991), 301; Roediger, "And Die in Dixie," 173.

28. Charles Joyner, *Down by the Riverside: A South Carolina Slave Community* (Urbana,

Ill., 1984), 138; Kingsley, *Treatise on the Patriarchal*, 13; John Michael Vlach, *By the Work of Their Hands: Studies in Afro-American Folklife* (Charlottesville, Va., 1991), 44–45.

29. Sobel, *World They Made Together*, 219–20; John S. Mbiti, *Introduction to African Religion* (London, 1975), 120; John Michael Vlach, "Graveyards and Afro-American Art," *Southern Exposure* 5 (1977): 162.

30. DuBose Heyward, *The Half-Pint Flask* (New York, 1929), 10–11; Vlach, "Graveyards," 161.

31. Interview with Washington Dozier, June 23, 1937, in Rawick, ed., *American Slave*, 2:1:334; Frey and Wood, *Come Shouting to Zion*, 23; Trial of Jack Pritchard, July 9, 1822, in Kennedy and Parker, eds., *Official Report*, 103–5, 47.

32. Interview with Emmaline Heard, December 8, 1936, in Rawick, ed., *American Slave*, 13:4:250–51.

33. Keith Thomas, *Religion and the Decline of Magic* (New York, 1971), 419; Ruth Richardson, *Death, Dissection, and the Destitute*, 2d ed. (Chicago, 2000), 15–16; Hodges, *Root and Branch*, 419. See also Daniel A. Cohen's chapter in this volume.

34. Thomas, *Religion and the Decline of Magic*, 587; C. Vann Woodward and Elisabeth Muhlenfeld, eds., *The Private Mary Chesnut: The Unpublished Civil War Diaries* (New York, 1984), 181–82.

35. Interview with Minerva and Anderson Edwards, n.d., in Rawick, ed., *American Slave*, 4:2:708.

36. William Sidney Drewry, *The Southampton Insurrection* (Washington, D.C., 1900), 102 n. 2.

Chapter 10. Immortal Messengers

1. See Elizabeth Reis, *Damned Women: Sinners and Witches in Puritan New England* (Ithaca, N.Y., 1997), 93–120.

2. David D. Hall, *Worlds of Wonder, Days of Judgment: Popular Religious Belief in New England* (New York, 1989). Drawing a distinction between "religion" and the "supernatural" is, of course, somewhat artificial; for the purposes of this chapter, "supernatural" is defined broadly to mean extraordinary communication from otherworldly sources: devils, angels, or God.

3. Robert Bruce Mullin, *Miracles and the Modern Religious Imagination* (New Haven, Conn., 1997), 9–25. For arguments about the end of an angelic age, see Henry Lawrence, *An History of Angells, being a Theological Treatise of our Communion and Warre with Them* (London, 1649).

4. Ibid., 16.

5. See Walter W. Woodward, "The Magic in Colonization: Religion, Science, and the Occult in the Colonization of New England" (Ph.D. diss., University of Connecticut, 2000). See also Patricia A. Watson, *The Angelical Conjunction: The Preacher-Physicians of Colonial New England* (Knoxville, Tenn., 1991).

6. *The Diary of Cotton Mather*, ed. Worthington Chauncey Ford, *Collections of the Massachusetts Historical Society*, 7th ser., 7(1911–12): 86–87. On the dating of the angel sighting, see David Levin, "When Did Cotton Mather See the Angel," *Early American Literature* 15 (1980–81): 271–75; also Kenneth Silverman's review of Mather's *Paterna*, in *Early American Literature* 15 (1980): 80–87.

7. Increase Mather, *Meditations on the Glory of the Heavenly World* (Boston, 1711), 130. On the Puritan mistrust of miracles in the modern age, see Robert Bruce Mullin, *Miracles and the Modern Religious Imagination* (New Haven, Conn., 1997), 9–25.

8. Cotton Mather, *The Angel of Bethesda: An Essay Upon the Common Maladies of Mankind* (Barre, Mass., 1972), 51–52.

9. Ibid., 53.

10. Increase Mather, *Coelestinus. A Conversation in Heaven, Quickened and Assisted with Discoveries of Things in the Heavenly World. And some Relations of the Views and Joys That have been granted unto Several Persons in the Confines of it. Introduced by Agathangelus, Or, An Essay on the Ministry of the Holy ANGELS* (Boston, 1713), 13.

11. Ibid., 21.

12. Ibid., 24.

13. Increase Mather, *Angelographia, or A Discourse Concerning the Nature and Power of the Holy Angels, and the Great Benefit which the True Fearers of GOD Receive by their Ministry* (Boston, 1696), 10.

14. Mather, *Angelographia*, 16.

15. "Mather-Calef Paper on Witchcraft," *Proceedings of the Massachusetts Historical Society* 47 (1913–14): 240–68; quotations 266–67. See also Silverman, *The Life and Times of Cotton Mather*, 135–37.

16. Savage Papers, *Proceedings of the Massachusetts Historical Society* 44 (1910–11): 685.

17. Samuel Willard warned his parishioners, "We are to rest in the revealed will of God for our Hope, and not to pry into his secret will," and mandated, "leave Secret Things to the day of Revelation." See *The Mourners Cordial Against Excessive Sorrow: Discovering what Grounds of Hope Gods People have Concerning their Dead Friends* (Boston, 1691), esp. 73, 137.

18. Cotton Mather, *Diary*, 163

19. Cotton Mather, *Diary*, 163. For further thoughts on angels, see Cotton Mather, sermon notes, Boston, Massachusetts Church Records Sermon Notes 1690–94/5, September 3, 1693, American Antiquarian Society, Worcester, Mass.

20. Mather, *Angelographia*, 17. Emphasis added.

21. Rev. Joseph Standen to Rev. Benjamin Colman, February 1712/13, MHS Jenks Papers, Massachusetts Historical Society, Boston. My thanks to Sheila Mcintyre for bringing this story to my attention.

22. Anon., *The Heavenly Damsel: Or the Parents Blessing Being a true Relation of the Early Piety of a Young Damsel of Nine Years of Age* (Newport? 1755?). See also Joseph Emerson, V.D.M., *Early Piety Encouraged. A Discourse occasion'd by the joyful and triumphant Death of a Young Woman of Malden, Who died of the Throat-Distemper* (Boston, 1738). This is the story of a young girl on her deathbed, wishing for her death to come: " 'O Mother,' said she, 'I see CHRIST, and the Angels fluttering over me!' At another Time, she said, 'The Angels stand ready to carry me into Abraham's Bosom' " (26).

23. See esp. Nathan O. Hatch, *The Democratization of American Christianity* (New Haven, Conn., 1989) and Richard Rabinowitz, *The Spiritual Self in Everyday Life: The Transformation of Personal Religious Experience in Nineteenth-Century New England* (Boston, 1989).

24. Polly Davis, *A Faithful Narrative of the Wonderful Dealings of God Toward Polly Davis of New Grantham in the State of New Hampshire* (New Hampshire, 1792), 7. Historian Ann Kirschner examines the genre of spiritual visions which were especially popular during the Revolutionary era. See Kirschner, " 'Tending to Edify, Astonish, and Instruct': Published Narratives of Spiritual Dreams and Visions in the Early Republic" (paper presented to the McNeil Center for Early American Studies Seminar Series, March 23, 2001) 14. Some examples are Hezekiah Goodwin, "A Vision. . ." (New London, Conn., 1769); Miss Field, "The Glory of the Heavenly City. . ." (Philadelphia, 1785); "The Vision and Wonderful Experience of Jane Cish" (Newburyport, Mass., 1793); Aaron Warner, "A Remarkable Dream, or Vision" (Hart-

ford, Conn., 1801); Ebenezer Adams, "A True & Wonderful Relation of the Appearance of Three Angels, (Cloathed in White Raiment) to a Young Man in Medford . . . (Boston, 1761). On the relationship between politics and visionary literature, see Robert Girouard, "A Survey of Apocryphal Visions in Late Eighteenth-Century America," in Frederick S. Allis, Jr., ed., *Sibley's Heir: A Volume in Memory of Clifford Kenyon Shipton* (Boston, 1982), 39:191–219.

25. Davis, *A Faithful Narrative*, 9–10. On the ways in which eighteenth-century women were able to make a positive choice regarding their salvation, see Reis, *Damned Women*, 164–93. See also Richard Gildrie, *The Profane, the Civil, and the Godly: The Reformation of Manners in Orthodox New England, 1679–1749* (University Park, Pa., 1994), and Susan Juster, *Disorderly Women: Sexual Politics and Evangelicalism in Revolutionary New England* (Ithaca, N.Y., 1994).

26. On the widespread nature of dreams and visions, see Ann Taves, *Fits, Trances, and Visions: Experiencing Religion and Explaining Experience from Wesley to James* (Princeton, N.J., 1999), Mechal Sobel, *Teach Me Dreams: The Search for Self in the Revolutionary Era* (Princeton, N.J., 2000), and Leigh Eric Schmidt, *Hearing Things: Religion, Illusion, and the American Enlightenment* (Cambridge, Mass., 2000). For a rich account of one evangelical preacher's encounter with an angel, see Susan Juster, "The Angel Delusion of 1806–1811: Frustration and Fantasy in Northern New England," unpublished paper, 2001. On the Methodists, see John Wiggins, *Taking Heaven by Storm: Methodism and the Rise of Popular Christianity in America* (Oxford, 1998).

27. Ann Phillips, *A Vision of Heaven and Hell* (Barnard, Vt., 1812), 2.

28. *Testimonies of the Life, Character, Revelations, and Doctrines of Mother Ann Lee, and The Elders With Her, Through whom the Word of Eternal Life was opened in this day, of Christ's Second Coming, Collected from Living Witnesses in Union with the Church* (Albany, N.Y., 1888), 180.

29. Ibid., 177.

30. Ibid., 180–81. On the relationship between Shaker faith and spiritual sight, see Sally Promey, *Spiritual Spectacles: Vision and Image in Mid-Nineteenth-Century Shakerism* (Bloomington, Ind., 1993).

31. Ibid. See Susan Juster, "Neither Male nor Female: Jemima Wilkinson and the Politics of Gender in Post-Revolutionary America," in Robert Blair St. George, ed., *Possible Pasts: Becoming Colonial in Early America* (Ithaca, N.Y., 2000), 357–79. As many scholars have noted, Shaker sources are particularly problematic; skeptics published criticism and adherents penned veneration. But in these extant sources it is possible to see how Mother Ann Lee employed her visions to keep her followers on the straight and narrow. See Catherine A. Brekus, *Strangers and Pilgrims: Female Preaching in America, 1740–1845* (Chapel Hill, N.C., 1998), 98–101. Later permutations of Shakerism followed suit with respect to angel calls. In the 1870s and 1880s, Shakers organized spiritualist seances which hundreds of people attended. Out of closed cabinet doors came the voices and spirit angels of departed Shakers to remind supporters of what glory awaited them if they remained faithful and celibate, and to admonish them about the horrors they would likely encounter if they strayed and pursued carnal desires. Angels came not to individual hopeful worshippers, but to the leaders alone. See "A Brief Account of Ten Seances, Held at North Family, Mt. Lebanon, from May 13th to May 19th, 1878, for Materialization," Reel 3, Shaker Collection, New York Public Library.

32. Matthew Dennis, "Seneca Possessed: Colonialism, Witchcraft, and Gender in the Time of Handsome Lake," in Elizabeth Reis, ed., *Spellbound: Women and Witchcraft in America* (Wilmington, Del., 1998), 121–44.

33. Anthony F. C. Wallace, *The Death and Rebirth of the Seneca* (New York, 1969), 241.

34. Matthew Dennis, "Speech of Sose-Ha-Wa and the Code of Handsome Lake," in Colleen McDannell, ed., *Religions of the United States in Practice*, 2 vols. (Princeton, N.J., 2001), 1:394–408.

35. See, for example, Rev. Royal Washburn, "Angels," *The American Evangelist* (July 1828); George Clayton, Jr., *Angelology: Remarks and Reflections Touching the Agency and Ministration of Holy Angels; with reference to their History, Rank, Titles, Attributes, Characteristics, Residence, Society, Employments and Pursuits; interspersed with Traditional Particulars Respecting Them* (New York, 1851).

36. See Dr. A. D. C. Twesten, "Doctrine Respecting Angels," *Bibliotheca Sacra* (1844), 768–93. Theologians ascribed power to angels in obscure language, laced with Latin references and convoluted sentences, and ultimately admitted uncertainty.

37. Kirschner, "Tending to Edify, Astonish, and Instruct," 12.

38. Lewis Mayer, D.D., "The Scriptural Idea of Angels," *American Biblical Repository* 12 (October 1838): 374.

39. Emanuel Swedenborg, *A Brief Account of the Life of Emanuel Swedenborg, a Servant of the Lord and the Messenger of the New-Jerusalem Dispensation* (Cincinnati, Ohio 1827), 15–19; Swedenborg, *A Treatise Concerning Heaven and Hell, and of the Wonderful Things Therein, as Heard and Seen by the Honourable and Learned Emanuel Swedenborg* (Baltimore, 1812).

40. On the senses of Swedenborg's angels, see Schmidt, *Hearing Things*, 202–30.

41. J. Everett, *A Book for Skeptics: Being Communications from Angels, Written with their Own Hands; Also Oral Communications, spoken by Angels through a Trumpet, and Written Down as they were Delivered, in the Presence of Many Witnesses* (Columbus, Ohio, 1853), 14.

42. Frederick William Faber, *Ethel's Book; or, Tales of the Angels* (Baltimore, 1858), 51–52.

43. Ibid, 52–53.

Chapter 11. "In the Midst of Life we are in Death"

1. Diary of John L. Lewis, February 7, 6, 11, 12, 1830, Special Collections, New York State Historical Association, Cooperstown, N.Y. (NYSHA).

2. Ibid., February 14, 1830.

3. The themes of affliction found in New York materials were not specific to this region. On this point, see Lewis O. Saum, *The Popular Mood of Pre-Civil War America* (Westport, Conn., 1980).

4. Richard H. Steckel, "Stature and Living Standards in the United States," in Robert E. Gallman and John Joseph Wallis, eds., *American Economic Growth and Standards of Living before the Civil War* (Chicago, 1992), 265–308; Robert William Fogel, "The Conquest of High Mortality and Hunger in Europe and America: Timing and Mechanisms," Working Paper Series on Historical Factors in Long Run Growth, no. 16, National Bureau of Economic Research (Cambridge, Mass., 1990); Robert V. Wells, "The Population of England's Colonies in America: Old English or New Americans?" *Population Studies* 46 (1992): 85–102; Dora L. Costa, "Height, Weight, and Disease Among the Native-Born in the Rural, Antebellum North," *Social Science History*, 17:3 (Fall 1993): 355–83; Samuel H. Preston and Michael R. Haines, *Fatal Years: Child Mortality in Late Nineteenth-Century America* (Princeton, N.J., 1991).

5. Richard D. Arnold, quoted in Richard Harrison Shryock, *Medicine and Society in America: 1660–1860* (Ithaca, N.Y., 1960), 148. Holmes quoted in Edgar W. Martin, *The Standard of Living in 1860: American Consumption Levels on the Eve of the Civil War* (Chicago, 1942), 231. For descriptions of nineteenth-century medical practice,

see also Martin Pencak, *A Calculus of Suffering: Pain, Professionalism, and Anesthesia in Nineteenth-Century America* (New York, 1985); Judith Walzer Leavitt and Ronald L. Numbers, eds., *Sickness and Health in America: Readings in the History of Medicine and Public Health* (Madison, Wis., 1978); Regina Markell Morantz-Sanchez, *Sympathy and Science: Women Physicians in American Medicine* (New York, 1985); James Harvey Young, *The Toadstool Millionaires: A Social History of Patent Medicines in America Before Regulation* (Princeton, N.J., 1961); Susan E. Cayleff, *Wash and Be Healed: The Water-Cure Movement and Women's Health* (Philadelphia, 1987).

It should also be noted that this period witnessed a significant decline in fertility, with families averaging close to two fewer children born by the late antebellum era. What this meant for the strength of emotional bonds within families is hard to say, but one may imagine that early deaths became increasingly devastating. On fertility changes, see Nancy Osterud and John Fulton, "Family Limitation and Age at Marriage: Fertility Decline in Sturbridge, Massachusetts 1730–1850," *Population Studies* 30 (1976): 481–94; Richard A. Easterlin, "Factors in the Decline of Farm Family Fertility in the United States: Some Preliminary Research Results," *Journal of American History* 63 (September 1976): 600–614; Susan E. Klepp, "Revolutionary Bodies: Women and the Fertility Transition in the Mid-Atlantic Region, 1760–1820," *Journal of American History* 85 (December 1998): 910–45.

6. Emeline Hicks to Alice Barber, November 5, 1842, Barber Family Letters, Special Collections, New York State Library, Albany, N.Y. (NYSL).

7. Elizabeth Clark describes the changing perceptions of the purpose of pain. Abolitionists stressed that freedom from pain was a natural right, thus highlighting the concern of antebellum Americans for escaping the burden of pain and suffering. See " 'Sacred Rights of the Weak': Pain, Sympathy, and the Culture of Individual Rights in Antebellum America," *Journal of American History* 82 (September 1995): 463–93.

8. The dynamic of religious change, toward a softened Christianity that responded to affliction within increasingly affectionate homes, is explicitly laid out in Harriet Beecher Stowe, *The Minister's Wooing* (New York, 1859).

9. Diary of Anonymous Otsego County Farmer, November 11, December 11, 18, 1848, NYSHA.

10. Henry Clarke Wright, *Human Life: Illustrated in My Individual Experience as a Child, a Youth, and a Man* (Boston, 1849), 28, 30, 30–31. For a comprehensive account of Wright's life, see Lewis Perry, *Childhood, Marriage, and Reform: Henry Clarke Wright, 1797–1870* (Chicago, 1980).

11. Autobiographical sketch in Diary of George Kaercher, Kaercher and Packer Family Papers, Rare Book and Manuscript Department, Kroch Library, Cornell University (KLCU); "Journal of Peggy Dow," in *The Dealings of God, Man, and the Devil; As Exemplified in the Life, Experience, and Travels of Lorenzo Dow* (New York, 1850), 199–200.

12. Diary of William Pratt, January 7, 8, 10, 16, 1843, KLCU.

13. Ibid., January 17, 18, 1843.

14. Ibid., January 18, 22, 24, 1843.

15. Ibid., April 9, 16, 1843.

16. Diary of Susan Bibbens Fox, September 11, 1837, KLCU.

17. Ibid., May 26, April 21, 25, May 2, August 17, 1833; June 4, 1834; August 8, 1833; January 24, 1834.

18. Ibid., May 5, 1840; March 20, April 3, 20, 1841; May 28, 1833; August 29, 1837; July 1, 1840; March 28, 1842; July 11, September 24, 1843.

19. Silas Scott to Warham Scott, December 15, 1819, Scott Family Papers, NYSL; John Scott to Warham Scott, January 25, 1838, Scott Family Papers, NYSL.

20. Diary of Lucy M. Stoddard, January 1, December 31, January 22, March 18, 14, May 5, 1860, KLCU.

21. For some leading examples of historians' works that emphasize other social causes (economic, class, mobility, or political sources of anxiety), see Whitney R. Cross, *The Burned-Over District: The Social and Intellectual History of Enthusiastic Religion in Western New York, 1800–1850* (Ithaca, N.Y., 1950); Randolph A. Roth, *The Democratic Dilemma: Religion, Reform, and Social Order in the Connecticut River Valley of Vermont, 1791–1850* (New York, 1987); Paul Johnson, *A Shopkeeper's Millennium: Society and Revivals in Rochester, New York, 1815–1837* (New York, 1983); Donald G. Mathews, "The Second Great Awakening as an Organizing Process, 1780–1830: An Hypothesis," *American Quarterly* 21 (Spring 1969): 23–43; William G. McLoughlin, *Revivals, Awakenings, and Reform: An Essay on Religion and Social Change in America, 1607–1977* (Chicago, 1978); Robert H. Abzug, *Cosmos Crumbling: American Reform and Religious Imagination* (New York, 1994). For useful criticism of the dominant explanatory frameworks, and evidence for how ordinary converts do not easily fit into these theories of modernization, see Richard D. Shiels, "The Scope of the Second Great Awakening: Andover, Massachusetts, as a Case Study," *Journal of the Early Republic* 5 (Summer 1985): 223–46; George M. Thomas, *Revivalism and Cultural Change: Christianity, Nation Building, and the Market in the Nineteenth-Century United States* (Chicago, 1989); Curtis D. Johnson, *Islands of Holiness: Rural Religion in Upstate New York, 1790–1860* (Ithaca, N.Y., 1989). For a recent summary of problems (and suggested solutions) involved in quantifying the factors leadings to religious conversion, see Curtis D. Johnson, "Supply-Side and Demand-Side Revivalism: Evaluating the Social Influences on New York State Evangelicalism in the 1830s," *Social Science History* 19 (Spring 1995): 1–30.

22. The experience of Lucy Smith, the mother of the founder of Mormonism, is indicative of this process. As Richard L. Bushman puts it in *Joseph Smith and the Beginnings of Mormonism* (Urbana, Ill., 1984), "Lucy Smith solemnly promised to serve God with all her heart when an illness brought her close to death in 1803, and then was unable to find a pastor to suit her. She at last found a minister to baptize her without requiring church membership" (5).

23. Diary of Samuel S. Mariner, 1854, KLCU; Diary of Cornelia H. Smith, 1843, KLCU; Diary of Benjamin F. Gue, 1848–49, NYSL; Diary of John Bower, January 4, 1844, KLCU.

24. For those scholars who stress the importance of death and mourning rituals, and do not dismiss this development as strictly maudlin, see David E. Stannard, *The Puritan Way of Death: A Study in Religion, Culture, and Social Change* (New York, 1977); Charles O. Jackson, ed., *Passing: The Vision of Death in America* (Westport, Conn., 1977); Martha V. Pike and Janice Gray Armstrong, *A Time to Mourn: Expressions of Grief in Nineteenth Century America* (Stony Brook, N.Y., 1980); Philippe Aries, *The Hour of Our Death*, trans. Helen Weaver (New York, 1981); Gary Laderman, *The Sacred Remains: American Attitudes Toward Death, 1799–1883* (New Haven, Conn., 1996); Robert V. Wells, "Taming the 'King of Terrors': Ritual and Death in Schenectady, New York, 1844–1860," *Journal of Social History* 27 (Summer 1994): 717–35; Robert V. Wells, *Facing the "King of Terrors": Death and Society in an American Community, 1750–1990* (New York, 2000).

25. Ann Douglas, *The Feminization of American Culture* (New York, 1977), esp. 92, 255; Jane Tompkins, *Sensational Designs: The Cultural Work of American Fiction, 1790–1860* (New York, 1985), esp. xi, 130. Other works on antebellum sentimental culture include Mary P. Ryan, *The Empire of the Mother: American Writing About Domesticity, 1830–1860* (New York, 1982); Nina Baym, *Woman's Fiction: A Guide to Novels by and About Women in America, 1820–1870*, 2d ed. (Urbana, Ill., 1993); Nancy Schnog,

"Inside the Sentimental: The Psychological Work of *The Wide Wide World*," *Genders* 4 (Spring 1989): 11–25; Alice Fahs, "The Sentimental Soldier in Popular Civil War Literature," *Civil War History* 46 (June 2000): 107–31; and Shirley Samuels, ed., *Race, Gender, and Sentimentality in Nineteenth-Century America* (New York, 1992). Recently scholars have stressed the eighteenth-century roots of sentimental culture. This new work clearly challenges Douglas's argument that sentimentalism was devoid of intellectual complexity. For example, see Janet Todd, *The Culture of Sensibility: An Introduction* (New York, 1986); G. J. Barker-Benfield, *The Culture of Sensibility: Sex and Society in Eighteenth-Century Britain* (Chicago, 1992); Norman Fiering, "Irresistible Compassion: An Aspect of Eighteenth-Century Sympathy and Humanitarianism," *Journal of the History of Ideas* 37 (April–June 1976): 195–218; Jay Fliegelman, *Prodigals and Pilgrims: The American Revolution Against Patriarchal Authority, 1750–1800* (New York, 1982); and Andrew Burstein, *Sentimental Democracy: The Evolution of America's Romantic Self-Image* (New York, 1999).

26. Harriet Beecher Stowe, *Uncle Tom's Cabin, or Life Among the Lowly* (New York, 1851; rpt., 1968), 300–301.

27. Anonymous Account Book, Lintner Family Papers, NYSL.

Chapter 12. The Romantic Landscape

1. For the rural cemetery movement in America, see Blanche Linden-Ward, *Silent City on a Hill: Landscapes of Memory and Boston's Mt. Auburn* (Columbus, Ohio, 1989); Stanley French, "The Cemetery as Cultural Institution," *American Quarterly* 26 (March 1974): 37–59; Gary Laderman, *The Sacred Remains: American Attitudes Toward Death, 1799–1883* (New Haven, Conn., 1996); David C. Sloane, *The Last Great Necessity: Cemeteries in American History* (Baltimore, 1991), 44–95, Thomas Bender, *Toward an Urban Vision* (Lexington, Ky., 1975), 80–88; and Philippe Ariès, *The Hour of Our Death* (New York, 2000), 531–36.

2. Washington Irving, *Journals and Notebooks,* 1 (1803–6): 280. This and following references to Irving's writings are from *The Complete Works of Washington Irving,* ed. Henry Pochman, Herbert Kleinfeld, and Richard D. Rush (Boston, 1965–). See also *Journals,* 2 (1807–22): 323 (Paul); 4 (1826–29): 146 (Ferdinand); and *Letters,* 1 (1802–23): 694 (Charlemagne). For the Swiss churchyard, see "Rural Funerals" in *The Sketch Book,* 118, and *Letters,* 1 (1802–23): 213–14. For Bakewell churchyard and Winchester Cathedral, see *Journals,* 2 (1807–22): 73, 80–81, 84, 305. I am indebted to my research assistant, Robert Pittman, for his help in locating many of these references.

3. *Journals,* 1 (1803–6): 279–80. For the Protestant Cemetery, see Johan Beck-Friis, *Il Cimitero Acattolico di Roma* (Malmö, Sweden, n.d.) and Judi Culbertson and Tom Randall, *Permanent Italians* (New York, 1996), 43–56.

4. See Mark Twain, *Innocents Abroad,* chaps. 18, 26, 53–54. Both Irving and Twain draw on the Protestant tradition of mocking Roman Catholic devotional practices, particularly the veneration of relics, which had flourished since the days of Luther and had roots, even earlier, in the anticlerical humor of Chaucer's age.

5. *Journals,* 1 (1803–6): 190.

6. *Letters,* 1 (1802–23): 64–65, 69. Some remains of the Church of the Cordeliers, where Laura was interred in 1348, survive in Avignon today, but her tomb did not escape the church's destruction. See *Blue Guide to France* (New York, 1991), 842.

7. "Westminster Abbey," in *The Sketch Book,* 134–35, 146.

8. Ibid., 137, 139, 141.

9. Ibid., 137.

10. Ibid. John Wesley, by contrast, thought this monument one of only two in the abbey "worthy of the attention of a Christian." Esdale cites oral tradition as recording that Lady Nightingale had been felled by lightning. Katharine A. Esdake, *English Church Monuments, 1510–1840* (London, 1946), 75.

11. "Westminster Abbey," 138.

12. "Rural Funerals," 110; "The Widow and Her Son," 84. He described another rural funeral in the latter. See Andrew Burstein, *America's Jubilee* (New York, 2001), 101–2.

13. "Rural Funerals," 13–14. See Charles Dickens, *Oliver Twist* (1838), chaps. 5–6.

14. "Rural Funerals," 109–16.

15. "Westminster Abbey," 136. In Scott's case, the great author survived by several years the anxious earl of Buchan, who had assured him during a serious illness that funeral arrangements and a eulogy were ready and waiting. See "Abbotsford," in *The Crayon Miscellany*, 157–58; Philip McFarland, *Sojourners* (New York, 1979), 144; Dorothy Eagle, Hilary Carnell, and Meic Stephens, *The Oxford Literary Guide to Great Britain and Ireland*, 2d ed. (Oxford, 1993), 95. The greyhound monument is mentioned in "Abbotsford," 138.

16. "Newstead Abbey," in *The Crayon Miscellany*, 185–86, esp. 185; *Letters*, 2 (1823–38): 668, 684. The Byron family had lost ownership of Newstead Abbey before the poet's death, so that ruined church may not have been an option in any case.

17. *Journals*, 2 (1807–22): 60.

18. Pierre M. Irving, *The Life and Letters of Washington Irving*, 3 vols., in *The Works of Washington Irving* (Philadelphia, n.d.), 1:335–36.

19. For the origin of the ghost, see Henry A. Pochman, "Irving's German Sources in *The Sketch Book*," *Studies in Philology* 27 (1930): 477–507, and "Irving's German Tour and Its Influences on His Tales," *PMLA* 45 (1930): 1150–87. See also Daniel Hoffman, *Form and Fable in American Fiction* (New York, 1961), 83–96.

20. "Sleepy Hollow," in *Miscellaneous Writings, 1803–1859* 2:105.

21. *Life and Letters*, 1:36–37.

22. "The Legend of Sleepy Hollow," in *The Sketch Book*, 273. Several "originals" of Ichabod Crane are said to be buried elsewhere, including Samuel Youngs (Dale cemetery, Ossining) and Ichabod B. Crane (Asbury Church of the Nazarene Cemetery, Staten Island). See Culbertson and Randall, *Permanent New Yorkers* (Chelsea, Vt., 1987), 309–10; Friends of the Old Dutch Burying Ground, *Tales of the Old Dutch Burying Ground*, rev. ed. (North Tarrytown, 1992), 9, 19; Nancy Ellis and Parker Hayden, *Here Lies America* (New York, 1978), 148–49; Interview of William Lent, Old Dutch Churchyard, June 2001.

23. "Legend of Sleepy Hollow," 273–74.

24. Kathleen Eagen Johnson and Timothy Steinhoff, *Art of the Landscape: Sunnyside, Montgomery Place, and Romanticism* (Tarrytown, N.Y., 1997), 8–9.

25. "Legend of Sleepy Hollow," 273, 288–92; inscription, André Monument, North Nave Aisle, Westminster Abbey, London. Michael Meranze examines André's posthumous refashioning in Chapter 7 of this book.

26. "Sleepy Hollow," 107–9; "Legend of Sleepy Hollow," 289.

27. The county history dates the church to c. 1680–85 and the cemetery to c. 1645–55. Alvah French, ed., *The History of Westchester*, 2 vols. (New York, 1925), 1:287–88. The surviving inscriptions, the earliest dating to 1755, have been recorded in *The Old Dutch Burying Ground of Sleepy Hollow* (Boston, 1953), v, vii.

28. "Abbotsford," 127, 160–61.

29. See Kathleen Eagen Johnson, *Washington Irving's Sunnyside* (Tarrytown, N.Y., 1995), 11; Johnson, *Sunnyside*, 32; and Theodore Tilton, "A Visit to Washington Irv-

ing," *Living Age*, 815 (December 1859): 822–24. A few years after Irving's death, a popular engraving by Felix O. C. Darley depicted him surrounded by his literary friends in his study (according to Tilton, this was "a sacred place!"). Darley's *Washington Irving and His Literary Friends at Sunnyside* was printed in London in 1863. The print was also popular in America. In Philadelphia, Christian Schussele completed a painting, in 1863, after the engraving that is now in the collection of Historic Hudson Valley. The image portrays Irving surrounded by Tuckerman, Holmes, Simms, Halleck, Hawthorne, Emerson, Prescott, Willis, Bryant, Cooper, Bancroft, and Kennedy. See *Visions of Washington Irving: Selected Works from the Collections of Historic Hudson Valley* (Tarrytown, N.Y., 1991), 67–68.

30. Irving "dressed up" the house's history with more than "a little becoming fiction" in *Wolfert's Roost*, intended both to spin a legendary history of the house as well as to raise funds for its remodeling. See *The Adventures of Capt. Bonneville and Wolfert's Roost* (New York, 1896). John Deedy calls the house "a quaint architectural *ménage à trois* of the Dutch, Gothic, and the Romanesque" in his *Literary Places: A Guided Pilgrimage* (Kansas City, Mo., 1978), 31. Also see Johnson, *Washington Irving's Sunnyside;* Harold Dean Cater, "Washington Irving and Sunnyside, *New York History* 38:2 (April 1957): 123–66; Debra L. Clyde, *Sunnyside and Romanticism* (Tarrytown, N.Y., 1983), an unpublished typescript at Historic Hudson Valley Library; and Joseph T. Butler, *Washington Irving's Sunnyside* (Tarrytown, N.Y., 1974). I am grateful for the help supplied by Maria Gagliardi of the Historic Hudson Valley Library and Dina Rose Friedman and Greg Klein of Sunnyside.

31. Johnson and Steinhoff, *Art of the Landscape*, 18. Also see Robert M. Toole, *Sunnyside Historical Landscape Report* (unpublished report Tarrytown, N.Y., 1995), Historic Hudson Library, esp. 28–29 and fig. 44; Clyde, *Sunnyside and Romanticism;* Butler, *Washington Irving's Sunnyside* 28–37; Andrew Jackson Downing, *Landscape Gardening*, 2d ed., 38, quoted in Toole, *Sunnyside Landscape Report*, 30.

32. Toole, *Sunnyside Landscape Report*, 19.

33. *Letters*, 3 (1839–45): 108–9.

34. *Letters*, 2 (1823–38): 932. He expressed his grief and affection for Peter in a letter to his sister Sarah. See *Letters*, 2 (1823–38): 936–37; and 3 (1839–45): 333.

35. *Letters*, 3 (1839–45): 440.

36. Mathilda Hoffman lies in the churchyard of St. Marks-in-the-Bowery in Manhattan's East Village, where some family vaults (including hers) survive today. See Culbertson and Randall, *Permanent New Yorkers*, 36. Recent scholarship downplays the importance of Irving's relationship with Hoffman, which was certainly overromanticized in the century after his death. See Jenifer S. Banks, "Washington Irving, the Nineteenth-Century Bachelor," in Ralph Alderman, ed., *Critical Essays on Washington Irving* (Boston, 1990), 253–65.

37. Irving vowed to protect "the ashes of those I loved from desecration." See *Letters*, 4 (1846–59): 436–37; also see Shepherd Knapp, *A History of the Brick Presbyterian Church in the City of New York* (New York, 1909).

38. *Letters*, 4 (1846–59): 437.

39. Benson J. Lossing, *The Hudson from the Wilderness to the Sea* (New York, 1866), 325–26; Irving, *Letters*, 4 (1846–59): 437. The cemetery records do not support Lossing's account. The practice of burying two coffins in one grave would have been unlikely in Sleepy Hollow until almost a century later. See Interview of William Graham, Sleepy Hollow Cemetery, June 2001.

40. *Letters*, 4 (1846–59): 436–7.

41. See Irving Plot Diagram, Section 9/Lot 166 to 177, Lot Diagram Book, and Register of Internments, 1:154 (September 29, 1853), Sleepy Hollow Cemetery; Irving genealogical tables in Stanley Williams, *Life of Washington Irving* (New York,

1935), vol. 2, appendix; and photograph of Irving plot (as well as my own observation and photographs) in *Sleepy Hollow Cemetery at Tarrytown-on-the-Hudson* (New York, 1891), 12. See also *Letters*, 3 (1839–45): 109; Johnson, *Sunnyside*, 47; Toole, *Sunnyside Landscape Report*, 27–28.

42. See A. J. Downing, "Public Cemeteries and Public Gardens," in *Rural Essays*, 154–59; Jacob Bigelow, *A History of the Cemetery of Mt. Auburn* (Boston, 1840; rpt., Cambridge, 1988); Linden-Ward, *Silent City on a Hill;* "Address to the Inhabitants of Concord at the Consecration of Sleepy Hollow Cemetery," in *The Complete Works of Ralph Waldo Emerson* (Boston, 1903–4), ix, 435–36. Emerson, Hawthorne, Thoreau, Channing, and the Alcotts are all buried on "Authors' Ridge" in the Concord cemetery. The chronology of relevant dates strongly suggests that Concord's Sleepy Hollow was named for Irving's story.

43. *History of Westchester County*, 2:734; "Washington Irving, Capt. Storm Started Sleepy Hollow Cemetery," Tarrytown *Daily News*, October 7, 1958, copy at Sleepy Hollow Cemetery.

44. *Letters*, 4 (1846–59): 192; Sleepy Hollow Cemetery (1891), 2; *History of Westchester County*, 2:734; *Knickerbocker* 33 (June 1849): 548.

45. Ibid. By 1866, the cemetery advertised that "the Hudson River Rail Road brings this cemetery within an hour's ride of the Thirtieth Street station-house in New York City." See *Sleepy Hollow Cemetery at Tarrytown* (New York, 1866), 9–10.

46. One version of the "battle" fought here has a group of local patriots throwing up the redoubt to fire on a British frigate grounded on the mud flats in the Hudson below. Steuben P. Swartwout, "Recollections of Tarrytown," Letter 10, Tarrytown *Argus*, February 16, 1901, Historic Hudson Valley Library, Typescript/Pamphlet 974.72721T27s. Several New York City cemeteries were developed on the site of Revolutionary battles, which did no harm in lending heritage and patriotic sanctity to their appeal. Plaques in Manhattan's Trinity Church Cemetery commemorate the Battle of Washington Heights (1776), a marker in the Bronx's Woodlawn Cemetery memorializes a redoubt (1776) on Gun Hill, and "Battle Hill" in Brooklyn's Greenwood Cemetery refers to the Battle of Long Island (1776). John V. Butler, *The Churchyards of Trinity Parish* (New York, 1969), 83, 85; *Map of the Woodlawn Cemetery* (1981); and Mark M. Boatner, *Landmarks of the American Revolution* (Harrisburg, Pa., 1975), 284. Sloane wrongly suggests that only veterans could be buried on Sleepy Hollow's Battle Hill. This is contradicted by the physical evidence at the site. Sloan, *Last Great Necessity*, 80–81; Visit to Battle Hill section, Sleepy Hollow Cemetery, June 2001.

47. *Sleepy Hollow Cemetery at Tarrytown* (Tarrytown, N.Y., 1925), 9–15; *History of Westchester County*, 2:734. See *Permanent New Yorkers*, 305–27, for a tour of the cemetery's more famous inhabitants, who include Carl Schurz, Whitelaw Reid, Henry Villard, George Washington Hill, Elizabeth Arden, Vincent Astor, William Rockefeller, Mark Hellinger, and Major Bowes. By June 7, 2001, 41,472 people had been interred here. Register of Interments, Sleepy Hollow Cemetery. Samuel Gompers lies across Summit Avenue from the glade sheltering Andrew Carnegie's Celtic cross. To the north lies the inaccessible private family cemetery on the enormous Rockefeller estate.

48. "Sleepy Hollow," 110–13.

49. *Life and Letters*, 2:137–39. He used the $3,500 paid to him by the railroad to finance the construction of the Spanish Tower at Sunnyside. See *Visions of Washington Irving*, 47, 122–23; Toole, *Sunnyside Landscape Report*, 33.

50. *Letters*, 4 (1846–59): 48. The aqueduct's massive stone bridge over the Pocantico now forms part of the cemetery's northeastern boundary. Irish laborers had

indeed walked off the job at one point, though it was because of low wages rather than whiskey or violence. They did live in "shantys" provided by the contractor, and some were known to drink heavily. They were also unwelcome in many rural old Dutch and English parts of Westchester. Sing-Sing's village elders "clamped down" on their makeshift Catholic church (constructed on land purchased for that purpose) after the ground began to be used for burials. Gerard T. Koeppel, *Water for Gotham: a History* (Princeton, N.J., 2000), 201–2, 212–13, 226, 249–53. I am grateful to Joanne Goldman for background and sources on the aqueduct.

51. "A Letter of 'Geoffrey Crayon' to the Editor of *The Knickerbocker Magazine*" (March 1839), *Miscellaneous Writings,* 2:104.

52. "Address on the Death of Washington Irving, delivered to the Massachusetts Historical Society, December 15, 1859," in Henry Wadsworth Longfellow, *Poems and Other Writings* (New York, 2000), 800–801; J. M. [sic], "At Irving's Grave," *Children's Magazine* 32 (February 1860), 35–36. An early motorists' travel guide to the northeast recommended a visit to the old Dutch Church, adding that "our beloved Washington Irving" sleeps behind it. The guide illustrates the church on a route map and "Ichabod's Midnight Ride" in the margin of the text. See *Historic Tours in Soconyland* (New York, 1925), 5, 8, 26, 44. I am grateful to Barbara Cutter for lending me this source.

53. Lossing, *Hudson,* 324–25. The first grave is pictured in *Frank Leslie's Illustrated Newspaper,* December 17, 1859, 45, Historic Hudson Valley Library, Library of Graphics Collection. Also see *Sleepy Hollow Cemetery* (1866), 8–9.

54. William Smith, "Gravestone of Washington Irving," August 6, 1956, Historic Hudson Valley Library, Pamphlet 974.727722 D 1956s. A postcard of Irving's tomb, dated July 14, 1906, confirms that the present stone predates 1906. It also shows that a mound remained over the grave at that time (postcard in author's collection).

55. See Frederic A. Conningham, *Currier and Ives Prints: An Illustrated Check List* (New York, 1983), nos. 3439, 4124, 4572, 5550–51, 5891–93; Harry T. Peters, *Currier and Ives: Printmakers to the American People* (Garden City, N.Y., 1943), 33, plate 16. George Inness painted his canvas of *Sunnyside* in the 1850s. See *Visions of Washington Irving,* 43, 111, 124; Downing, "Hints to Rural Improvers," in *Rural Essays,* 111; Oliver Wendell Holmes, "Dr. Holmes' Remarks on the Death of Washington Irving" (1859), in *The Autocrat's Miscellanies* (New York, 1959), 93. James had been introduced to Irving by his father fifty-five years earlier. See Henry James, *The American Scene* (New York, 1907), 152.

56. Butler, *Washington Irving's Sunnyside,* 38. Surviving documentation is not detailed enough to reconstruct the precise layout of paths or placement of seats at Sunnyside. Many images exist from the nineteenth century, each differing in its picturesque details of the setting as demanded by the artist's own vision of Irving's house.

57. James, *The American Scene,* 150.

58. Lossing, *Hudson,* 349.

Contributors

Nancy Isenberg is Associate Professor of History and coholder of the Mary Frances Barnard Chair in Nineteenth-Century American History at the University of Tulsa. She is the author of *Sex and Citizenship in Antebellum America* (1998).

Andrew Burstein is Professor of History and coholder of the Mary Frances Barnard Chair in Nineteenth-Century American History at the University of Tulsa. He is the author of *The Inner Jefferson: Portrait of a Grieving Optimist* (1995), *Sentimental Democracy: The Evolution of America's Romantic Self-Image* (1999), and *America's Jubilee* (2001).

*   *   *

Daniel A. Cohen is Associate Professor of History at Florida International University. He is the author of *Pillars of Salt, Monuments of Grace: New England Crime Literature and the Origins of American Popular Culture, 1674–1860* (1993) and editor of *The Female Marine and Related Works: Narratives of Cross-Dressing and Urban Vice in America's Early Republic* (1997).

Thomas G. Connors is Assistant Professor of History at the University of Northern Iowa.

Matthew Dennis is Professor of History at the University of Oregon. He is the author of *Cultivating a Landscape of Peace: Iroquois-European Encounters in Seventeenth-Century America* (1993) and *Red, White, and Blue Letter Days: Identity, History, and the American Calendar* (2002).

Douglas R. Egerton is Professor of History at Le Moyne College. He is the author of *Gabriel's Rebellion: The Virginia Slave Conspiracies of 1800 and 1802* (1993) and *He Shall Go Out Free: The Lives of Denmark Vesey* (1999).

Nicholas Marshall is Assistant Professor of History at Marist College. He is working on a book based on his doctoral dissertation, "The Dissonant

Society: Gain and Suffering, and the Rise of an Improving Class in Rural New York, 1815–1860."

MICHAEL MERANZE is Associate Professor of History at the University of California, San Diego. He is the author of *Laboratories of Virtue: Punishment, Revolution, and Authority in Philadelphia, 1760–1835* (1996) and editor of Benjamin Rush, *Essays: Literary, Moral, and Philosophical* (1988).

ELIZABETH REIS is Assistant Professor of Women's Studies and History at the University of Oregon. She is the author of *Damned Women: Sinners and Witches in Puritan New England* (1997). She is also editor of *Spellbound: Women and Witchcraft in America* (1998) and *American Sexual Histories* (2001).

JULIA STERN is Associate Professor of English at Northwestern University. She is the author of *The Plight of Feeling: Sympathy and Dissent in the Early American Novel* (1997).

LAURA M. STEVENS is Assistant Professor of English at the University of Tulsa. She is completing her first book, *"The Poor Indians": Missionary Writings and Transatlantic British Sensibility, 1642–1776.*

ROBERT V. WELLS is the Chauncey Winters Professor of History and Social Science at Union College. He has published six books, most recently *Facing the "King of Terrors": Death and Society in an American Community, 1750–1900* (2000).

Index